Library of
Davidson College

VOID

STUDIES IN GDR CULTURE AND SOCIETY 6

Selected Papers from the Eleventh New Hampshire Symposium on the German Democratic Republic

Editorial Board:
Margy Gerber, Chief Editor
Christine Cosentino
Volker Gransow
Nancy A. Lauckner
Christiane Lemke
Arthur A. Stahnke
Alexander Stephan
W. Christoph Schmauch

UNIVERSITY
PRESS OF
AMERICA

LANHAM • NEW YORK • LONDON

Copyright © 1986 by

University Press of America,® Inc.

4720 Boston Way
Lanham, MD 20706

3 Henrietta Street
London WC2E 8LU England

All rights reserved

Printed in the United States of America

Co-published by arrangement with the
International Symposium on the
German Democratic Republic

ISBN (Perfect): 0-8191-5469-5
ISBN (Cloth): 0-8191-5468-7

All University Press of America books are produced on acid-free paper which exceeds the minimum standards set by the National Historical Publications and Records Commission.

TABLE OF CONTENTS

Acknowledgments   v

Preface   vii

Arthur A. Stahnke. Progress and the GDR Economy: GDR Economic Performance and its Measurement   1

Pieter A. Boot. The GDR Economy between East and West: Problems and Opportunities   17

Karl-Heinz Röder. The Perception of the United States in GDR Policy and Society: Preconditions and Possibilities for Dialogue   31

Dietrich Staritz. <u>Untertänigkeit</u>: Heritage and Tradition   37

Lyman H. Legters. The Abrogation of Politics: Pseudo-Marxism in the GDR and Eastern Europe   49

Mike Dennis. Degradation or Humanization? Work and Scientific-Technical Progress in the GDR   59

Irene Dölling. Social and Cultural Changes in the Lives of GDR Women - Changes in their Self-Conception   81

Christiane Zehl Romero. Changing Patterns of Male and Female Identity in Recent GDR Prose   93

Rüdiger Pieper. Official Policy and the
   Attitudes of GDR Youth towards Marriage
   and the Opposite Sex as Reflected in the
   Column "Unter vier Augen" — 109

Carol Poore. Illness and the Socialist
   Personality: Philosophical Debates and
   Literary Images in the GDR — 123

Gerd Labroisse. Fortschritt in der DDR-
   Literaturkritik der 80er Jahre - ein
   ambivalentes Phänomen? — 137

Günter Erbe. Moderne, Avantgarde und
   Postmoderne: Zur neueren Rezeption in der
   Literaturwissenschaft der DDR — 157

Anna Chiarloni. The Museum of Hope:
   The Poems of Richard Pietraß — 173

Dennis R. McCormick. Wolf Biermann and
   "die zweite deutsche Exilliteratur":
   An Appraisal after Nine Years — 187

Contributors to Studies in GDR Culture
   and Society 6 — 205

Acknowledgments

The editors wish to express their thanks to Dietz Verlag in Berlin for granting permission to use the cartoons reproduced in the article by Mike Dennis.

Thanks go also to Judith Pouget for her help with the preparation of the manuscript.

Preface

The fourteen papers collected here are the revised versions of papers presented at the Eleventh New Hampshire Symposium on the German Democratic Republic, which took place at the World Fellowship Center near Conway, N.H. from June 21-28, 1985.

The 1985 Symposium was attended by approximately sixty-five academicians and others with expertise on the GDR from seven countries. Some thirty-three papers and presentations were given during the week-long interdisciplinary program.

That Volume 6 is somewhat more slender than previous volumes in the series is mainly attributable to the program structure of the 1985 Symposium, which included panel discussions for the first time. Although a stimulating modus for the Symposium itself, panel discussions proved to be less favorable for the volume, since written statements frequently did not materialize subsequently from the oral remarks.

    Margy Gerber
    Chief Editor

    Christine Cosentino
    Volker Gransow
    Nancy A. Lauckner
    Christiane Lemke
    Arthur A. Stahnke
    Alexander Stephan
    W. Christoph Schmauch,
      ex officio

Progress and the GDR Economy:
GDR Economic Performance and its Measurement

Arthur A. Stahnke

The idea of progress and its achievement has been of obvious importance to the political leadership of the GDR. At the theoretical or ideological level, the Socialist Unity Party has repeatedly claimed to be the agent directing the progression of society toward communism and has used this claim to legitimize both government policy and its own right to rule. Politically, purported progress, especially in economic performance, has been held up as proof that the Party's claims are being realized, with social benefit for all. Moreover, to the extent to which the citizenry has accepted the argument of the elite, economic progress has been a means of increasing and maintaining general public support for the new political order.

Yet, economic progress is a concept not without ambiguity, especially when it is applied to non-technical or non-quantifiable matters. Even where the focus is on comparatively concrete and measurable phenomena, as with the analysis of economic performance that follows, determining whether significant progress has been achieved is not necessarily a simple or straightforward task. For example, as is well known, Western students of the GDR economy have differed consistently and sometimes heatedly over the proper interpretation of the available data on GDR economic performance; some have allegedly seen substantial progress, while others have emphatically disagreed.[1]

At least part of the reason for this lack of consensus has stemmed from the paucity and/or poor quality of the GDR data with which Western analysts must work. The Informationspolitik of the East German Party/State elite seems too often intent upon identifying and magnifying the positive, while concealing or minimizing failure and shortcomings; well-founded frustration (and here there is consensus in the West) has evoked criticism of this policy as foolishly restrictive and perhaps even counterproductive to the GDR's own interests.

Another source of evaluative disagreement over evidence of progress in the GDR economy has been a function of using different indicators as the decisive measures. For example, an optimistic assessment can almost certainly be obtained from a cataloging of official growth rates, while a more pessimistic conclusion can be drawn from productivity or product quality comparisons between the GDR and Western industrialized states, assuming they can be made on a systematic basis.

In the following, I will discuss several ways in which we can--and often do--measure GDR economic performance, and will then fit the relevant data into those measures and evaluate both the method and the performance record. Though only very cautious generalizations about the GDR's overall economic progress will be made, the exercise should at least aid in clarifying the extent to which we have evidence on the subject and what that evidence might imply.

Perhaps the most obvious and commonly used measure of economic performance is the calculation of macro-growth rates like Gross National Product (GNP) or National Income (NI) on an annual basis; one can then compare a given year with the following or the preceding. Western economists are familiar with these indicators and use them to show whether, or to what extent, more goods and services have been produced or utilized in a country from year to year. Socialist leaders are, if anything, even more prone to report their countries' growth rates over time and to imply or state outright that such evidence of growth is an indication of progress.

Table 1 displays the GDR record as regards two of its standard measures, Produced National Income (PNI) and Industrial Goods Production (IGP), for the years from 1961 to the present. From the data presented there one can say that the GDR economy has grown at a fairly consistent, substantial, but somewhat declining rate. Indeed, GDR economists and publicists have frequently compared their economy's growth in PNI with GNP growth rates in Western countries to demonstrate, inter alia, that socialism is superior to market economies.[2] Such claims and comparisons should not be accepted uncritically, for the GDR's methods of computing its growth rates are not the same as those we use in the West, and the methods result in the deriving of comparatively higher rates of growth.

TABLE 1: GDR MACRO-ECONOMIC GROWTH RATES (Average Annual %, 1961-1980; Annual %, 1981-1984)

	PNI	IGP	GNP
1961-1965	3.4	6.0	NA
1966-1970	5.2	6.5	3.2
1971-1975	5.4	6.5	3.5
1976-1980	4.2	5.0	2.4
1981	4.8	5.1	2.4
1982	2.5	3.6	.5
1983	4.4	4.1	NA
1984	5.5	4.2	NA

Key: PNI = Produced National Income
      IGP = Industrial Goods Production
      GNP = Gross National Income

Sources: PNI and IGP calculated from Statistisches Jahrbuch der DDR 1984 (Berlin: Staatsverlag der DDR, 1984); GNP taken from Thad Alton, Occasional Papers, Nos. 75 and 76.

Though we do not have the data necessary to calculate the GNP for the GDR, serious estimations have been made by Thad Alton and his associates and the results of their work have been included in the first table. As can be seen, Alton's figures are on the order of 2% below the official GDR growth rates (e.g., 2.4% GNP growth in 1981, as against 4.8% PNI). Even so, GDR annual GNP growth has probably averaged about 3% over the past 25 years, and on the order of 2.5% over the past decade--not a bad record, by any means. A fair assessment would conclude that substantial progress has been made on this dimension.

Simple growth in the size of an economy does not necessarily translate into improved living standards for the populace. It is therefore important to examine data showing trends in personal income and the availability of consumer goods. Though the GDR publishes many data here, their utility for our purposes is often limited or obscure. Nevertheless, some interesting conclusions can be drawn from the available data.

Table 2 shows annual and average annual increases in the average monthly income of workers in state enterprises, and similar increases in country-wide retail trade totals. These figures tell us something

TABLE 2: GDR MONTHLY INCOME AND RETAIL GROWTH RATES
(Aver. Annual %, 1961-80; Annual %, 1981-84)

	Aver. Monthly Income	Retail Trade
1961-1965	2.8	2.6
1966-1970	3.6	4.6
1971-1975	3.5	5.1
1976-1980	2.8	4.1
1981	1.6	2.5
1982	2.7	1.0
1983	1.3	.5
1984	NA	4.3

Source: Calculated from *Statistisches Jahrbuch der DDR 1984*.

about trends in consumer purchasing power and the totality of available goods at the sales counters.

As can be seen (taking the data at face value), the greatest increases were registered during the period 1966-1975, as was the case with Produced National Income, while the most recent decade shows much more modest growth rates (approximately 2% annually for the years 1981-1983). Moreover, the growth rates for income and retail trade were substantially lower for the entire period of 1965 to the present than were those for Produced National Income and Industrial Goods Production. Thus it is clear that personal consumption growth has not progressed as rapidly as the economy has grown; the gap has been on the order of 1.5-2.5% in most years.

It is also a fact that over the past several years prices for consumer goods have been raised substantially--by a variety of devices,[3] so that at least part of the increases in personal consumption have been negated by de facto inflation. The Deutsches Institut für Wirtschaftsforschung in West Berlin, certainly not the most critical observer of GDR economic affairs, has asserted that for at least some years in the 1980s the standard of living in the GDR may actually have declined, and that, at least until 1984, stagnation rather than progress has most likely obtained on this dimension.[4] At the same time, the preliminary figures for 1984 and 1985 at least suggest that the economy has "turned the corner," and that, after a time lag, the GDR consumer is now beginning to benefit from the successes of the 1980s, though at a rate still below that of the overall economy.[5]

Of course there are other indicators of improved welfare as well. For example, increased consumption of meat and other dietary delights, greater availability of durable consumer goods, more and better housing, and increased social services are all worth examining. For present purposes, it will suffice to show data only on durable consumer goods and social service payments, for in regard to the consumption of edibles the GDR has long shown a pattern which one would expect of an industrial society, and its housing program has been given ample attention elsewhere.[6] Suffice it to say that GDR citizens eat too much meat and butter, and that almost 125,000 new dwelling units have been constructed and an additional 50-75,000 units modernized annually since 1980.

As to durable consumer goods (see Table 3), the data show first of all that nearly every household must now have at least one washing machine, a television set, and a refrigerator. Presumably the same can be said of irons, radios, and other small electrical appliances. Any future progress here would have to be qualitative rather than quantitative. As to autos, the story of long waits between the time an order for one is placed and its delivery is well-known; for us the data are interesting because they show that ever more Trabbis are on the road, and that the rate of increase is not much lower now than it was in the 1970s.

TABLE 3: DURABLE CONSUMER GOODS IN THE GDR
(per 100 Households)

	Personal Autos	Refrigerators	Washing Machines	TV Sets
1955	.2	.4	.5	1.2
1960	3.2	6.1	6.2	18.5
1965	8.2	25.9	27.7	53.7
1970	15.6	56.4	53.6	73.6
1975	26.2	84.7	73.0	87.9
1980	38.1	100.8	84.4	105.0
1981	40.2	114.2	87.7	108.8
1982	42.1	118.8	90.8	111.4
1983	43.7	129.0	94.4	114.1

Source: Statistisches Jahrbuch der DDR 1984, p. 277.

Turning to social services, Tables 4 and 5 show (average) rates of increase in state subsidies and budget allocations. One must interpret these statistics cautiously, for they conceal substantial fluctuations from year to year, and their degree of correlation with an improved standard of living is substantially less than one-to-one. Yet, it is striking that they all show a similar pattern, with sharply lower annual growth rates in recent years. They seem to confirm that GDR citizens are generally only slightly better off now in economic terms than they were at the beginning of the current five-year plan.

Thus, progress here has not been noteworthy, or even comparatively good.

TABLE 4: SERVICES (SUBSIDIES) FROM SOCIAL FUNDS
(Average Annual and Annual Increases in %)

1972-1975	1976-1980	1981	1982	1983
9.1	7.2	10.6	4.8	1.5

Source: Calculated from <u>Statistisches Jahrbuch der DDR 1984</u>.

TABLE 5: BUDGET OUTLAYS FOR PUBLIC SERVICES
(Average Annual and Annual Increases in %)

	Education	Culture	Health	Social Security + Pensions
1961-65	3.8	4.3	2.9	4.2
1966-70	6.0	6.2	3.8	4.9
1971-75	7.4	12.8	6.1	7.4
1976-80	3.5	3.2	3.9	6.7
1981	7.8	6.2	5.1	.7
1982	3.3	2.3	9.3	2.9
1983	1.5	2.3	1.8	.1

Source: Calculated from <u>Statistisches Jahrbuch der DDR 1984</u>.

Another measure (or set of measures) of economic progress that is of particular importance in the case of the GDR centers on its foreign trade performance. The GDR, as a small and resource-poor country, is highly dependent upon foreign trade, both to obtain a variety of products essential to its most basic needs (e.g., petroleum), and to provide it with the advantages of economic specialization. At present, roughly 30% of its Produced National Income is exported, and a similar share of its domestic needs is met through imports.[7] Over time, the percentage has been rising.

Two types of progress here are at least very desirable and probably essential for the long-term economic well-being of the GDR. The first constitutes the engineering of an export surplus so that its net external debt, in favor of the West as well as the Soviet Union, can be reduced and ultimately eliminated. Its net indebtedness to the West increased from about $1 billion in 1970 to $10-11 billion by the end of 1982, while its cumulative trade imbalance vis-à-vis the USSR for the years 1975-1982 was on the order of over 14 billion Valuta Marks (or 25% of GDR-USSR total trade turnover for 1982).[8]

GDR economic statistics for foreign trade are probably the most inadequate of all. Nevertheless, they do show, as do the "mirror" statistics of its trading partners, that, since about 1981, the GDR has progressively improved its trade balance and has thus made a good beginning in solving its debt problem. The data in Table 6 show the trend through 1983.

It is worth noting, however, that the GDR's success in this endeavor has been achieved in good part through the strict control of its imports. As Table 6 shows, imports from the "Non-Socialist-World" were held roughly constant over the years 1981-1983, which in fact would translate into actual reductions in quantities purchased, for the figures are at current rather than constant prices. The data for imports from the "Socialist World" do show some increases, but they can mostly be accounted for by inflation. Thus we can see the high costs of economic progress in dealing with the problem of indebtedness, for the impact of reducing imports portends serious negative consequences for future economic performance.

The second type of progress sought in the foreign trade sector concerns the composition of GDR exports to the "Non-Socialist World," particularly to OECD countries. Ideally, the GDR would most importantly export finished products and industrial goods to the West, as it presently does within the CMEA. This would permit it to expand its production in sectors where its economic advantages are thought to be greatest, and it would also reduce the pressures to export the raw materials and semifinished goods it would prefer to further process or refine at home. The prestige factor is also involved: the GDR claims to be a mature industrialized country, and as such should have a foreign trade structure with other industrial states similar to those between Western industrialized states.

TABLE 6: GDR FOREIGN TRADE TOTALS FOR SELECTED YEARS
         (in Billion Valuta Marks)

	1970	1975	1980	1981	1982	1983
Socialist Countries						
Import	14.1	26.1	40.1	44.9	47.9	50.6
Export	14.2	25.7	39.7	43.6	48.0	54.0
Balance	.1	-.4	-.4	-1.3	.1	3.6
Non-Socialist Countries						
Import	6.2	13.1	22.9	22.1	22.0	25.6
Export	5.0	9.4	17.4	22.3	27.2	30.2
Balance	-1.2	-3.7	-5.5	.2	5.2	4.6
Total						
Import	20.4	39.3	63.0	67.0	69.9	76.2
Export	19.2	35.1	57.1	65.9	75.2	84.2
Balance	-1.2	-4.2	-5.9	-1.1	5.3	8.0

Source: Calculated from Statistisches Jahrbuch der DDR 1984.

For a variety of reasons, economic and political, GDR exports to the West have not featured industrial goods very prominently. As shown in Table 7, its sale of investment goods to the Federal Republic has remained constant over the past 25 years at about 10% of total value. Since that special trade relationship accounts for about 55-60% of total GDR trade with the West, the stagnant results are clearly disappointing.

As to trade with the other OECD countries,[9] the record is somewhat better, as shown in Table 8. For

TABLE 7: COMPOSITION OF GDR "EXPORTS" TO THE FEDERAL REPUBLIC (in %)

	RM + SG	IG	CG	FS	Total
1961-65	51.0	10.5	22.0	16.2	99.7
1966-70	30.9	13.6	29.4	25.6	99.5
1971-75	38.5	10.7	30.6	19.5	99.3
1976-80	47.3	10.6	27.1	14.3	99.3
1981	57.1	9.6	21.4	11.2	99.3
1982	55.8	10.0	23.0	10.6	99.4
1983	54.7	10.5	23.3	10.9	99.4

Key: RM + SG = Raw Materials and Semifinished Goods
 IG = Investment Goods
 CG = Consumer Goods
 FS = Foodstuffs

Source: Deutsches Institut für Wirtschaftsforschung, Handbuch DDR-Wirtschaft, 4th ed. (Reinbek: Rowohlt, 1984), Table 60, pp. 409-10.

1982, the last year for which I have data, the share of investment goods as a percentage of all GDR exports to that group of partners had risen from 29.7% (for the years 1975-1980) to 37%. If we "guesstimate" the overall trend here (i.e., for both inter-German and GDR-OECD trade),[10] we find that Investment Goods as a percentage of total GDR exports to the West increased by about 2.3% over the years 1975-1982. That may be progress, but just barely.

A final and perhaps decisive measure of progress in GDR economic performance is that of improvement in productivity or efficiency terms. GDR spokesmen would term this "intensification" or growth by "intensive means." Anyone who has more than a passing knowledge about current GDR economic performance and strategy is aware that intensification or economic growth through intensive means is seen there as the absolute requirement for the 1980s. The reasons for this view

TABLE 8: COMPOSITION OF GDR EXPORTS TO OECD COUNTRIES
(in %)

	RM + SG	IG	CG	FS	Total
1971-75	38.3	31.6	10.3	19.1	99.3
1976-80	35.5	29.7	9.7	26.6	99.5
1981	25.2	32.9	8.9	32.5	99.5
1982	24.7	37.0	9.5	28.4	99.6

Key: RM + SG = Raw Materials and Semifinished Goods
      IG = Investment Goods
      CG = Consumer Goods
      FS = Foodstuffs

Source: Handbuch DDR-Wirtschaft, Table 52, p. 401.

are not difficult to discern. In the early years of the GDR experiment, economic growth was possible by means of expanding the labor force, using ever larger quantities of material inputs, and increasing plant capacity and other capital investment. More recently, however, these means have become less and less an option, either because of absolute limits (as with labor) or increasing relative costs.

It is clear that, in a general crude sense, the GDR, since 1980, has made some real progress in achieving economic growth--even under adverse circumstances--through intensification. The growth rates since 1980 were achieved with virtually no increases in the use of material inputs, with only .8% annual increases in the labor force (.7% in industry), and with relatively constant investment levels. It is possible, however, to look a bit more closely at this crucial dimension, and, in doing so, to test the validity of the many claims of startling success made by numerous GDR luminaries.

The most positive results here seem to have been achieved in the more efficient use of material inputs. As shown in Table 9, the annual reduction rates in the use of energy and raw materials per unit value of output have nearly doubled since 1975: from 3.6%

for 1976-1979, to 6.2% for 1980-1983. Over the same period of time, electricity usage per unit output dropped at fairly constant rates (about 2.8-3% annually). Finally, total energy consumption for all purposes also showed a very favorable trend; whereas in 1976-1978 usage increased about 3% annually, it remained constant for the years 1979-1981, and actually dropped slightly in 1982 and 1983.

TABLE 9: ENERGY AND RAW MATERIALS USAGE
(Annual Increase in %)

A. Industry Only; Usage per Unit Output

	1976	1977	1978	1979	1980	1981	1982	1983
Electricity Only:	-2.3	-3.5	-2.4	-3.7	-3.8	-2.7	-2.7	-2.8
All Key Energy + Raw Materials:	-3.4	-2.4	-3.7	-5.1	-5.3	-5.6	-7.5	-6.5

B. Total Energy Consumption in the GDR

1976	1977	1978	1979	1980	1981	1982	1983
3.9	2.3	2.4	1.4	-1.2	.3	-1.7	-.1

Source: Statistisches Jahrbuch der DDR 1984, p. 151.

These figures must certainly be interpreted positively. Nevertheless, they are not necessarily indicators of scientific and technological progress, though they might be. That is, they could reflect either miniaturization in television sets or simply thinner shoe soles, weaker Weinbrand, or shorter skirts. Fortunately, we are able to use three additional measures which offer a somewhat better basis for making assessments of GDR productivity gains. They are labor productivity, capital productivity, and capital intensity.[11] Though each is a crude indicator by itself, collectively they can provide some signs of trends.

The results are shown in Table 10. The first point of note is that the rate of increase in labor productivity has dropped progressively from an average annual growth rate of 6.1% for the years 1966-1970, to 2.6% for 1982. The upturn in 1983 (to 3.4%) was still well below the years 1976-1980 (4.6%) when general economic performance was only mediocre. These figures are even more sobering when one recalls that the hours worked per week by GDR employees were reduced more significantly during the 1976-1980 period than they have been since, and when one also notes that increases in capital intensity remained relatively high at 5% or above until 1983. Clearly, much remains to be done here, and if we take the measure the government itself holds up as the goal (that labor productivity should increase at a rate higher than that of capital intensity), there is still a gap of 1% for 1983, which is larger than for any previous year, or five-year period, except for the year 1982.

TABLE 10: PRODUCTIVITY INCREASES
(in Annual or Average Annual %)

	Labor	Capital	Capital Intensity
1961-65	5.9	-.5	6.6
1966-70	6.1	1.6	4.8
1971-75	5.2	-.3	5.5
1976-80	4.6	-.4	5.2
1981	4.2	-1.2	5.0
1982	2.6	-2.9	5.0
1983	3.4	-1.3	4.4

Key:
Labor Productivity = PNI (Indust.) ÷ Indust. Workers
Capital Productiv. = PNI (Indust.) ÷ Fixed Assets
Capital Intensity = Fixed Assets ÷ Indust. Workers

Source: Statistisches Jahrbuch der DDR 1984, pp. 148f.

The second point is that capital productivity shows a similarly negative trend, from modest declines for the decade of the 1970s (i.e., -.3% growth for 1971-1975, and -.4% for 1976-1980) to -1.2% for 1981, -2.9% for 1982 and -1.3% for 1983). Though it may seem striking that absolute decreases in productivity have been recorded, the much more important point is that the rates have declined and are substantially inferior to those of the 1960s and 1970s.

Finally, we should note that 1983 shows notable improvement over 1982, and the preliminary results for 1984 suggest that the upward trend continued and continues to the present time. It may be that in retrospect, 1982 will appear as an exception and therefore not weigh so heavily in our assessments about GDR economic performance in the 1980s. For now, however, it is one of three or four years for which we have data.

So what are we to conclude about progress in the GDR economy? We seem to be faced with the problem of the half-filled glass of water: is it half-full or half-empty? On the one hand, Produced National Income has been growing, the trade balance has been improving, and some progress has been achieved toward intensive growth. On the other hand, consumer welfare has improved much more modestly, and productivity results continue to be rather disappointing.

I should like to conclude with a somewhat paradoxical statement and a prediction. In my view, the GDR economy has performed very well during the 1980s, better than we had any reason to expect. But that does not mean that the economic strategy for the 1980s has succeeded or will succeed, or that progress has been notable, for the circumstances under which the GDR has operated have been terribly severe. Sometimes athletes perform marvelously well and still lose; sometimes in crisis situations, "staying even" is a real achievement. The GDR has probably done a little better than "staying even" under very difficult circumstances, not all of which were of its own making, and doing so has been a considerable accomplishment.

As to the prediction: the GDR economy will probably perform as well in the short and middle run as it has in the recent past. But again, whether such a performance will result in significant progress is another question, for it is not at all likely that the GDR will join Western industrialized nations at the pinnacle of economic performance when it comes to product quality, technological innovation, or even per capita income. And such are the goals, whether stated or not, toward which progress must be made by the GDR economy.

Notes

1 For example, the Deutsches Institut für Wirtschaftsforschung (DIW) in West Berlin generally makes the more positive assessments of GDR economic performance, while the Forschungsstelle für Gesamtdeutsche Wirtschaftliche und Soziale Fragen, also in West Berlin, generally sees things in the GDR more negatively. The DIW publications on the GDR are to be found in its Wochenbericht, its Vierteljahrshefte zur Wirtschaftsforschung, and in special monographs. The Forschungsstelle publishes a monthly called FS Analysen.

2 One of the more extreme examples of this type of comparison is to be found in Erich Hanke, Ins nächste Jahrhundert: Was steht uns bevor? (Leipzig/Jena/Berlin: Urania, 1984). Hanke projects from the past to show that the USSR will overtake the USA in industrial production in 1986, or, if the US should avoid economic crisis, in 1993. Even more astonishing, he foresees the achievement of equal labor productivity by the Soviet Union in the year 2005. He is somewhat less specific about the GDR's progress in overtaking the Federal Republic. (See pp. 108ff.)

3 Probably the most significant method used to raise prices is minor product modification, combined with significant up-pricing.

4 See Wochenbericht, 50, No. 5 (1983), 54.

5 The annual fulfillment reports are published by the GDR in February of the following year. I have used the data from the Statistical Yearbooks instead because they measure growth in constant prices. The fulfillment reports, on the other hand, are in cur-

rent (and also rising) prices.

6 See Manfred Melzer, *Wohnungsbau und Wohnungsversorgung in beiden deutschen Staaten: ein Vergleich* (Berlin: Duncker und Humblot, 1983); also, "The GDR Housing Construction Program: Its Problems and Successes," in *Studies in GDR Culture and Society 5*, ed. Margy Gerber (Lanham: University Press of America, 1985), pp. 53-68.

7 It is impossible to be precise here because Produced National Income is measured in (domestic) Marks, while foreign trade activity is computed in Valuta Marks; the relative worth of the two types of Marks is not public knowledge, nor is it calculable.

8 The DIW's *Handbuch: DDR-Wirtschaft* sets the 1982 GDR hard currency debt at $8.39 billion. Jan Vanous, on the other hand, sets the corresponding figure at $11 billion. See "Macroeconomic Adjustment in Eastern Europe in 1981-83: Response to Western Credit Squeeze and Deteriorating Terms of Trade with the Soviet Union," in *East European Economics: Slow Growth in the 1980s*, published by the Joint Economic Committee of the U.S. Congress on October 28, 1985 (Washington: GPO).

9 OECD, or Organization of Economic Cooperation and Development, includes the 24 major Western industrialized countries.

10 The statistical problem with combining inter-German and GDR-OECD trade figures is that the Federal Republic keeps its inter-German trade figures separate from its foreign trade data, and categorizes the two differently as well.

11 These measures are not computed as one usually does in the West. For example, labor productivity would better be measured by calculating the hours it takes to produce a certain good or value. However, we do not have these data for the GDR. The crucial assumption here is that the data are no better or worse from year to year.

The GDR Economy between East and West:
Problems and Opportunities

Pieter A. Boot

The GDR has traditionally been thought of as Moscow's German ally, not only in view of its political-military position in the Warsaw Pact, but also because of its political-economic position in the Council of Mutual Economic Aid.[1] Geographically, on the other hand, the GDR is the most Western member of the East bloc countries. Not only is it situated on the border between East and West; its special relationship with the FRG represents a door to the West. And beyond these givens, the GDR has recently mounted a campaign to improve its political (and economic) relations with Western countries--not only with the Federal Republic, but with Austria, Italy, and other countries as well.

The aim of this paper is to explore and explain the position of the GDR economy between East and West and the GDR's recent economic policy in regard to both the CMEA and the West. I will first address the problems and the opportunities the GDR has with the CMEA and with the USSR; and secondly, the problems and opportunities of the GDR's economic relations with Western Europe. We will see that the GDR is trying to stimulate economic ties with both the West and the CMEA. The success of this policy is not guaranteed, however. My main argument will be that healthy economic relations with the West are needed to both solve the problems and realize the possibilities of cooperation within the CMEA, but that these same problems and possibilities restrict the development of good relations with the West.

Problems and Opportunities within the CMEA

The first problem is that the CMEA is in serious trouble. One can argue that this has always been the case, but new problems have arisen in recent years, or, to be more exact, illusions have eroded. After the 1969 Summit Council of the CMEA most East European leaders, including the GDR leadership, had hopes of attaining a "planned integration" of their economies by means of joint investment projects and coordinated, long-term planning of various products (e.g., agricultural and engineering goods, nuclear energy, turbines). This turned out to be somewhat optimistic, and in 1978 the so-called target approach was chosen, in which "major common output targets would be selected in response to forecasts of probable future demand levels for the region as a whole and individual countries."[2] This approach proved to be too ambitious as well, and in the end the coordination of production and the use of crucial primary goods remained.

This does not mean that the CMEA's record was entirely negative, but the East European leaders were left without an ideal which they could reasonably hope to realize in the near future. The 1984 Summit Council of the CMEA announced no new integration programs. And the fortieth session of the CMEA Council in Warsaw in June 1985 brought about no breakthroughs. In the months before this meeting all interested member states had tried to prepare a new "comprehensive program for scientific and technological development," but the long communiqué at the end of the meeting did not speak even of an agreement in principle. It mentioned, to be sure, an increase in mutual trade and the obligation of member states to export products of better quality, but such statements are nothing new.

Under the new Soviet party leader Gorbachev, the closer coordination of economic policies within the CMEA has become a major Soviet preoccupation. Confronted with the centrifugal tendencies of countries in the socialist bloc and the challenge of the American SDI program, it is pushing a compromise idea based on the Soviet concept of integration. Although the June 1985 session had decided to discuss "details of a combined technical development" in 1986, the prime ministers of the member states met again already in December 1985 to approve a comprehensive program on scientific and technical progress up to the year 2000.[3] This program is based on national concepts, which of course means that the Soviet scientific and technical complexes will in essence become the leading ones for the comprehensive program.[4] The program holds out the prospect of doubling productivity by the year 2000. Intense cooperation and extreme efforts will be necessary to accomplish this, given the "fast and in many instances startling development of modern science and technology."[5] Another reason is the impact of Western sanctions.[6]

The Comprehensive Program outlines cooperation in five directions:

- the introduction of electronics in all economic fields (one of the aims of the measures is to decrease the use of materials and energy, compared with national income, by 50-65%);

- complex automation, with the aim of speeding up (esp. auxiliary) production and transport and ensuring a more constant use of capital goods;

- the accelerated development of nuclear energy;

- the introduction of new materials and technologies;

- the accelerated development of biotechnology.[7]

These directions are not new. They were announced in general terms by GDR economists some years ago.[8] Several steps have already been taken. In the electronics industry a rather effective system of concentration has been implemented whereby the participating countries carve out suitable niches for themselves without totally destructive infighting. In biotechnology things are developing rapidly. The Soviet Union now has what is perhaps the largest microbiological industry in the world.[9] GDR and Soviet scientists and engineers cooperate closely in single-cell protein production (which may become an important source of cattle fodder). Striking, too, are the directions of useful cooperation which are not mentioned, for example, a conceived program in telecommunications that would go well beyond simply producing standardized data communications hardware, or cooperation in agriculture, which was one of the priorities declared at the June 1984 summit.[10]

Problems and Opportunities vis-à-vis the USSR

The GDR's crucial CMEA partner is of course the USSR. Its foreign trade turnover with the USSR exceeds the turnover with the other socialist partners altogether (39% compared with 27% in 1984). Of all exported GDR engineering goods, 70% go to the USSR; 40% of the GDR patents granted to foreign countries have been granted to the USSR.[11] An important interaction exists between Soviet pure research and GDR applied research.

Using the analogy of relations between developed and developing countries, Abonyi and Sylvain speak of a socialist dependency, "a relational inequality of one way domination" between the USSR and East European countries.[12] The GDR leadership, like the leadership of the other East European countries, is dependent on the Soviet Communist Party. This does not mean that the GDR (or the other Soviet bloc countries) has no room to manoeuvre; one cannot use a deterministic model in which everything depends on Moscow. Much depends on the strategy chosen by the leaders; their margins will be broader when the Soviet leadership is divided, as seems to have been the case in 1984, and narrower when a strong leader comes to power.

In its economic relations with the USSR, four issues are important for the GDR: energy, prices, technology, and trade balances. First, large and constant oil deliveries to the GDR from the USSR are not guaranteed. The USSR faces an augmented domestic demand and a stagnation in energy production (oil production decreased in 1984; coal production has stagnated for several years; only gas production is increasing). This led the Soviet Union to reduce its oil exports to the GDR by 10% in 1984. Since then, however, Soviet oil deliveries have been stable and promise to have the same volume in the period 1986-90.

After the first international oil crisis in 1973 Soviet oil prices remained relatively low. A lively debate has been held on the amount of the USSR's "implicit subsidies" to the CMEA countries and, especially, to the GDR.[13] This has changed in the meantime: while world-market oil prices have decreased in recent years, CMEA energy prices will reach a maximum in 1986. In general, however, one can say that the GDR buys its oil cheap in the USSR, given the export prices it gets--although this advantage was greater in the period 1975-83 than it is today. A host of non-price commercial conditions (like credits, forced re-exports, scarce hard and abundant soft goods) play a role also. And GDR investment contributions (e.g., investment in Soviet pipelines) are a substitute for a sharp rise in prices. However, no Western experts doubt that, in purely commercial terms, GDR-Soviet trade is favorable to the East Germans, when compared with world-market conditions. This has nothing to do with a Soviet "blueprint" for CMEA subsidization; it is due to the development of relative world-market prices in the 1970s and the specific monetary relations within the CMEA.

In the foregoing section, the increasing importance of GDR technology deliveries to the Soviet Union was mentioned. According to computations I made in an earlier study,[14] the percentage of these technology-intensive exports (e.g., engineering goods, instruments, optical goods, and some chemical products) rose constantly in the 1970s (from 33.4% in 1970 and 48.9% in 1975 to 57.2% in 1980). Judging by the recently signed GDR/Soviet "Long-term Trade Agreement," this share will rise even further.[15] This strengthens the position of the GDR in the CMEA. On the other hand, it will require maximum effort on the part of the GDR, for it entails a high level of investment and the import of advanced technology from the West (see next section). The technology deliveries to the USSR are thus both a problem and an opportunity for the GDR.

A final problem is the trade balance with the USSR. In the 1970s the USSR permitted the GDR considerable trade deficits, the second highest in the CMEA after Poland. In the early 1980s these deficits reached their zenith, and the Soviet Union pressed the GDR to reduce them, especially by increasing its exports. The result was a rapid reduction of the imbalance--from 643 million TrR (foreign trade ruble) in 1982 to 202 million in 1983 and 114 million in 1984--and a probable surplus in 1985.[16] In the years 1981-84 GDR exports to the USSR increased by 44%, while the deliveries to the other socialist partners grew by only 23%.[17] The total GDR debt to the USSR is some 15 billion Valuta Marks and is to be paid back, for the most part, within the next five years.

In summary, one can say that the GDR's economic problems with the USSR are not negligible. Even after the energy prices begin to decrease in 1986, a continuing trade surplus will still be necessary to pay off the debt, and technical cooperation will require imports from the West.

Problems and Opportunities vis-à-vis the West

In contrast to the 1960s, GDR leaders are now convinced that the CMEA cannot solve all their problems. Attempts to improve the functioning of the CMEA will go on, but the expectations are modest, and solutions are being sought elsewhere, i.e., in economic relations with the West. The GDR does not want its CMEA trade to preclude trade with Western countries. It is well aware of what has been called "the increasing dollar content of ruble exports and the increasing ruble content of Western exports."[18] Healthy trade with Western countries is a condition for an ongoing increase in intra-CMEA exports because of the heightened share of Western components in exports to other socialist countries (and vice versa).

The volume of GDR trade with the industrialized Western countries represents about 27% of its total foreign trade (1983 figures). At first glance, this would appear to be an average share, but in reality it is rather low, given the GDR's proximity to important Western centers.[19] On the other hand, the GDR is the only East European country whose share of exports to industrialized market economies rose in the period 1980-84.

In the late 1970s and early 1980s the trade deficit and mounting debts in convertible currency were probably the main concerns of GDR economic leaders. These problems have lessened in the meantime. After chalking up great deficits in the late 1970s, the GDR began to develop a steady surplus: 5.20 billion Valuta Marks in 1982; 4.69 billion VM in 1983; and 3.85 billion VM in 1984.[20] The surplus in convertible currency (or awarded loans) with developing market economies has remained steady at about 2 billion VM; the rest was gained in trade with the developed

Western countries.

This impressive record was made possible by the restriction of imports (esp. in the period 1980-82) and the increasing of exports. The surplus has enabled the GDR to reduce its convertible currency debts. Net loans from Western banks, for example, dropped from 8.6 billion US-dollars in June 1981 to 3.4 billion dollars in June 1985. The GDR's total net Western debt, including inter-German trade credits (Swing) and supplier credit is 3-3.5 billion dollars higher.

The debt reduction did not significantly affect the GDR's economic growth rate, which remained superior not only to that of many of its CMEA partners but to that of many Western countries as well. Private consumption rose an average 3.2% from 1981-85, according to the (albeit inflated) official figures. Investments, on the other hand, stagnated, and the GDR faces massive future capital investment requirements if it is to remain internationally competitive. The crucial question is whether or not the GDR has been competitive in Western markets in recent years. Did the GDR succeed in ensuring a continuous delivery of modern technology, or did these imports simply serve to decrease temporary shortages? Has the GDR economy been able to export goods of greater quality, or has it been forced to deliver low-priced products and raw materials which are in scant supply at home?

Investigating the composition of GDR trade with the West is not as easy as one might think, since the GDR does not publish detailed figures, and Western sources ordinarily exclude trade with the Federal Republic in their calculations. The FRG gives statistics, but classifies them in a different way. I have attempted to put the pieces together.

The GDR imports mainly agricultural products (24% of the total in 1982) and processed industrial goods (56%) from OECD members, and exports chemicals, manufactured goods, machinery and transport equipment, as well as increasing amounts of oil and oil products to the industrialized West (4.7% of exports in 1978; 29.2% in 1982). The above figures do not include the Federal Republic. Oil products are exported mainly to the Scandinavian countries; chemical goods, to Yugoslavia and the EC countries; engineering goods and transport equipment, mainly to Yugoslavia, Greece, and Spain.

One asks how the energy-poor GDR can export oil. The main reason is the GDR's energy-saving policy. An indication of this is given by the figures on consumption of "important materials and energy," which, compared with the national product, decreased by an average 4% annually between 1976-80 and an average of 6.2% between 1981-84.[21] The Deutsches Institut für Wirtschaftsforschung in West Berlin estimates that GDR oil consumption decreased from 15.1 million tons in 1980 to 9.6. million in 1984.[22]

Generally speaking, the GDR exports raw materials and semi-manufactured articles to the most developed Western countries, and more sophisticated products to states in an earlier stage of development, where competition is less severe. For example, Yugoslavia receives about 20% of the GDR's OECD exports, but more than 40% of its machinery and almost 100% of its office machinery exports to the West.[23]

Inter-German trade makes up about one-half of the GDR's trade with Western developed countries. Agricultural imports from the FRG are less important than those from other OECD countries, but the GDR imports relatively more oil and oil products, iron, steel, and non-ferrous metals from the FRG. This is partly due to favorable finishing possibilities: the GDR buys oil (in 1983, for a total of 676 million VM) and non-ferrous metals from the FRG, and sells processed petroleum (in 1983, for 1573 million VM) and finished metal products.[24] GDR exports to the FRG include relatively more agricultural goods (food for West Berlin, for example) and industrial consumer goods. Table 1 shows GDR trade with the OECD and the FRG combined.

In 1975 the GDR had a relatively sophisticated export profile, with a healthy share of final products (e.g., clothing, furniture) and machinery. Although the share of engineering goods in its Western imports was somewhat higher than in its exports, it was still extremely low compared with that of other CMEA countries (e.g., Czechoslovakia, 38.8%; Poland, 39.8% of OECD imports in 1975). In 1982 GDR exports showed a high level of raw materials. This can be explained only in part by deliveries of pro-

TABLE 1: FOREIGN TRADE OF THE GDR TO ALL OECD COUNTRIES (including Inter-German Trade), Product Groups in % of Total Foreign Trade

	GDR Export		GDR Import	
	1975	1982	1975	1982
Agricultural Products and Beverages	17.0	7.2	12.5	18.8
Mineral Fuels	10.2	30.0	3.5	7.2
Other Raw Materials	9.6	7.9	5.9	5.0
Chemicals	13.0	13.1	21.0	15.4
Manufactured Goods	14.8	14.4	26.8	22.2
Machinery and Transport Equipment	15.7	13.0	22.9	18.4
Miscellaneous Manufactured Products	22.2	9.1	6.1	8.4

Source: Computed from OECD, Trade by Commodities, Vols. 1 and 2 (Paris, 1977, 1984) and Statistisches Bundesamt, Warenverkehr mit der DDR und Berlin (Ost), December 1976, 1983, recomputed to SITC code.

cessed petroleum to West Berlin, since that share of exported petroleum and petroleum products to other OECD countries was high (29.2%) as well (caused by deliveries to Scandinavia). The share of machinery and final goods decreased dramatically. The decreasing percentage of imported engineering goods indicates that the GDR was less in a position to import Western technology than before--due to the necessity of buying agricultural goods (mostly in the form of feed for animals).

The above observations confirm the conclusions drawn by Andras Inotai in his study of the CMEA's share of the FRG's import market in the second half of the 1970s:[25] namely, that, although the CMEA countries, with the GDR in the forefront, launched an export offensive in the hope of reducing their trade balance deficits, their relative market position deteriorated. In this study of the market shares of eighteen countries (six CMEA members, four Southern European countries, and eight newly industrializing countries), the GDR accounted for 16.3% of the manufactured products delivered to the FRG in 1975, but only 11.8% in 1980. The decrease in the market share of end products was just as extensive: from 11.3% to 8.3% (p. 93).

All of this implies, on the one hand, that the GDR is doing rather badly in its trade with Western countries, and, on the other, that trade with the West is important, especially for reducing existing shortages and in the interest of re-export. The imports of (technically advanced) engineering goods are relatively low and are targeted for special priority projects. This situation strengthens a "dual structure" of GDR industry. A few enterprises are oriented toward Western markets; the imported technology trickles down only partially to the other branches of industry. This is an unfavorable situation.

Most enterprises are more involved with CMEA economic integration than with ongoing contacts with the West. Of course, they want to import from the West; however, the technical, organizational, and behavioral skills, knowledge, and connections at the enterprise level have exerted an increasing influence on actual enterprise management--which is aimed at integration within the CMEA, not with the West. There is a strong, more or less spontaneous tendency to maintain and expand these structures. Even if GDR policymakers try to induce a more Western-oriented policy, one has to appreciate the realities at the micro-level.

This means that the "administrative reform," although undoubtedly having positive results, cannot be judged as complete. This "reform" aims at improvement of the organizational structure of planning and management (constitution of relatively large enterprises--<u>Kombinate</u>--with responsibilities in the field of research, production, marketing, and foreign trade), improvement of planning methods (balances, norms, control) and of the system of economic levers (prices, wages, other monetary incentives). Given certain conditions--esp. a foreign-trade policy facilitating imports of modern technology on all levels of industrial production--learning processes with positive consequences for the efficiency of socialist economic planning within the GDR system's own functional limits should indeed be possible. One may include that this condition and the success of the reform are mutually dependent. In order to keep its position of most advanced East European economy, the GDR has both to increase its trade with Western countries--especially its imports of technology--and to go on with its "administrative reforms."

Assessment

In this article, I analyzed some problems and opportunities of the GDR's international economic situation and policies. The basic position is one of socialist dependence. Within the CMEA, the problems are the stagnation in cooperation and the Soviet pressure to deliver more goods, especially products of higher quality. Opportunities manifest themselves in the apparent Soviet need to modernize its economy--a situation in which the GDR will be a very useful partner--and in the new Soviet leadership, which seems to grant its socialist partners more room for manoeuvring within their economic policy and system. The Gorbachev leadership looks approvingly at the recent organizational changes in the GDR economic system, above all at the Kombinate and the relatively weighted system of success indicators and norms for material and energy use.26

Now that it has realized a foreign trade surplus in convertible currency for several years, and greatly reduced its net debt, the GDR may be in a position to halt the ongoing loss of market shares in manufactured products in the West. It should be possible to consolidate this position by means of continued organizational change and a balanced policy of investments and technology imports for priority projects. Given the fact that the market economies are experiencing a wave of technical change, competition on export markets in the West will be severe. If the deterioration of the structure of foreign trade with Western countries can be halted, this would be an impressive success for the SED leadership. My assessment is that, partly because of the new accents in foreign policy, this possibility cannot be excluded.

Notes

¹ This is documented, for example, in the title of David Childs's new book Moscow's German Ally (London: Allen & Unwin, 1983).

² Jozef M. van Brabant, "The Global Recession and Socialist Economic Integration in the 1980s," Osteuropa Wirtschaft, 29, No. 3 (1984), 207.

³ The extraordinary meeting had been announced at the 117th session of the CMEA Executive Council in November. Quick approval was important, as the program was to be part of the new five-year plans.

⁴ "Koordiniertes Handeln zur Schaffung modernster Technik," Neues Deutschland, 17 December 1985, p. 5.

⁵ Boris Ladygin, "CMEA: Focus on Technological Teamwork," New Times, No. 52 (1985), p. 7.

⁶ Vladimir Obchinnikov, "Mezhdunarodnoe Obozrenie," Pravda, 29 December 1985, p. 4; and Hans-Georg Haupt and Renate Neumann, "Ökonomische Interessen der Mitgliedsländer des RGW im Prozeß der sozialistischen ökonomischen Integration," Wirtschaftswissenschaft, 33, No. 2 (1985), 163. Although some observers hold the view that Western sanctions have not been very effective, Mitchell Kellman disagrees in his recent study, "The Crumbling Embargo? Evidence of OECD Cohesiveness from the Composition of Manufactured Exports to the USSR," Comparative Economic Studies, 27, No. 2 (1985), 66.

⁷ "Komplexprogramm des wissenschaftlich-technischen Fortschritts der Mitgliedsländer des RGW bis zum Jahre 2000," Neues Deutschland, 19 December 1985, pp. 6-7.

⁸ Christa Luft, "Zur Durchsetzung von Intensivierungsmaßstäben bei der Teilnahme der Kombinate an der sozialistischen ökonomischen Integration," Wirtschaftswissenschaft, 32, No. 2 (1984), 171-77.

⁹ Anthony Rimmington, Issues in Soviet Biotechnology: The Case of Single-Cell Protein, paper read at the NATO colloquium, Brussels, April 1985,

pp. 1 and 8.

10 The Romanian party leader Ceauşescu has charged that the Comprehensive Program deviates from the priorities declared at the June 1984 summit. Cf. Radio Free Europe/Radio Liberty, Situation Report Romania, No. 1, 10 January 1986, p. 1.

11 Gaspar Graziani, Comecon, domination et dépendences (Paris: F. Maspero, 1982), p. 124.

12 Arpad Abonyi and Ivan J. Sylvain, "CMEA Integration and Policy Options for Eastern Europe: A Development Strategy of Dependent States," Journal of Common Market Studies, 16, No. 2 (1977), 142.

13 Cf. Josef C. Brada, "Soviet Subsidization of Eastern Europe: The Primacy of Economics over Politics?" Journal of Comparative Economics, 9, No. 1 (1985), 80-92.

14 Pieter A. Boot, Economische planning in de DDR (Utrecht: Elinkwijk, 1984), p. 167.

15 "Langfristiges Abkommen im Handel mit der UdSSR 1986-90," Neues Deutschland, 28/29 December 1985, p. 1.

16 These are Soviet figures. See, e.g., Christian Meier, "Sowjetische Außenwirtschaft 1983/84 unter außenpolitischer Restriktion?" in Berichte des Bundesinstituts für ostwissenschaftliche und internationale Studien, No. 24 (June, 1985), p. 34.

17 Computed from Statistisches Taschenbuch der Deutschen Demokratischen Republik (Berlin: Staatsverlag der DDR, 1985), p. 100, and United Nations, Monthly Bulletin of Statistics, July 1985, p. xxxvii.

18 See Laszlo Csaba, "The Role of CMEA in the World Economy in the 1980s," The ACES Bulletin, 26, Nos. 2-3 (1984), 2.

19 Pieter A. Boot, "European Trade Patterns, The Case of European Community, EFTA and CMEA," in Andrzej Stepniak and Michael R. Will, Structural Changes in the European Community (Gdansk/Saarbrücken: Uniwersitet Gdanski/Universität des Saarlandes, 1985), pp. 279-94.

20 Statisches Taschenbuch der DDR 1985, p. 100.

21 Statistisches Taschenbuch der DDR 1985, p. 54.

22 Deutsches Institut für Wirtschaftsforschung, "Der Primärenergieverbrauch in der DDR und seine Struktur," Wochenbericht, 20 December 1985, p. 579.

23 More extensively discussed in Pieter A. Boot, "The German Democratic Republic between East and West: The Margins of Socialist Dependencia," Research Memorandum, No. 8508 (University of Amsterdam, 1985), pp. 11-16, 21.

24 I will not treat here additional advantages of inner-German economic relations such as annual payments of the FRG Treasury (1-1.3 billion DM annually), profit from Intershop and Intertank, obligatory money exchange for tourists, interest-free Swing credits, West German tax breaks for imports from the GDR, and so on. Cf. the East German economist Hermann von Berg, Die Analyse: Die Europäische Gemeinschaft - das Zukunftsmodell für Ost und West? (Cologne: Bund Verlag, 1985), pp. 194-97.

25 Andras Inotai, The FRG'S Import Market for Manufactured Products: CMEA; Southern European and Developing Countries (Budapest: Hungarian Scientific Council for World Economy, 1982).

26 Heinz Timmermann, "Gorbatschow zeigt außenpolitisches Profil. Kurskorrekturen oder Konzeptionswandel?" Berichte des Bundesinstituts für ostwissenschaftliche und internationale Studien, No. 38 (October 1985), pp. 13, 45 (footnote 64).

The Perception of the United States
in GDR Policy and Society:
Preconditions and Possibilities for Dialogue

Karl-Heinz Röder

I would like to address three aspects of the image of the United States in GDR policy and society: 1) the view of the role of the United States in the fight against fascism; 2) the increasing interest in U.S. society within the GDR population; and 3) the realization of the necessity of dialogue and collaboration with the United States.

On April 12, 1985, the fortieth anniversary of the death of Franklin D. Roosevelt, an article lauding Roosevelt as one of the architects of the anti-Hitler coalition appeared in Neues Deutschland.[1] The article quotes from Roosevelt's undelivered last speech, which he had intended to give on Jefferson Day, April 13, 1945, the day after his sudden death. The speech, which may be considered his legacy, contains the following passages:

> The once powerful, malignant Nazi state is crumbling. . . . But the mere conquest of our enemies is not enough. . . . Today we are faced with the preeminent fact that, if civilization is to survive, we must cultivate the science of human relationships-- the ability of all peoples, of all kinds, to live together and work together, in the same world, at peace.[2]

As Roosevelt stressed, the greatest challenge to be met by the postwar generation was the establishing of a lasting peace. Was this an utopian idea then? And, in view of the wars waged in the last forty years and the current tense international situation, is it even more utopian today?

We cannot close our eyes to reality: the postwar situation, especially as regards Allied relations, did not develop as Roosevelt and many other Americans, and millions of people in the Soviet Union and elsewhere had hoped. At the same time, however, the idea of coming closer together--despite the differing economic and political systems--and of warding off existential dangers--today it is the possibility of nuclear holocaust--is very alive and is gaining momentum.

I was reminded of this recently when, on the occasion of the fortieth anniversary of the link-up of U.S. and Soviet troops at the Elbe, I spoke with American veterans who, as members of the 9th U.S. Army, had been present in Torgau in April 1945. I also met with U.S. Air Force veterans who had been imprisoned in a P.O.W. camp near Barth/Rostock during the war and who had been liberated by the Soviets. The camp had contained 7,500 members of the U.S. Air Force and 1,500 members of the British RAF.

I spoke with these veterans about the reception they had been given by the GDR population forty years later. They reported that the people they had met while traveling in the GDR--people with differing levels of education and from various social groups--had all emphasized their appreciation of the United States' contribution to the fight against fascism and the ending of World War II and had indicated their desire for improved relations, especially between the United States and the Soviet Union. Not a few of the veterans, incidentally, changed their view of the GDR as the result of their visit.

A second factor contributing to the image of the United States as an antifascist force is the fact that a number of well-known Germans, notably writers and artists who took up residence in the GDR after the war, had found refuge in the United States in the period from 1933 to 1945.[3] Moreover, a number of books and films with antifascist and antiwar themes by American authors have appeared in the GDR, and American plays with these themes have been performed. The role the United States played in the liberation of the German people from fascism is thus still remembered in the GDR. The antifascist efforts of the United States have informed its image in the GDR. This is however only one aspect of the image, which is highly complex and contradictory. This leads me to my second point.

In recent years the GDR population has shown much greater interest in receiving serious and detailed information about the society, economy, and policies of the United States. Living in a country that is strategically located in Central Europe, on the border between the Eastern and Western social and political systems and military alliances, the GDR people are highly sensitive to political events. They clearly realize that the development of the world in general and of Europe in particular is decisively determined by the United States, as the major political, economic, and military power of the capitalist world. And they are also well aware of the fact that the United States, as one of the Siegermächte of WW II, is present in the Federal Republic and West Berlin. The heightened international tensions following the NATO Doppelbeschluß, the stationing of a new generation of missiles in Western Europe, and the American decision to develop the SDI project have led to the need for more information about U.S. policies, including not only SDI but also Central America, in particular Nicaragua, and the withdrawal of the United States from UNESCO. These developments are regarded with dismay in the GDR and, in contrast to the antifascist activities outlined above, influence the image of the United States in a negative way.

The international tensions and the danger of nuclear war have led to the realization of the necessity of dialogue and collaboration with the United States, the third point of my paper. The GDR is of course well aware that bilateral relations with the United States cannot be considered independently of the state of affairs between the United States and the Soviet Union. This does not mean, however, that the GDR has to sit by until the relations between the United States and the Soviet Union have improved. The GDR does not share the view that it is up to the big powers alone, as the only countries with the necessary means at their disposal, to improve international relations; the world situation depends largely, of course, on them, but it does not depend only on them.

The smaller nations of the world can and must play an active role in improving the international situation and reducing the danger of war.

Given this fact, the GDR is presently pursuing a very active "Socialist Europe policy." Its major elements, which can also be applied to the GDR's policy toward the United States, are the following:

- The GDR attaches great importance to dialogue between the leaders of the socialist and capitalist countries.[4] Such dialogue is currently being conducted--in some cases, intensively--between the GDR and Denmark, Norway, Sweden, and Finland, and with Austria, Italy, France, Great Britain, and, last but not least, the Federal Republic. Political dialogue on a high level with the United States, which was interrupted in 1984, has also been resumed. Such dialogue is constructive and fruitful if both sides respect each other and accept as a given the membership of each side in their respective alliances. Progress in bilateral relations is evidenced in the cooperation of the GDR with a number of West European countries. Such cooperation contributes to the improving of the general political climate between East and West.

- Dialogue is seen as a means of preparing the way for the expansion of relations in economic and trade matters, as well as in other areas such as environmental protection. That progress has been made here can be seen in the improved economic and trade relations between the GDR and West European countries.[5]

- A decisive factor in the improving of international relations is the further development of contact in the areas of science and culture. More knowledge about the history, culture, and language of the countries involved is essential for better political relations.

For some time now, the GDR has been using the term "coalition of reason and realism" in its political declarations.[6] This term expresses the idea that it is possible to bring about the active cooperation of all forces that are determined to avert the danger of nuclear war and to safeguard peace. Essential prerequisites are that the partners not try to impose their own ideology or their own political standpoint upon the other, and that political consensus not be made the precondition for cooperation in the question of world peace. The coalition of reason and realism means that all differences, whether political, ideological, or religious, be put aside in the interest of peace: even ideological and political opponents have a common interest in survival.

I feel that this is a practicable platform for solving the most important global problem facing mankind today. In the fact that it overcomes differences in its effort to combat the common enemy, nuclear war, the coalition of reason and realism contains the idea of the anti-Hitler coalition, which worked together, in spite of national differences, to defeat fascism. The anti-Hitler coalition was successful. It goes without saying that the world we live in today is not that of forty years ago. The problems of our world require different solutions. A coalition of reason and realism can find such new solutions in regard to peace, and this is the main problem on our minds today.

Notes

[1] Klaus Steiniger, "Einer der Architekten der Antihitlerkoalition," Neues Deutschland, 12 April 1985, p. 6.

[2] Franklin D. Roosevelt, "'Let Us Move Forward with Strong and Active Faith' - Undelivered Address Prepared for Jefferson Day. April 13, 1945," in The Public Papers and Addresses of Franklin D. Roosevelt. 1944-45 Volume, ed. Samuel I. Rosenman (New York: Harper & Brothers, 1950), p. 615.

[3] See Eike Middell, Exil in den USA, Volume III of Kunst und Literatur im antifaschistischen Exil 1933-1945 (Leipzig: Reclam, 1983).

[4] Erich Honecker, Zu einigen aktuellen Fragen der Innen- und Außenpolitik der DDR (Berlin: Dietz, 1984).

[5] See Statistisches Jahrbuch der DDR 1984 (Berlin: Staatsverlag der DDR, 1984), pp. 87ff.

⁶ Erich Honecker, "Wir wirken für weltweite Koalition der Vernunft," <u>Neues Deutschland</u>, 21 February 1985, p. 1.

Untertänigkeit: Heritage and Tradition

Dietrich Staritz

This paper addresses a problem which at best has only been touched upon in the literature dealing with the development of the GDR.[1] Answers will be sought to the question of what has happened in the GDR to that legacy of German history which--intentionally using an old word--I will call Untertänigkeit. I am referring to the syndrome of authoritarian (authority-fixated) attitudes, mind sets, and patterns of interaction which, although they developed differently in various layers of society, became common modes of behavior for the majority of Germans, independent of social status. There is a general consensus of opinion about their origin and consolidation in social history: they are the result of the specific circumstances of the development of German society, the consequence of a modernization process which for the most part was urged by the authorities and only seldom--and always for short periods of time--determined by democratic principles.[2] There is more disagreement over the view that this German road into the industrial age facilitated the establishment of national socialism in German society, that it contributed to the fact that the Nazi Volksgemeinschaft was able to develop strong contours between 1933 and 1945, and furthered the acceptance of the leader-follower principle in not insignificant portions of German society. In my opinion, these considerations are not implausible.[3]

It is not clear in which concrete attitudes and orientations of the Germans in the Soviet Zone of Occupation after the war this legacy of German history is reflected. No specific studies on the Soviet Zone are available. There is little reason however to assume that the attitudes of these Germans were essentially different from those ascertained in Germans living in the Western zones. One must of course take into consideration that a large percentage of the actively engaged national socialists left the Soviet Zone already before the Red Army entered the area, and that the revolutionary changes in the social structure which were immediately introduced in the East were not without influence on the attitudes of the people. Still, it is unlikely that these developments evoked a sudden change in concepts and patterns of orientation, and thus it seems permissible to use data which were collected in West Germany as indicators of an all-German consciousness, that is, an East German consciousness as well. The data quoted here are from the American Zone of Occupation and were gathered by means of opinion polls taken by the U.S. Military Administration.[4]

This material is startling at first glance (only): it shows a clear continuity of authoritarian views and--albeit in a refracted form--the continuing close relationship of the Germans to defeated fascism. This is discernible above all in the answers to questions which were devised to ascertain past political activity and the degree of current dismay: in 1946, 87% of those interviewed admitted that they had lost confidence in Hitler only at the end of the war; at the same time, 74% denied any personal responsibility for the war and blamed--as the majority of this generation still does today--Hitler alone, against whose regime, according to just under half of the people questioned, the "little" people couldn't have done anything anyway, and against whom, in the view of another 40%, nothing should have been done, since it was the duty of all citizens to obey the orders of the State.

The apparent contradiction of these answers can undoubtedly be partially attributed to the circumstances of the canvassing, which encouraged deception rather than candor, and partly to the stubbornness with which many Germans (probably as a means of explaining their having adhered to fascism for twelve years) clung to the belief that national socialism was a "good" idea which had been "badly carried out." In twelve surveys undertaken between November 1945 and December 1946, an average 47% of the people questioned shared this view; 12% had no opinion, and only 41% considered national socialism to be entirely negative. This attitude corresponded conversely to the Germans' interest in democracy, which--with the material want of the postwar period--had decreased even more: 60% preferred a government that offered economic security and good prospects for personal gain over one that guaranteed free elections, freedom of speech, freedom of the press, etc.[5]

Findings such as these correlate in their tendency with the impression formulated by representatives of the working-class parties in the Soviet Zone after 1945 when they warned against using membership in the Nazi party or its organizations as the sole measure of German involvement in national socialism, or when they, as the KPD leadership did, repeatedly spoke of the "verschüttete Klassenbewußtsein" of the workers,[6] i.e., presumed that the fascist ideology had deeply penetrated the German people, even the working class. But if the Western powers optimistically banked on formal reeducation programs--at first and not for long--and then on the long-term persuasive powers of democratic institutions and procedures, leaving the socio-economic basis of traditional Untertänigkeit and of German fascism untouched, the Soviet Union and the German communists one-sidedly trusted in socio-economic change and, for the most part, paid no heed to democracy training in democratic institutions.

The reason for this is probably primarily to be found in the concept of revolutionary change that the Soviet Military Administration and the German communists followed. Here a political understanding dominated that relied more on the effectiveness of disciplined organization than on the direct participation of individuals or democratically structured collectives in the decision-making processes; the overcoming of subordination was at best a long-range goal of the transformation and not a method of the process of transformation. On the contrary, according to the dominant view, which had been vigorously shaped by Stalin, the overcoming of the old class society was possible only with the compliant integration of individuals and their collectives in the--ideally--monolithic party, with their acceptance of a vanguard of the revolution and its leadership. The old type of subordination, which had evolved culturally and socially, been trained, and traditionally expected, was replaced by the call to acquiesce in a subordination that was legitimized by revolutionary theory, whereby the old internalized subordination was to encourage the acceptance of the new.

To be sure, intensive participation training would scarcely have been possible with a less rigid concept either. After all, the occupying power, the antifascist parties and organizations, and the administrative apparatus had reason to fear that broad democratic participation could be misused by those who had made the Nazi regime possible or even supported it up to the very end. This concern undoubtedly figured in their reliance on traditional Untertänigkeit.

In many regards it thus appears as if authoritarian attitudes were used--nolens, volens--to stabilize the new social order and its political system, as if they had not only been preserved more or less intact but been able to gain in strength and establish themselves on an even broader social basis. It is true of course that the often cited "activists of the first hour," party cadres, old labor union functionaries or previously unorganized workers sometimes broke out of the old Untertänigkeit--for example, when they expropriated or took over abandoned enterprises in 1945. And it is true that the farm workers and small farmers lost some of their submissiveness when they parcelled out the land that had been expropriated in the course of the (decreed) Bodenreform. However, their self-determination training took place with the benevolent approval of a new government which--especially after the introduction of central planning (1948)--demanded strictest subordination and discipline, dissolved the autonomous representative bodies of the workers (the Betriebsräte)--thus putting an end to the wide-reaching Mitbestimmung in industry, and transformed the labor unions into mass organizations of Stalinist design.[7]

The majority of East Germans had experienced the post-fascist new beginning very differently than the few who were politically active. After all, in 1946 more than half of all the Germans in the Soviet Zone belonged to those age groups which, with their voting behavior, had brought Hitler to power. In 1950, more than two-thirds of the GDR population was still made up of Germans who had been socialized either in the

Empire, the Weimar Republic, or the Third Reich.[8] Only a third of the population, the generation of young people up to the age of twenty, could be expected to accept the new order relatively quickly. To be sure, only somewhat less than half of the older population had voted for Hitler; the others--especially in the SPD and KPD strongholds of Middle Germany and Berlin--had remained loyal to their parties. All the same, this did not prevent the feeling of <u>Volksgemeinschaft</u> that developed in the period between 1933 and the end of the war and which made it possible to continue the war until 1945.

The necessity of minimizing the influence of the older generation in the restructuring of society, in particular of isolating those who had directly participated in the Nazi system, was perceived by all antifascists, and, in view of the power structure in existence after 1945, it wasn't difficult to do so. In a measure backed by the Soviet Military Administration, the old propertied elite had been dispossessed and stripped of its power. The denazification process prevented the access of Nazi sympathizers to the State, administrative offices, and public culture. By 1948 more than half a million people had been removed from the schools, courts, economic and all other management positions. They either joined the work force or went West.

The new administrative apparatus was by and large comprised of young people who ordinarily came from socially and culturally underprivileged sections of society. They became the heart of the new bureaucracy, as did the new teachers, people's judges and people's prosecuting attornies, the new enterprise managers, etc. The positions of authority were given to members of the Unity Party, and by 1948 nearly 44% of the employees in all branches of the state apparatus were members of the SED, which was being transformed at the time into a party of the new type. In regard to the social origins of the government employees, the working class was dominant (46.4%). Only about a fourth came from the middle class (salaried personnel, just over 14%; civil servant families, a little over 11%). This tendency continued in the 1950s, but then levelled off.[9]

For the majority of the new state servants the social climb produced very few immediate advantages.

Professional civil service and its privileges had been abolished; salaries usually ranged lower than those in industry; and appreciable social prestige was only seldom attached to the new position. Chances for advancement and attaining power were predicated above all on political Akkuratesse and discipline, that is, on qualities which had essentially determined the old political culture and which now helped safeguard the new order's ability to function. Submissiveness, punctilious execution of instructions, and strict orderliness were required once again; the climate of bureaucracy was fostered. This process took place, to be sure, under different political circumstances and on a new social basis, but it produced a comparable mentality: submissive, wary of responsibility, and power-conscious—and this more widespread than ever before in Germany, for now it dominated not only the classic public services but also the entire economy.

The education reform supported this process. Its goal was the "overcoming of the education privilege" of the old upper layers of society and the educating of a "new intelligentsia," which was to be trained to meet the demands of the increasingly hierarchical structures; the new intelligentsia was to be derived especially from the classes of the workers and peasants. The preferential admission of workers' and peasants' children to institutions of higher learning was in keeping with this goal. Special courses which were to prepare young adults from these backgrounds for study at the university—the subsequent Arbeiter- und Bauernfakultäten (ABF)—were introduced already in 1946. Graduates of this program made up a large part of the cadre reservoir from which the cadres were drawn who, since the 1960s, have increasingly dominated the political and cultural "command bridges." They, like the other "upward bound" members (Aufsteiger) of the revolutionary phase, reflect and inform the social profile and the social mentality of GDR society, its social and political style. Although the reality is far removed from the programmatically fixed ideal of the domination of workers and peasants, people from this milieu administer policy on all levels of the hierarchy, and the sum of their old values and new experiences determines the climate of the GDR just as do the political and ideological goals proclaimed by the core of the power elite at the head of the Party and State, who--incidentally--for the most part themselves stem from these same social classes.[10]

This climate was strengthened by a paternalistic cadre policy. Since the 1950s long-range cadre plans have been prepared in all enterprises and offices; all willing and able employees are to commit themselves in cadre conversations to individualized, precise "Kaderperspektiven," in which levels of qualification (e.g., courses, additional training, university study), trial assignments, future places of work, and areas of activity are agreed upon. This authoritarian-solicitous personnel policy produced results: for one thing, it laid the foundation for a feeling of social security, fostered the traditional Aufsteigermentalität, strengthened the orientation toward consumerism, and, last but not least, helped to legitimize--at least partially--the bureaucratic climate of administration. At the same time, however, it led in many cases to a renouncing of individual initiative and to adaptation to prescribed behavioral patterns and career models, i.e., to renewed practice in submissiveness.[11]

Comparable tendencies shaped the efforts of the SED in regard to its authority in cultural matters in the GDR. Although, since the 1960s--in the shadow of the Wall--the Party and State had concentrated on the economic efficiency of GDR society, they didn't want to relinquish their cultural leadership role: thus the Party--in keeping with its self-definition as vanguard--continued its lecturing and its attempts to inject its consciousness into the population; as a means of monitoring its success, it appealed to the population to profess its political consciousness and not only demonstrate it in the sphere of production. The result--or so it appears--was a deepening of the already manifest split of social consciousness into a public and a private sphere: not because the demands of the SED grew, but rather because--after August 1961--the possibility of criticizing GDR society by leaving it no longer existed and this critical potential now saw itself obliged to make its way in the social climate of the GDR--if necessary, in free spaces (Freiräume), self-made but tolerated by the authorities, between the official norms and individual orientations. The result was an authoritarian convention that apparently determines the political and social behavior of many GDR citizens up to this very day: the demands of the multiform authority are to be complied with, and are treated as legitimate, provided that they require nothing more than formal compliance. And vice versa: the State, whose representatives themselves for the most part grew up with this convention, accepts this formality as content, as long as the plan, the order, and thus it itself sustains no injury. The private "niche," identified by Günter Gaus in the 1970s as an essential sphere for GDR Germans, was the consequence of this "as if" clause of the social contract.

Only since the beginning of the 1970s has there seemed to be a chance to gradually dissolve this handed-down submissiveness and GDR-specific authoritarianism. For one thing, those age groups that grew up during fascism or during the revolutionary phase of GDR society are now in the minority: people over fifty represent only a scant one-eighth of the GDR population today; those born after August 13, 1961, on the other hand, almost one-third. In comparison with the older population, they are much less influenced by the repressive and lean postwar period, are accustomed to the net of social services and a certain standard of living, and they seem more willing to question tradition than are their elders. The norms that were internalized by the generations of their parents and grandparents and the traditional way of living are no longer a matter-of-course for them. Many seem open to alternatives, and a few attempt to realize them--in spite of the warnings of the Party and the State, and the admonitions of the majority.

Secondly, since the worldwide recognition of the GDR, and since its participation in the discussions on security and cooperation, the international conventions on the granting and honoring of human rights have gained influence in the GDR. Since Honecker's signing of the Helsinki Treaty in 1975, they have served many people as a means of legitimizing their demands on the State. This happens most frequently, to be sure, in regard to the freedom to travel, i.e., to move to the West, and strongly challenges the SED's perception of its role in society. In the long run, however, this challenge may lead to a respecting of international norms and thus contribute to the liberalizing of the authoritarian norms that are presently valid.

Thirdly--finally and most importantly, the SED, under pressure to make good its leadership claim, has had to adapt itself to GDR society, in spite of its efforts to preserve its political exclusivity. Thus the vanguard, the self-named cultural innovator and Hegemon, is influenced by a political culture which the SED itself could only partially shape and in which for that reason old values and new GDR-specific values, concepts, and behavioral patterns come together. The Party is thus succumbing to a tendency toward (in the view of the Party leadership, a better word would probably be: the danger of) becoming politically and culturally a part of society. This, too, has undoubtedly contributed to the fact that some perspectives have been redefined and become more commonplace. Instead of the earlier dominance of extensive theoretical designs, "real socialism" now stands in the foreground. And that means pragmatic, concretely measurable goals, as they clearly appear in the concept and practice of the unity of economic and social policy. This in turn increases the need for consultation with society rather than the need for bureaucratic-authoritarian administration. It strengthens (objectively) the necessity of societal participation, at least in economic and social policy decisions. The expertise of the mass organizations (e.g., the unions), production units (enterprises, LPGs), production collectives (brigades), and individuals (e.g., academicians) is needed now more than ever before.

The question whether this objective constraint to increase consultation and participation can actually be socially productive, whether it leads to broader forms of participation and helps decrease submissiveness and authoritarianism--two central elements of the old Untertänigkeit--must go unanswered here. For one thing, it depends on whether the Party leaders perceive in these developments a threat to their leadership claim; it also depends on the extent to which society demands consultation and participation, and in which spheres. At present it seems that the Party, now as ever, is inclined to be cautious; and in spite of the incipient rethinking of values, it also appears as if the interest of society in the achievements of the socialist welfare state and in the freedom to travel is still stronger than its interest in participatory goods. Both attitudes reflect Erbe and Tradition--to use GDR terms, i.e., the legacies of the authoritarian old society and traditions of the socialist new society: the inheritance of a power structure which was tailored to the vanguard and the tradition of the political culture which it helped form. The chances of a swift overcoming of Untertänigkeit--or once again formulated in Marxist-Leninist terms--of the formation of universally developed personalities are, seen in this way, not very good.

Translated by Margy Gerber

Notes

[1] Most recently by: Rolf Badstübner, "Die Geschichte der DDR unter dem Aspekt von Erbe und Tradition," Zeitschrift für Geschichtswissenschaft, 33, No. 3 (1985), 339ff; Helmut Hanke and Thomas Koch, "Zum Problem der kulturellen Identität. Anregungen für eine Diskussion," Weimarer Beiträge, 31, No. 8 (1985), 1237ff.

[2] Cf. e.g., Ralf Dahrendorf, Gesellschaft und Demokratie in Deutschland (Munich: Piper, 1968), passim.

[3] See, for example, Martin and Sylvia Greiffenhagen, Ein schwieriges Vaterland. Zur politischen Kultur Deutschlands (Frankfurt: Fischer, 1981), pp. 74ff.

[4] Public Opinion in Occupied Germany. The OMGUS-Surveys, 1945-1949, ed. Anna J. Merrit and Richard L. Merrit (Urbana/Chicago/London: University of Illinois Press, 1970).

[5] The question about the quality of national socialism was repeatedly asked in later opinion polls. In 1977, 26% of those polled agreed to the statement: "National socialism was basically a good idea which was badly carried out"; 72% disagreed. In the age group over 50, the relation was 32% to 66%; 2% of the entire sample as well as of the sub-group refused to answer. Cf. Martin and Sylvia Greiffenhagen, p. 334.

⁶ Cf., for example, "Aufruf des ZK der KPD vom 11. Juni 1945," in Um ein antifaschistisch-demokratisches Deutschland. Dokumente aus den Jahren 1945-1949, ed. Ministerium für Auswärtige Angelegenheiten der DDR, Ministerium für Auswärtige Angelegenheiten der UdSSR (Berlin: Staatsverlag der DDR, 1968), pp. 56ff.

⁷ Cf. Dietrich Staritz, Sozialismus in einem halben Lande. Zur Programmatik und Politik der KPD/SED in der Phase der antifaschistisch-demokratischen Umwälzung in der DDR (Berlin: Klaus Wagenbach, 1976), pp. 102ff.

⁸ Cf. Dietrich Staritz, Geschichte der DDR 1945-1985 (Frankfurt/Main: Suhrkamp, 1985), pp. 54ff.

⁹ In 1950, 48% of the government personnel and 54.3% of the "local state officials" came from working-class backgrounds. Cf. Klassenkampf. Tradition. Sozialismus. Von den Anfängen der Geschichte des deutschen Volkes bis zur Gestaltung der entwickelten sozialistischen Gesellschaft in der Deutschen Demokratischen Republik. Grundriß, ed. Zentralinstitut für Geschichte der Akademie der Wissenschaften der DDR (Berlin: Deutscher Verlag der Wissenschaften, 1978), p. 558. As can be learned from internal Party material, the portion of working-class cadres on the local level reached 61.1% in 1958. Among the new personnel, however, only one out of three came from a working-class background at that time. Cf. "Rede von Anton Plenikowski vor der 36. Tagung des SED-Zentralkomitees (10./11. Juni 1958)," copy at the Arbeitsbereich Geschichte und Politik der DDR of the University of Mannheim.

¹⁰ It would be an underestimation of the influence of the old society to assume that those Aufsteiger from the old lower class who were traditionally oriented towards the values of middle-class culture and whose political socialization had been strongly influenced by the unquestionably authoritarian structures of the social democratic and communist workers' movement brought to their new positions completely new, less authority-fixated attitudes.

¹¹ Once, in 1963, this was even addressed by the SED. In a communiqué on youth policy the Politbüro assumed an almost revolutionary stance when it re-

leased the following: "Solche jungen Menschen, die aus Angst vor einer 'übergeordneten' Meinung unehrlich und heuchlerisch geworden sind, die ihr eigenes Denken zurückhalten und stets auf Anweisungen von oben warten, sich äußerlich anpassen, werden . . . in der Praxis kaum Großes leisten können, weil dort schöpferische und kämpferische Sozialisten, aber keine kleinmütigen Seelen, Streber und Karrieristen gebraucht werden." (<u>Dokumente</u> <u>der</u> <u>SED</u>, Vol. IX [Berlin: Dietz, 1965], 679ff.)

The Abrogation of Politics: Pseudo-Marxism
in the GDR and Eastern Europe

Lyman H. Legters

Toward the end of his life, Engels made a fascinating admission about the work that he and his intellectual partner had done and left behind as their joint legacy. He conceded that politics had probably been slighted in their theoretical work, explaining this by pointing out that, in the context of prevailing 19th century discussion, it had seemed more vital to insist upon the primacy of underlying economic realities.[1]

Many students of Marxism have noted the neglect of political considerations and of the very processes of politics in the corpus of theory that Marx generated; and some have been led to rather strange conjectures about Marxism and politics in an attempt to close the gap. It comes at least as an item of refreshing candor to find Engels acknowledging this neglect. Any sound intellectual historian would of course appreciate such an acknowledgment that theoretical offerings are only understandable with reference to what the debate was all about and, as a correlative, accept the notion that texts, so examined, do not automatically yield final or absolute rank-ordering of the components of a body of theory. By the same token, any student of 19th century social movements might well be relieved by the admission, for it narrows what is otherwise a rather glaring gulf between what Marx and Engels wrote and what they practiced in their highly political, indeed insistently political, careers. All of us who till the contemporary academic vineyard could also record a measure of chagrin at the same time, for we are thrown back upon a procedure, legitimate and necessary though it is, that is among the slipperiest with which we have to work, that of extrapolating authentic meanings from a combination of what was stated, what was left unsaid, and what was merely implied.

The simplest and most direct way of approaching the problem from within Marxist theory is to note the unwritten volume of <u>Das Kapital</u>, adumbrated in the <u>Grundrisse</u> and mentioned in correspondence, that was to deal with the state.[2] Like other unwritten volumes, the ones that were to treat the world market and international trade, this omission left an opening for subsequent generations of Marxian theorists to fill. One can acknowledge straightaway that one gap has been filled more satisfactorily than the other. The extension of theory to cover the world market took the form of the theories of imperialism that emerged in the second generation, associated with Lenin, Luxemburg, Hilferding, and Bukharin. These contributions unquestionably took into account matters that Marx could not have anticipated, but they were conceived and presented in perfectly acceptable Marxist fashion as contributions coherent with the main body of Marxist theory. Moreover, as Lenin made quite explicit in his study of imperialism, they were also theories of international politics.

Work by Marxists on the state and politics has not served in equal measure to close the other gap. Gramsci is sometimes named as the author of a Marxian theory of politics, and the recognition is well-deserved even though it has not precipitated a development of theory commensurate with the investigations of imperialism. Still, like the others, Gramsci's contribution is an extension of Marxian thought intended to cohere with original Marxism even while taking new experience into account.

These fairly unstartling observations point to the misplaced conjectures and anticipations, mentioned at the outset, associated with the neglect that Engels admitted. It would seem that some observers imagine that if there were a full-blown Marxian theory of politics it would stand in parallel relationship to the critique of capitalism as a sort of companion edifice.[3] It is perhaps understandable that students of politics might wish for such an arrangement that would give parallel weight to their subject. But it is of course a profound misapprehension of Marx's project. We have no way of stating with any confidence what might have appeared in those missing volumes. We can be quite sure, however, that they would not have altered the underlying structure of Marx's theory. In that sense, it is appropriate to view Gramsci's and Lenin's extensions of theory as surrogates for things that Marx did not quite get to (needless to add, one can also criticize them as inadequate performances) but not to regard them as independent, self-contained bodies of theory that fall short of meeting expectations--misplaced ones, as I am contending--of a politics equatable with the original economics.

Indeed, this is already a distorted and distorting way of talking about Marxism, for it was a single project, not a set of compartmental investigations, some of which came closer than others to completion. Accordingly, it is altogether permissible--unless one detects outright inconsistencies--to search Marx's works and his conduct for the germs of a politics that is presumed to be coherent with his overall theory and critique of capitalism.

From the actions of Marx and Engels in their own time and from the strategic recommendations they offered to their followers, we can derive a good deal of illumination about the weight they did assign to politics, at least the bourgeois or prerevolutionary politics with which they had to deal. The list of demands with which Marx was armed when he reached Cologne in 1848 displays a definite inventory of what the working class might reasonably strive for politically within the framework of a capitalist social order.[4] And the quite similar catalogue contained in the <u>Manifesto</u> suggests not only the political content of revolutionary praxis but also, quite significantly I think, a putative continuity of political aspiration from the prerevolutionary class struggle to the inauguration of a socialist politics in the postrevolutionary period.

There can be no serious question about the centrality that Marx assigned, precisely in this passage from bourgeois to postrevolutionary politics, to the abolition of private property. Along with that, I would want to argue, went a plain expectation that democratization and socialization must be pursued concurrently. But the point I want to stress in the present context is rather the hint of continuity, the suggestion that a revolutionary seizure of power, watershed event though it certainly is, does not necessarily imply a radical discontinuity in the content of any appropriate political program. On the contrary, the overwhelming weight of Marx's view of history implies that a revolutionary class will begin to develop and seek to implement elements of its program in the prerevolutionary phase.

The notion with which we seem to be more familiar, the one that may, for many, be an intuitively more fitting one for a proletarian victory and smashing of the bourgeois state, is that postrevolutionary politics should prove to be altogether different in kind from bourgeois politics. Lenin's insistent distinction between the phoniness of bourgeois democracy and the authentic democracy that socialism would bring in its train matches up rather tidily with our intuitive assignment of qualitative difference between prerevolutionary and postrevolutionary politics. And Marx, it must be acknowledged, had his visionary moods when he was lured or lulled into a portrayal of politics, as manifestation of class struggle, giving way to some kind of harmonious administrative routine once class struggle is truly eliminated during the transition to socialism and classlessness.

An intermediate or transitional period was foreseen of course, both by Marx and by his followers, the primary political feature of which would be in effect a prolongation of oppositional politics in the form of eliminating the class enemy with its threat of counterrevolution. Beyond that, politics would consist of the working out, within the proletarian party, of policies and decisions surrounding the introduction of a socialist program. The harshest theoretical view of internal party politics available, Lenin's democratic centralism, foresaw inner-party discussion followed by loyal adherence to the policies adopted.[5]

Leaving aside the conflict-ridden arena of international politics, wherein the first instances of revolutionary triumph would be counterposed to a hostile capitalist world, the prevailing attitudes toward postrevolutionary politics came perilously close to reducing politics to administration. Beyond the point when counterrevolution was effectively stamped out, a positive politics tended to be viewed largely, in the Soviet case, in terms of inner-party deliberation on the introduction of socialism. (The persistence of a purely oppositional view of politics may shed some light, incidentally, on the need to depict all revivals of true political clash as counterrevolutionary tendencies rather than as straightforward disagreements among the revolutionary leaders; the possibility of, and indeed the need for, a different kind of postrevolutionary politics is what I shall be arguing for a bit further on.)

To follow this line of thinking a bit further, it appears that this conception, what I call the denial of politics, has been the dominant one in Eastern Europe since 1917. Whatever the reasons--whether purely symbolic, or because the Leninist theory of prerevolutionary organization required it, or merely because prerevolutionary politics in that region lacked even the limited malleability that Marx and Engels could discern in the Europe of 1848 or 1871 or 1875--the reigning view seems to have been that any of the characteristics of political clash or conflict would be a reproach to the attempt to introduce socialism, perhaps an actual impediment, perhaps a sign of failure, but in any case a sign of insufficient concentration on the task at hand.

This train of thought brings us quickly to the German Democratic Republic, if only because, within this reigning conception of postrevolutionary politics, it has been one of the great success stories of the postwar world. Someday we are going to recognize Walter Ulbricht as a master of this denial of politics, conceivably Honecker as well (notwithstanding the great differences between his style and that of his predecessor). I think it is very important for Western observers to recognize not just that Eastern Germany as an occupied territory was especially susceptible to Soviet dictation but also that the government installed there after World War II registered an admirable technical command of the procedures implicit in this view of politics: since 1953 no other ruling party of the Soviet bloc has outstripped the GDR in its ability to contain political tensions within its own ranks, to offer requisite elbowroom for potentially explosive social forces without risking public outburst or upheaval, to seek out its own distinctive path without threatening the senior alliance partner. No mean achievement.

Other things being equal (as they never are), I would prefer to emphasize this triumph of skill and technique over the notions of obedience and even servility that are habitually invoked to account for the position of the GDR within the Soviet orbit. In a world imprinted by Henry Kissinger's or Zbigniew Brzezinski's style of moral assessment, technical accomplishment according to established rules is not to be minimized.

But I have used a harsh term--pseudo-Marxism--in my title, and it requires me to retrace my steps to the point at which I first intimated that a denial of politics might be a false understanding of Marxist teaching. If you examine my usage thus far, you will discover that I am construing politics as the clash and working out <u>in public</u> of discrepant interests irrespective of the mode of production or property relations prevailing in a given social order. I am quite willing to grant the Marxian anticipation that a postrevolutionary politics can, and perhaps ought to, look quite different from the class-based politics of the prerevolutionary period. I will also grant that a plebiscitary democracy, practiced from the first day of the transfer of power to a working-class party, would be a fairly certain recipe for defeat. What I will not grant, invoking all of the available clues from a decidedly non-utopian original Marxism, is the indefinite postponement of democracy or, more pointedly stated with reference to the revolution and/or surrogates for revolution in Eastern Europe, the assumption that the revolutionary event, in addition to suppressing the class interests of the old order, creates homogeneity or univocality within a now ruling proletariat.

The silent element in this discussion so far has been the assumption that interests can only be class interests. No Marxist would argue that class interests ought to figure indefinitely in postrevolutionary public affairs. But are there no other kinds? Did Marx really imagine that the elimination of class interests, problematical as that is in itself, would equal the establishment of universal harmony, the reduction of public affairs to administrative routine? I have admitted that he sometimes spoke that way. But did he really suppose that the dialectic of history would be superseded once class divisions were fully eradicated, that history would come to a standstill? I don't think so. I think the most we can say is that interests of another sort, tensions and dislocations arising elsewhere than in issues of class, would become the stuff of human affairs. And that implies a continuation of politics. It also validates the Marxian emphasis, already cited, on democracy as an essential accompaniment of socialism. For democracy, self-governance, remains the requisite procedure, even if socialism does succeed in eliminating class struggle and class interest, for resolving whatever remains of disparate interest in a complex society.

The technical accomplishment of managing conflict and social tension, behind the scenes, as it were, becomes, then, approximately the same kind of feat whether it is done under capitalism or under socialism. The conspicuous difference is that the latter seeks, and the former eschews, Marxian precepts as a mode of validation or legitimation. Whether Marx's anticipations were right or wrong is of course arguable. The point is that his admittedly fragmentary vision of the postrevolutionary society, and his not so fragmentary sense of how a postrevolutionary praxis might measure the suitability of governing policies and programs, offer a starting point for the sharpest possible criticism of postrevolutionary history.[6]

Since the absence of politics (in the special sense that I am urging), or its failure in most of the cases where it has reasserted itself, has been the norm in Eastern Europe's postrevolutionary record, the pattern hardly needs elaboration here. It may, however, be useful to instance some of the resurgences of politics in the postwar period, in addition to acknowledging the differing interests that show through the Soviet intraparty debates of the 1920s. The most dramatic by far was of course the Prague Spring of 1968 when the "human face" of a revived democracy so well expressed both a return to defensible Marxism and an intolerable challenge to the Soviet model. A more enduring example, albeit one that is periodically disfigured by repressive measures, is the Yugoslav evolution since its break with the Soviet Union. Church-party relations in Poland offer an instance in which politics revived within a limited sector of a society's public sphere, to be followed by an episode--the Solidarity movement--in which the whole society was engulfed by politics. And the gradual relaxation in Hungary after 1956 exemplifies another manner in which politics was readmitted on a limited scale. Space does not permit any sort of documentation of correlation, but I should like to suggest a striking "coincidence": the times and places that disclose a renewal of politics in the sense of recognizing a play of discrepant interests in public are also the times and places in which a serious Marxism has surfaced. The philosophers of Czechoslovak democracy, the Praxis group in Yugoslavia, the so-called Lukács school in Hungary, and the independent (though repressed) voices of critical Marxism in Poland--these correspond remarkably to the isolated revivals of politics.[7] Without a documented analysis one cannot fully establish a relationship-- the surface possibility that a revival of politics has permitted a renewal of serious Marxist thought or the more intriguing possibility that Marxist intellectual renewal has helped to revive politics--but I suspect a mutual interplay and reinforcement.

What seems, then, to count as emblems of "success" in the terms of centrally managed socialism turn out in a Marxian critical perspective to be prophylaxis against the introduction of authentic participation and democratic handling of public affairs. Therewith the irony is complete: what a genuine Marxian viewpoint would regard as signs of longterm viability and constructive movement through the transitional stages are precisely the developments that the reigning party has arrested in the interests of a smooth management of centrally directed and controlled change.

In that light, I would propose that the real Marxian challenge to the GDR and its neighbors has not been answered because the issue has not been properly framed: the task is not to supplant politics with routine administration, but rather to invent an appropriate politics.

Notes

¹ From a letter to J. Bloch, dated 21/22 September 1890. The exact wording is as follows: "Marx and I are ourselves partly to blame for the fact that the younger people sometimes lay more stress on the economic side than is due to it. We had to emphasize the main principle, vis-à-vis our adversaries, who denied it, and we had not always the time, the place or the opportunity to allow the other elements involved in the interaction to come into their rights." As quoted in Ralph Miliband, Marxism and Politics (Oxford: Oxford University Press, 1977), pp. 9-10.

² For a discussion of Marx's Aufbauplan, see Martin Nicolaus's Foreword to his translation of the Grundrisse (London: Allen Lane, 1973), pp. 52ff.

³ Commenting upon the fragmentary sources in original Marxism for a theory of politics, Miliband cautions "that the most careful textual scrutiny will not yield a smooth, harmonious, consistent, and unproblematic Marxist political theory" (p. 5). This absence of a straightforward approach to politics may help to account for the tendency of critics, especially the more hostile ones, to take Soviet political practice as acceptable evidence for what ought to count as Marxian political theory.

⁴ Reprinted from the original in Heinrich Billstein and Karl Obermann, Marx in Köln (Cologne: Pahl-Rugenstein, 1983), pp. 156-57.

⁵ Although it came to hand too late to figure in my paper, a similar line of argumentation about Lenin and politics can be found in A. J. Polan, Lenin and the End of Politics (London: Methuen, 1984).

⁶ The central philosophical point of this argument is nowhere better stated than in Carol C. Gould, Marx's Social Ontology (Cambridge: Harvard University Press, 1978) where the possibility of deriving norms from Marx's corpus of theory is well established. On the historical plane, one needs only to point to the voluminous body of explicitly Marxian criticism directed by East European theorists at their own societies. One of the best examples would be George Konrád and Ivan Szelényi, The Intellectuals on the Road to

<u>Class Power</u> (New York: Harcourt Brace Jovanovich, 1979); for the GDR, Rudolf Bahro, <u>Die Alternative</u> (Cologne/Frankfurt: Europäische Verlagsanstalt, 1977) comes immediately to mind.

⁷ Again, the literature is already immense—in English and German. All I can do is mention a few of the most pertinent authors of the critical commentary: Marković and Stojanović from Yugoslavia, Agnes Heller and Konrád from Hungary, Bauman and Kołakowski from Poland, Kosík and Svitak from Czechoslovakia. The GDR contribution tends to be weaker, but we are all familiar with the voice of Robert Havemann, <u>Ein deutscher Kommunist</u> (Reinbek: Rowohlt, 1978).

Degradation or Humanization?
Work and Scientific-Technical Progress in the GDR

Mike Dennis

Contemporary labor process debates in the West have focused once more on the extent to which work in capitalism is gradually degraded, as many elements of knowledge, responsibility, and judgment are taken from the worker and tasks become programmed, routinized, and specialized. The worker lacks an interest in his job and comes to experience a sense of meaninglessness and unimportance. Degradation is attributed, in varying degrees, to technology and management strategies of control. The microprocessor, for example, permits the incorporation of a wide range of human skills and intelligence into machines and facilitates the standardization and fragmentation of tasks in the office. I wish to examine, mainly on the basis of GDR research undertaken in the 1970s and early 1980s, whether similar symptoms of the degradation of work can be traced in the GDR and how humanization of work schemes--job enrichment, job enlargement, semi-autonomous work groups--have been utilized to modify the rigid technical division of labor and to create "progressive" work contents.[1]

At its Tenth Congress in 1981 the SED announced its economic strategy for the 1980s, which was to enable the GDR to maintain stable economic growth in the face of a mounting cumulative debt to the OECD countries, higher energy prices (especially for Soviet oil imports), rising military expenditure, and the more costly extraction of domestic raw materials such as lignite. The central place in this strategy is occupied by the further modernization and automation of production techniques through the application of microelectronics, electronic data processing, and industrial robots. Forty to forty-five thousand robots are to be in operation by the end of the 1981-1985 Plan and, although the GDR cannot dispense with imported Western technology, a determined effort is being made to build up the country's own microelectronics industry, especially the production of microelectronic components. The question now is whether complex mechanization and automation can be reconciled with the humanization of work. Do numerically controlled (NC) and computer numerically controlled (CNC) machines, industrial robots, visual display terminals, and continuous processing reduce workers to mere spectators or minders of machines? Or do they release workers for more creative, stimulating, and satisfying work tasks?

It has, of course, long been recognized by labor scientists in the GDR that serious problems are associated with the introduction of automated techniques: the creation of boring, repetitive jobs, the underutilization of qualifications, and the persistence of disparities between manual and intellectual work. The growing awareness of such problems led to a dampening of those high expectations, in the 1960s, of the scientific-technical revolution. The accession to power of Honecker coincided with a more sober approach to the possibilities of science and technology. The concept of scientific-technical revolution was played down and that of scientific-technical progress emphasized. And as Hartmut Zimmermann has observed, "the scientific-technical revolution was officially interpreted as a long-term and even self-contradictory process. . . ."[2]

Although it is now accepted that work problems similar to those in capitalism also prevail in socialism, at least while the material base is being laid for the establishment of communism, the GDR still adheres to an optimistic long-term view of the interrelationship between work and technology: first, in communist society, towards which the GDR is supposed to be progressing, the traditional division of labor will be dissolved and creative work will become possible for everyone; and secondly, even in actually existing socialism itself, capitalist techniques or forms may be used to promote the goals of socialism. This position rests on the view, as expressed by Fritz Macher, professor at the University of Dresden, that "Technology is neither good nor bad, neither progressive nor reactionary."³

In other words, there is no single technologically determined consequence. Good and bad uses depend on the way technology is designed and applied, and on the socio-economic system. To quote Weidig and Prager:

> Generalising one can and must say that the scientific-technological development influences, promotes, accelerates, or delays only such economic and social processes which are rooted in the relevant socioeconomic system of the society.⁴

The GDR's transformation of ownership relations, from private to social, is therefore decisive for the application of technology. According to this interpretation, so-called capitalist techniques or forms acquire a new social content with the creation of socialist economic relations. On the other hand, the humanization of work schemes such as job enlargement, job enrichment, and semi-autonomous work groups introduced in the FRG and elsewhere in the 1970s cannot resolve the fundamental contradictions of the capitalist mode of production. Work cannot be organized in a humanistic way in a system characterized by private ownership and by exploitation and antagonistic relations. However, whereas the "new" job designs are basically devices to enhance profits and maintain the capitalist system, they can, or so it is argued, be utilized to counteract monotony, job dissatisfaction, and labor turnover in a socialist society. I should like to focus first on these problems before seeking to evaluate the GDR's own humanization of work schemes.

Although the level of qualification of the GDR work force is extremely impressive, a considerable proportion of the workers (about 25%) does not make full use of its qualifications: 12% of all university cadres and 22% of all foremen (Meister), according to a 1981 report, were employed in jobs which did not match their level of qualification; 18% of all skilled workers were employed as semi-skilled or unskilled labor.⁵ This mismatch may occur as a result of inadequate vocational guidance, family considerations, and other factors not directly related to the workplace. However, and this is central to our inquiry, while a higher technological stage may produce a growing need for higher levels of qualification, it may also, especially in the stage of partial automation, downgrade certain tasks.

The 1973 Sociological Investigation (conducted between 1970 and 1972 at three large enterprises and then repeated one year later at twenty-seven enterprises)[6] permits an insight into this problem (see Table 1). The highest proportion of skilled workers was located in the stage of partial mechanization; a decline in the ratio occurred in the next two stages and then there was a partial recovery in full automation. Partial automation was characterized by the highest percentage of semi-skilled and partly skilled workers. In short, higher qualifications and higher stages of technology do not necessarily coincide.

TABLE 1: TECHNOLOGICAL STAGES AND THE QUALIFICATIONS OF PRODUCTION WORKERS (in percentages)

	Un-skilled	Semi-skilled	Partly skilled	Skilled
Manual	16	19	9	56
Partial mechanization	5	12	5	78
Full mechanization	10	20	8	62
Partial automation	4	24	14	58
Full automation	7	17	7	69

Source: Werner Fitze, Norbert Pauligk, and Henning Schleiff, <u>Wissenschaftlich-technischer Fortschritt - Sozialistische Arbeit - Persönlichkeit</u> (Berlin: Dietz, 1976, p. 104)

Other data from this important investigation revealed the existence of a serious contradiction between workers' actual qualifications and job requirements: whereas about 70% of production workers in the stage of partial automation were skilled workers, only about 55% of the latter were actually required.[7] This discrepancy was observable in the other four technological stages as well.

Another important question is: to what extent does the application of complex mechanization and automation coincide with creative mental activities? Significant differences emerged in the 1973 Sociological Investigation when level of qualification and technological scale were related to work contents such as receptive-mental demands, non-algorithmic demands, and being tied to the technology. Unskilled, semi-skilled, and partly skilled workers were at a clear disadvantage (see Table 2). Moreover, GDR sociologists have identified a correlation between the mental content of work and societal and leisure activities. In central industry almost twice as many production workers with exacting mental work participate in the innovators' movement than those with less exacting work. And, generally speaking, the 1973 Investigation established that the higher the level of qualification, the more likely a worker's involvement in public affairs. For example, 64.2% of the foremen, but only 29.4% of the production workers in basic processes held a public office.

What further evidence do we have of the degradation of labor? There is little doubt that for many the experience of work has involved a loss of skills and discretion. As machines take over the functions performed by workers at higher intellectual levels, workers come to feel that they are no longer stretched. Fritz Macher has described two aspects of monotony at work: where an individual performs a purely supervisory role within an automated system and where s/he has to carry out the same functions time and again, as in assembly plants.[8] Classic examples of workers performing little more than monitoring functions occur in the chemical industry and among NC- and CNC-machine operatives in machine tools.

The introduction of numerical control machine tools is a frequently quoted example of deskilling. The tasks of an operator of conventional lathes in small-batch production require a high degree of skill, and the operator enjoys considerable freedom of control over his job. He assists with the planning of the production of a part, setting up the machine, and controlling its operation. With the arrival of numerical control these tasks may be transferred to separate production preparation departments such as technology, programming, and toolsetting. The tasks left to the machine operator are frequently of a routine nature, for example, feeding and unloading the machine. The discretion of operators can be fur-

---

TABLE 2: WORK CONTENTS ACCORDING TO LEVEL OF QUALIFICATION AND TECHNOLOGICAL STAGE

A. Qualification	Receptive mental demands	Non-algorithmic decisions	Being tied to the technology
Unskilled	1.89	1.11	2.70
Semi-skilled	2.23	1.23	3.08
Partly skilled	2.33	1.24	3.00
Skilled	2.94	1.72	3.75
Foremen	3.93	2.65	2.37
B. Technological Stage			
I	2.51	1.50	2.61
II	2.58	1.66	2.67
III	2.47	1.29	3.19
IV	2.83	1.49	3.37
V	2.51	1.31	3.03

1 = very little, very low
5 = very much, very high

Source: Hansgünter Meyer, "Eine Retrospektive auf soziologische Untersuchungen zur Entwicklung der Struktur der Arbeiterklasse in der DDR 1970 bis 1973," in *Jahrbuch für Wirtschaftsgeschichte,* II (1981), 317.

ther eroded by the introduction of the new generation of computer numerical control and direct numerical control. With CNC-machine tools the computer is programmed to control the operation of the machine. Various published and unpublished surveys by Weiß, Mirche, Torke, Plath, Näke, Saalfrank, and Müller have confirmed a widespread deskilling of lathe operators and a separation between conception and execution as a result of the introduction of numerical control in machine tools and machine construction. Dietrich Weiß has depicted the rigid technical division of labor in gloomy terms. The NC-lathe operator is reduced to feeding, unloading, and supervising the machine; he exercises no control over the utilization of the machine, the work flow, and the use of tools. The impoverishment of his activity may lead to a loss of interest in his work, job dissatisfaction, and a high labor turnover.[9] Another worrying feature is the linkage between an undemanding job and illness: workers with less mentally stimulating activities are more likely to be ill for a longer period than those with more exacting activities.[10]

If we turn now to continuous processing in the chemical industry, we can see that the automatic control of key variables such as temperature pressure, density, and flow rate have tended to replace manual work. An effective utilization of instruments is achieved through central control, whereby one centrally located control room is used for the indication, recording, and regulation of the process variables. Process control may also take place from control rooms in the production process itself; this represents a lower stage of technical development. As the instruments normally provide the key indicators, the plant operatives' job has increasingly been reduced to that of monitoring or checking the process parameters. This can be illustrated by Gerhard Schmidt's data on work tasks at twelve enterprises.[11] Monitoring accounted for 23.8% of operatives' working time at partly mechanized, 39.8% at fully mechanized, and 68.2% at fully automated plants. Supervision or monitoring entails a reduction in the operatives' direct influence on the production process as well as prolonged periods of inactivity. Consequently, when production is running normally, work is basically monotonous and affords few opportunities for creative activity. And, especially among skilled workers, discrepancies exist between their relatively high level of qualifications and job demands. On the other hand, as operatives' alertness is impaired by long periods of inactivity, they are frequently unable to react quickly and efficiently to a sudden disturbance in the normal flow or to an emergency. This discrepancy between the normal and the abnormal can lead to considerable mental strain, job dissatisfaction, and a health risk. Having surveyed some of the 1970 research, a brief examination of more recent data will now be undertaken.

Industrial robots will, it is hoped, not only reduce unhealthy jobs and arduous physical labor but also increase labor productivity. Improvements are anticipated in work content too. Robots are to relieve workers, often semi-skilled and in lower wage groups, of those repetitive manual tasks which are frequently associated with a high labor turnover. Despite such hopes, recent empirical investigations have revealed an increase in the routinization of work, job monotony, and mental strain at robotic work places. This is illustrated by one well-designed investigation into the manufacture of panniers.[12] The robot transported the work tool for welding. The workers were left with servicing, control, and handling functions, including the highly repetitive task of placing the individual parts into a magazine. This task represented 40.3% of work time and imposed relatively low demands on skill and qualifications. In a study of the application of robots to preassembly and assembly tasks, Eberhard Kruppe, director of the Scientific Work Center of the electrical industry in the GDR, found that in only two out of fourteen cases were job design solutions conducive to personal development. The so-called operators merely performed the residual functions from the previous activity. Kruppe was highly critical of job designations such as "operation" and "supervision," as they gave a false picture of the job. The impoverishment of work content can be gauged by his finding that in only two out of fourteen cases did the operators perform tasks in line with a skilled worker's level of qualification. Work content characteristics were also examined. Out of the thirteen characteristics, only two were rated as adequate but several groups of characteristics such as "intellectual demands," "scope for action," and "variety of work tasks" were deemed unsatisfactory. A general problem encountered in the application of robotics is the frequent failure to design an integrated system; this results in "islands of automation" which reduce workers to the performance of simple and monotonous auxiliary tasks such as machine loading, packing, and sorting.

Visual display terminals (VDTs) are the standard means of communication between people and computerized equipment, and one can anticipate their more rapid development in the GDR. Initial research in the GDR supports Western findings that the use of VDTs can lead to problems of eye strain, headaches, backaches, skin inflammation, concentration difficulties, fatigue, stress, monotony, and social isolation. Considerable effort is being expended on devising ways of reducing glare and noise, improving keyboard design, providing opportunities for regular breaks, and so on. A recent investigation by the Psychology Section of the Humboldt University at three machine construction enterprises has pinpointed various difficulties experienced by semi-skilled women workers who had the task of off-line data input.[13] The study shows that the introduction of VDTs led to a decline in the proportion of creative work and job autonomy. Although a decline had taken place in the proportion of routine jobs, this was not so pronounced as among the highly qualified technologists. Routine calculations and time-consuming inquiries had decreased for the latter. Finally, although the technologists' autonomy remained virtually the same as before the introduction of VDTs, opportunities for creative activities had increased.

Clearly, then, we have the preconditions for humanization of work programs. Fritz Macher describes the problem well:

> The great political and moral responsibility that rests on society as a whole and on managers in particular has as its basic characteristic the fact that we are dealing with people who have spent ten years at school, followed by two or three years of vocational school, and often have other qualifications as well. Nothing can be worse for them than to be stuck in a job where they feel they cannot use all this knowledge. This leads to discontent at work and to job-switching which is very expensive.[14]

The progressive forms of job design such as job enrichment, job enlargement, and semi-autonomous work groups are clearly intended to enhance job satisfaction, reduce labor turnover and illness, increase labor productivity, and improve product quality. Jobs are to become more interesting and varied. These designs are similar to those developed in the large capitalist enterprises in the USA and Western Europe--Atlas, SAAB, Volvo, Olivetti, Fiat. Still, GDR social scientists insist that, if used correctly and critically, bourgeois methods can be applied in the GDR too. It is, of course, no accident that the programs, first launched in the 1970s, have been concentrated in industries such as chemicals and machine tools, which play a key role in the GDR economy. Over 80% of the GDR's machine-tool production in the 1970s was exported, and in 1983 the GDR stood in sixth place in terms of estimated world production and third in world exports.

One well-known study in machine tools was conducted by Mirche and Torke. They established that the most progressive work contents--for example, productive mental demands and task discretion--were found more frequently among operators on conventional lathes than those on linked-transfer lathes and NC-lathes with a rigid division of labor (see Table 3). The activities of operation and supervision involved few creative inputs and were essentially reactive, whereas preparation/setting, judged to be crucial to progressive work, was characterized on the conventional lathes by greater variety and creativity. An attempt was therefore made to modify the division of labor on NC-lathes, for example, by incorporating repairs, programming, and tool presetting into the tasks of the operatives (see Table 4). Greater opportunities for creative work now became possible.

The aim of semi-autonomous working groups is "to provide a job which is complete in the sense that a group sees it through from beginning to end and also has the responsibility for planning, co-ordinating, and evaluating its own work activities, within broad constraints reached through the participation of group members in joint decision-making with their superiors."[15] Such groups are important for combating monotony, dequalification, and obstacles to interpersonal communication on the assembly line, where a low level of knowledge is sufficient for the execution of

TABLE 3: INDEX OF LEVEL OF MENTAL DEMANDS

	Preparation/ setting up	Operation	Supervision
Conventional lathes	1.00 *	0.10	0.05
Linked-transfer lathes	0.64	0.12	0.16
NC-lathes with a rigid division of labor	0.64	0.05	0.05
NC-lathes with a flexible division of labor	1.06	0.10	0.08

* The basic value of 1.00 was allotted to the activity "preparation/setting up" on conventional lathes and represents an appropriate indicator for determining progressive work contents.

Source: Dietrich Torke, "Möglichkeiten der Bewertung von Arbeitsinhalten," <u>Sozialistische Arbeitswissenschaft</u>, 21, No. 6 (1977), 437.

simple tasks. Detailed studies conducted in the GDR in the 1960s indicated that the repetitive work rhythm enhances stress and leads to nervous exhaustion and other psychic illnesses. Negative effects on life outside work have also been traced: repetitive work inhibits the pursuit of mentally stimulating leisure activities. The argument of Hans Joachim Zimmermann, in the late 1960s, that the performance of societal functions is a means of enhancing job satisfaction and combating dequalification was criticized by Helmut Gregor on the grounds that the workers would regard this kind of participation as a "necessary evil." Work itself should be made more creative. Zimmermann, however, insisted that the assembly line could not be dispensed with as it offered opportunities for enhancing productivity:

A rejection of specialization, the division of labor and rationalization, including technological methods such as the assembly line, would mean that socialism was relinquishing the development of modern socialist productive forces, automation and finally the completion of socialism itself.[16]

TABLE 4: COMPARISON OF WORK TASKS ON NC-LATHES

	Variant A (rigid division of labor)	Variant B (flexible division of labor)
Preparation:		
- Programming	−	+
- Tool presetting	−	+
- Direct preparation of machine	−	+
Setting	+	+
Operation, esp. feeding and loading	+	+
Observation/control	+	
Correction of faults	+*	+
Searching for faults	−	+
Repairs	−	+

Key: + signifies the incorporation (− the absence) of the activity in the work task.

+* = partly incorporated

Source: Mirche and Torke, p. 120.

A recent assessment of the application of the cell system (<u>Nestmontage</u>) at factories in machine, automotive, and instrument construction demonstrated significant increases in labor productivity and manpower economies (see Table 5). Equipment costs tended to increase rather than decrease, partly because of

TABLE 5: TECHNOLOGICAL EFFECTS OF THE CELL SYSTEM AND THE ASSEMBLY LINE

	Workers		Labor productivity of cells relative to A.L.	Reject and error quota		Area costs of cells relative to A.L.	Equipment costs of cell relative to A.L.
	A.L. No.	Cell No.	A.L.=100%	A.L. %	Cell %	A.L.=100%	A.L.=100%
Car gears	9	2	137.0	3.4	0	80.1	85.4
Headlights	4	1	112.0	2.9	1.4	89.3	91.5
Moped engine	26	3	149.0	44.8	3.0	105.2	210.0
Keyboard	31	4	119.0	34.8	2.5	119.4	108.0
Impulse meter	11	4	110.0	–	–	74.6	145.5
Small armature	10	1	166.0	7.0	1.0	103.0	175.0
Electric switch	6	1	118.0	–	–	78.3	23.9
Washing machine	17	3	133.0	7.5	4.2	115.5	353.0

Source: Helmut Enderlein, Ulrich Makert and Joachim Tannhauer, "Gestaltung progressiver Arbeitsinhalte im Montageprozeß," in: Winfried Hacker and Harald Raum, eds., Optimierung von Arbeitsanforderungen (Berlin: Deutscher Verlag der Wissenschaften, 1980), p. 85.

the need for more specialized tools. The labor force benefited from the greater variety of tasks, less monotony, and a more balanced expenditure of energy. But, as is emphasized by Heidrun Radtke, the cell system certainly cannot be regarded as a ready-made substitute for the assembly line.[17]

The principles of progressive job design in the chemical industry include the transfer of routine operations to technical equipment, the incorporation of production preparation, maintenance, servicing, and laboratory tasks into the plant operatives' work, and collective organizational forms of work.

In order to counteract monotony, Kund and Schmidt advocated, in the 1970s, job enlargement through the incorporation of cognitive elements into plant operatives' tasks.[18] One application of this principle occurred at the Leuna Works "Walter Ulbricht": tasks usually performed by laboratory personnel, for instance, taking samples, were transferred to the operatives. It is frequently recommended by labor scientists that operatives should perform maintenance and repair tasks, an indication of the growing need for labor in this area. In 1982, 29.8% of all workers in the chemical industry were involved in maintenance and repairs, the third highest category after water and energy. Whereas in 1969 maintenance tasks represented 8% of plant operatives' working time, this figure had increased between three and four times by 1978. Finally, one interesting method which is being developed by labor scientists at the Technische Hochschule "Carl Schorlemmer" in Leuna-Merseburg seeks to relate the degree of difficulty of work tasks to the jobs of skilled workers. A key target is that work with "an average degree of difficulty" should constitute 60% to 70% of work operations.[19] This method has been applied to the reallocation of low-level leadership functions and tasks. The following benefits are envisaged: increases in productivity, an enlargement of plant operatives' work content, and a lighter work load for lower administrative staff. As a high proportion of operative tasks entails a low to average degree of difficulty (34% and 53% respectively), it is considered that favorable conditions exist for the transfer of shift leaders' functions such as representing the collective on outside bodies as well as shutting down and starting up the plant.[20]

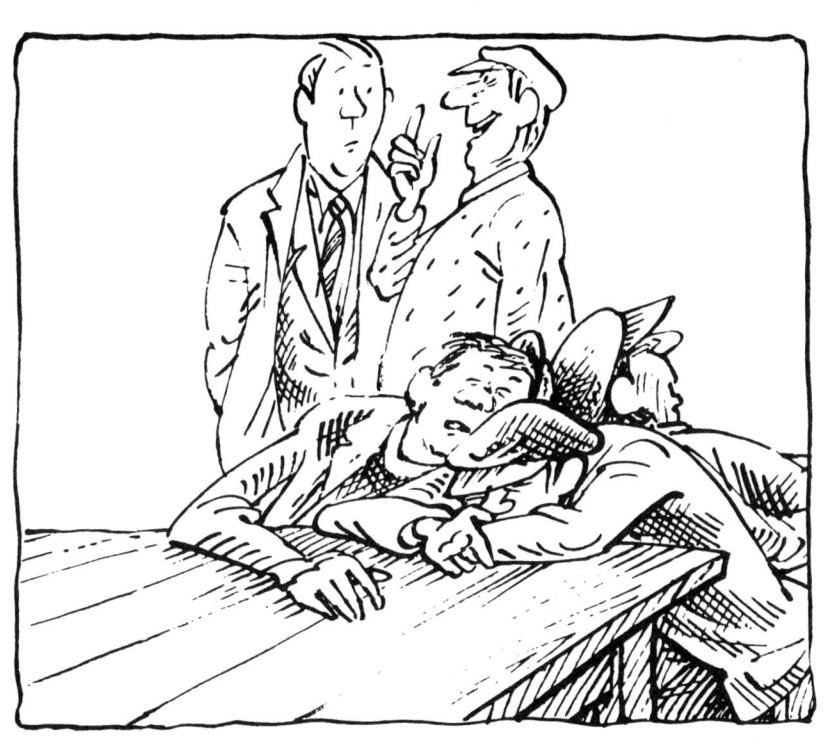

("Na ja, aber Sie sollten uns mal als Feierabendbrigade erleben!")

Naturally, the humanization schemes and measures proceed far from smoothly in the chemical industry. The organizational guidelines for redesigning work places are sometimes inadequate. Too much emphasis is placed on job enlargement, which, according to Schmidt and Kund, mainly involves the addition of simple tasks to existing ones; and too little attention is paid to job enrichment.[21] Furthermore, engineers and designers tend to neglect advancements in work content in favor of improvements in health and safety.

It should be pointed out that projects for the implementation of progressive work contents have not been introduced on a widespread scale; this is particularly true of job enrichment schemes. Even the need to counteract monotony on the assembly line has been described as a long-term task. Cost is undoubtedly one of the major factors determining the limited application of new forms of work organization. Helge Wendt of the Technische Hochschule "Otto von Guericke," Magdeburg, has warned that resources would be overstretched and economic growth jeopardized if the implementation of progressive work contents was attempted too hastily and in too ambitious a manner.[22] It is in fact openly admitted by labor scientists that economic criteria frequently enjoy priority over projects to improve work contents, even though a unity allegedly exists between the social and economic aspects of technological innovations. Quite recently Gottfried Schneider and several colleagues at the Central Institute for Vocational Training in Berlin intimated that consideration is now being given to reducing operatives' opportunities for intervention as operational errors have been responsible for significant economic losses in machine tools.[23] About 21% of damages to machine tools arose from such errors. It is extremely difficult to estimate the kind of costs which would be entailed in a comprehensive campaign to improve work contents; however, we do have some idea of the costs required to eliminate those working conditions which represent a threat to health and safety. Gerhard Lippold estimated that 82 million Marks would have been needed in 1972, a figure which was 2.4 times higher than total investments for that year.[24]

Which other factors constrain humanization of work schemes? Scientific management experts frequent-

("Auch beim Rauchen eingeschlafen?" - "Ja"
"Im Bett?" - "Nee, auf Arbeit!")

ly lament the tendency of managers and technologists to view innovations as a technical/technological issue and the design of progressive work contents as a residual matter. Progressive changes are sometimes, according to Mirche and Torke, only a response to worker dissatisfaction as expressed in a high labor turnover.[25] Such negative attitudes may well be storing up problems for the future as it is difficult and expensive to introduce progressive work contents retrospectively. However, labor scientists are obliged to admit that they experience great difficulty in devising a set of clear and precise criteria for evaluating and implementing changes in work contents, especially when they are dealing with a complex series of variables such as lot size, the division of labor, individual and/or collective forms of work organization, and so on. Ingeborg Henning also recognizes that sociologists and social psychologists need to offer practical advice and to operationalize concepts such as "job dissatisfaction" and "attitude to scientific-technical progress."[26] A more positive response might then be elicited from the foremen who have the day-to-day responsibility for the organization of work.

Finally, there are indications that some managers and workers are less than enthusiastic about the new schemes. Enterprise managers, as Mirche and Torke reveal, sometimes oppose change since workers with creative work contents are often critical of and impatient with deficiencies in work organization and impose greater demands on management. Skilled workers, in Schmidt's opinion, may seek to maintain traditional boundaries between jobs in order to resist an erosion of their status and skills.[27] Furthermore, new technology and new forms of work organization may be viewed as part of a strategy to increase work intensity rather than to improve the quality of working life.

New automated technology cannot be regarded as heralding a "brave new world of work," not even in state socialism. Although certain skills and qualifications (e.g., programming, designing) are in greater demand, deskilling and monotony occur on a widespread scale. The polarization between conception and execution runs counter to the official goal of narrowing the gap between production workers and the intelligentsia. Job enrichment and semi-autonomous working groups, it might be argued, are little more than sophisticated alternatives to direct forms of intervention in those "free spaces" or niches which many workers have created for themselves at their place of work. The network of personal relationships and communications in which some workers are enmeshed is illustrated by the GDR cartoons reproduced here.[28] This kind of "Arbeitsbummelei" represents a deviation from the officially approved norm of a disciplined and responsible attitude to work.

On the other hand, changes in work organization are not simply cosmetic; they do seem to influence various aspects of work content and requirements. Job enrichment and other designs, exemplifying the principle of "responsible autonomy," allow the possibility that "changes in organisation of work or decisions about work may increase the power which workers may exercise to act within the labor process according to their own judgment and their own will. . . ."[29] In certain sectors, for example, the chemical industry and machine tools, attempts have been made since the mid-1970s to implement the strategy of responsible autonomy. However, responsible autonomy, it should be emphasized, does not entail a change in the fundamental relations of production. Between the two poles of direct control and responsible autonomy, but also beyond them, lies the contested terrain, explored by Bust-Bartels, Klinger, Böhme, Markowsky, and others, of labor rationalization and job security, wages, work load, shift rotas, physical working conditions, and work norms.[30]

Notes

I wish to thank the Nuffield Foundation and the School of Humanities and Cultural Studies, Wolverhampton Polytechnic, for their generosity in granting me support at various times for this and other research.

[1] A good survey of the GDR literature on this topic is to be found in Günter Erbe, <u>Arbeiterklasse und Intelligenz</u> (Opladen: Westdeutscher Verlag, 1982).

² Hartmut Zimmermann, "The GDR in the 1970s," Problems of Communism, 27 (March/April 1978), p. 8. It should, however, be noted that the concept of the scientific-technical revolution is currently experiencing a revival.

³ "Man versus technology? Interview with Professor Macher," Prisma, No. 4 (1982), p. 31.

⁴ Rudi Weidig and Eberhard Prager, "The Preparation of the Working People for the Application of Microelectronics in the Industry of the German Democratic Republic," in Jan Berting, Stephen Mills and Helmut Wintersberger, eds., The Socio-Economic Impact of Microelectronics (Oxford: Pergamon, 1980), p. 90.

⁵ "Rundtischgespräch," Deutsche Zeitschrift für Philosophie, 31, No. 3 (1983), 320.

⁶ For details see Hansgünter Meyer, "Eine Retrospektive auf soziologische Untersuchungen zur Entwicklung der Struktur der Arbeiterklasse in der DDR 1970 bis 1973," in Jahrbuch für Wirtschaftsgeschichte, II (Berlin: Akademie, 1981), 299.

⁷ Erbe, p. 166.

⁸ "Man versus technology?" p. 33.

⁹ Dietrich Weiß, "Analyse des Einsatzes von unverketteten NC-Werkzeugmaschinen zur Ableitung von Maßnahmen für die Erhöhung der Effektivität unter besonderer Beachtung des Bedienens," Dissertation, Technische Universität Dresden, 1979, pp. 36-38.

¹⁰ Horst Mirche and Dieter Torke, "Analyse und Gestaltung des Arbeitsinhalts im Zusammenhang mit dem wissenschaftlich-technischen Fortschritt," Dissertation, Technische Universität Dresden, 1978, p. 146.

¹¹ Gerhard Schmidt, "Arbeitswissenschaftlicher Beitrag zur aufgaben- und objektbezogenen Ausrichtung der berufsspezifischen Weiterbildung des Anlagenpersonals in der chemischen Industrie," Dissertation, Technische Hochschule für Chemie "Carl Schorlemmer," Leuna-Merseburg, 1973, p. 120; see also Rainer Deppe and Dietrich Hoß, Sozialistische Rationalisierung (Frankfurt/M.: Campus, 1980), pp. 284-85.

[12] See Mike Dennis, "The Red Robots Are Here!" GDR Monitor, No. 12 (Winter 1984/85), pp. 9-11.

[13] Hartmut Wandke and Elke Wetzenstein-Ollenschläger, "Psychologische Probleme beim Einsatz rechnergestützter Bildschirmarbeitsplätze in der Produktionsvorbereitung," Zeitschrift für Psychologie, Supplement 5, 1983, pp. 102-07.

[14] "Man versus technology?" p. 34.

[15] Peter Warr and Toby Wall, Work and Well-being (Harmondsworth: Penguin, 1975), p. 128.

[16] Hans Joachim Zimmermann, "Probleme der persönlichkeitsfördernden Gestaltung des Arbeitsprozesses und der Überwindung von Tendenzen der Arbeitsmonotonie," Dissertation, Institut für Gesellschaftswissenschaften beim ZK der SED, Berlin, 1968, p. 97 (my translation). See also Helmut Gregor, "Wechselbeziehungen zwischen biologischen und gesellschaftlichen Wesensmerkmalen und Eigenschaften des Menschen unter den Bedingungen der Fließbandarbeit," Dissertation, Humboldt Universität, Berlin, 1970, pp. 18-19, 179, 183, 245.

[17] See Autorenkollektiv headed by Rosemarie Winzer, Körperliche und geistige Arbeit im Sozialismus (Berlin: Dietz, 1980), p. 194.

[18] Joachim Kund and Gerhard Schmidt, "Erfordernisse und Möglichkeiten zur Erhöhung des Anteils schöpferischer Arbeit des Bedienungspersonals von Chemieanlagen," Sozialistische Arbeitswissenschaft, 16, No. 6 (1972), 459, 468-69.

[19] Joachim Kund and Gerhard Schmidt, "Arbeitswissenschaftliche Vorgaben zur Gestaltung von Arbeitsaufgaben und Ausführungsbedingungen bei Anlagenprozessen," Sozialistische Arbeitswissenschaft, 25, No. 4 (1981), 270.

[20] See, for example, Hans Joachim Aust and Gerhard Schmidt, "Veränderung der vertikalen Arbeitsteilung in Produktionsbereichen - bessere Nutzung des gesellschaftlichen Arbeitsvermögens," Sozialistische Arbeitswissenschaft, 25, No. 5 (1981), 336-37, 341.

21 Joachim Kund and Gerhard Schmidt, "Arbeitswissenschaftliche Vorgaben," p. 268.

22 "Rundtischgespräch," p. 323.

23 Michael Guder, Peter Lorenz, Gerhard Pogodda and Gottfried Schneider, "Zur inhaltlichen Ausgestaltung der Facharbeiterberufe unter dem besonderen Aspekt der beruflichen Disponibilität," Forschung der sozialistischen Berufsbildung, 18, No. 2 (1984), 53.

24 Gerhard Lippold, Die materiellen Arbeitsbedingungen der Werktätigen (Berlin: Tribüne, 1975), pp. 228-29.

25 Mirche and Torke, p. 243.

26 Ingeborg Henning, "Aufgaben und Probleme beim effektiven Einsatz von Soziologen im Betrieb," Informationen zur soziologischen Forschung in der DDR, 28, No. 1 (1984), 47; Wolfgang Holle, "Arbeitsmethodengestaltung zur arbeitswissenschaftlich begründeten Montageprojektierung," Dissertation, Technische Hochschule Ilmenau, 1978, p. 27.

27 Mirche and Torke, p. 243; Deppe and Hoß, p. 270; Schmidt, p. 122.

28 The source of the two cartoons is: Peter Kroh, Jürgen Schmollak and Karl-Heinz Thieme, Wie steht es um die Arbeitsdisziplin? (Berlin: Dietz, 1984), pp. 79 and 89.

29 Andy Friedman, "Responsible autonomy versus direct control over the labour process," Capital and Class, No. 1 (Spring 1977), p. 45.

30 Bernd Markowsky's brief account of conflicts at the work place is a GDR counterpart to the experiences of Miklos Haraszti in Hungary. See Thomas Auerbach et al., DDR-konkret. Geschichten und Berichte aus einem real existierenden Land (West Berlin: Olle and Wolter, 1978), pp. 38-45. Fred Klinger's views are presented in his article "Soziale Auswirkungen und lebensweltliche Zusammenhänge der sozialistischen Rationalisierung," in Ilse Spittmann-Rühle and Gisela Helwig, eds., Lebensbedingungen in der DDR. Siebzehnte Tagung zum Stand der DDR-Forschung in der Bundesrepublik Deutschland 12. bis 15. Juni 1984 (Cologne: Wissenschaft und Politik, 1984).

Social and Cultural Changes in the Lives of GDR Women - Changes in their Self-Conception

Irene Dölling

Women who were between twenty and forty years of age at the end of World War II and who, in the immediate postwar period, went out to work because they were widowed or remained unmarried as a result of the war, are ordinarily old-age pensioners today. Their daughters are now between thirty and fifty years of age, and their granddaughters often have families of their own. Thus there are three generations of women in the GDR today for whom work outside the home has been a determining factor in their lives, three generations who were drawn into the process which changed the social situation of women in the GDR at various points of time and development. Today, forty years after the war, this process is characterized by: equality as regards profession, education, wages, and legal standing; job security; the right to determine the time of birth and number of children; women's exit from the narrowness of the household; and a social policy designed to improve conditions so that "eine Frau von ihren gleichen Rechten auch in vollem Umfang Gebrauch machen kann."[1] Today women are present in all spheres of public life. Not the fact <u>that</u> women have highly qualified jobs and responsible positions is considered remarkable today, but that so few do. Some one-half of the students studying at GDR universities are women, at technical colleges they make up 84% of the student body, but only 7.4% of the professors and lecturers are women.[2]

How have these changes affected women's lives? Have they eradicated the traditional disadvantages? Or have they added to the burden of women's chores in the household and of bringing up the children? Have they brought women a new, self-determined understanding of themselves and their role? Or do contemporary women, like their grandmothers, consider the welfare of the family and the functioning of the household to be their prime responsibility? Do they seek happiness above all in marriage and family and regard work merely as a financial necessity? These questions cannot be answered with a simple yes or no. Historical changes in ways of living, in relations between the sexes, in individual attitudes, in needs and aims in life, come about through long and contradictory processes. The emergence of something new is influenced not only by changed conditions, but also by those factors which change only in part or not at all. Changes take place within the stable, traditional cultural forms and norms by means of which people regulate their daily lives. People react to changes, relate to them, and modify their own behavior within these cultural forms.

The analysis of these interrelations is the subject matter of the theory of culture, the scientific discipline in which I work. We understand the theory of culture as a philosophical discipline that examines the interconnections between social relations and the possibilities individuals have for development. We investigate above all the circumstances and relations in which individuals live their daily lives, in which they are active, and in which their needs and abilities are developed. Under socialism, too, these social conditions are still different for men and women. Therefore, the relations between the sexes are an essential element of the cultural processes, and one of the tasks of the theory of culture is to analyze them. In the last few years my work has centered around this subject. In this context, I want to discuss some aspects of the changes in the lives and self-image of women in the GDR. As empirical evidence I will use both sociological and statistical data and GDR literature.[3] I will present this paper in the form of three questions.

1. <u>Emancipation through labor?</u>

In her novel <u>Die Alleinseglerin</u>, Christine Wolter uses an image which in my opinion describes the situation of women in the younger and middle generations in the GDR today:

> Es gibt beim Segeln, genauer gesagt in der Regatta, eine Situation, die man die "aussichtslose Position" nennt. . . . Stell dir vor, dort vor dir segelt ein anderes Boot, das nimmt dir den Wind und wirft dir dazu seine Bugwellen entgegen, so daß du gebremst wirst. Du kannst aber auch nicht zurück, weil hinter dir ein anderer ist und neben dir noch einer, dem du den Wind nimmst und der deshalb nicht schneller werden kann. Auch er hindert dich, einfach auszubrechen, weil er von dir gehindert wird. . . . Merkwürdigerweise rät die Seglererfahrung, nicht zu wenden, nicht auszubrechen: keine Manöver. Eine Regattaregel sagt, man sollte in der "aussichtslosen Position" bleiben, das ist meist besser, man kann dann immer noch in der Gesamtwertung ganz vorn liegen. Die Frage ist eben nur, ob einem die hoffnungslose Stellung und ihre Möglichkeiten klar sind.[4]

That sounds, to be sure, very sober and free of illusions; still, the tone is not resigned. To come to the realization that one cannot have everything here and now can sharpen the senses for what is possible under the present conditions. This can be a productive incentive to make the most of what one has and to deal better with the conditions of one's life and one's own expectations. It can prevent both the senseless expenditure of energy and blindness vis-à-vis the possibilities created by the construction of socialist society, a blindness caused by frustrated hopes for quick and radical change.

In which ways have the changes actually altered women's lives and what will the future bring? This has been a focal point both of literature--especially literature written by women--and of science in recent years. The mere fact that women are discussing this question with such urgency is a sign of the basic changes in their lives. Sociologists say that the compatibility of work and family life is characteristic of the present-day self-image of women in the GDR. Going out to work has become a matter of course. Evidence of this is the fact that some 90% of all women capable of doing so go out to work. For today's teenagers working for a living is to a very large extent a basic part of their plans for the future. It is interesting to note that a considerably higher percentage of girls have a positive attitude towards women's working outside the home than do boys.[5]

The women of the current middle and younger generations have different motives for wanting to work than their mothers and grandmothers had. The latter were usually forced to work for financial reasons. Well into the 1950s, the overwhelming majority of women worked as unskilled labor. For example, around 1950 only about 5% of the women working in industry had some type of qualification. Their daughters and granddaughters usually have better qualifications and vocational training. Today men and women aged forty and younger have an equal level of competence.[6] For women, this has meant not only the extension of their experience by entering social production; increasingly, it has also entailed the augmented development of their abilities, skills, and knowledge. Linked to this is a tendency toward increased emphasis on the qualitative side of their work--for themselves and for society. In addition to an interest in good wages, the content of the work has become a major factor in job motivation.

These changes encourage women's self-confidence, which has developed over three generations and is based on economic independence, on doing socially useful work--and this as well as men, and on the public support women receive when they claim their rights. The tape-recorded interviews published by Maxie Wander show that women of all social strata and in various professions are developing a new identity. The actual changes in their lives have meant that the traditional conception of male dominance, of the "female role" in marriage and in the family are at least being questioned and are causing problems in the relations between the sexes. Women are now defining themselves less in terms of their function within the family. As Helga Königsdorf writes in "Hochzeitstag in Pizunda," "Ich wage jetzt das große Abenteuer. Ich begebe mich auf die Suche nach mir selbst."[7]

A part of this search--for women of the second and third generations it is a determining factor--is the realization that equal rights and work outside the home do not directly lead to the social equality of the sexes. The division of labor into blue- and white-collar jobs, i.e., professions with varying levels of qualification, cannot yet be abolished. Linked to this is the division of labor between the sexes in the sphere of social production. This means that women are concentrated in the less qualified, largely menial jobs that are not particularly well-paid and which correspond to the "typically feminine" functions in the household and family. Such jobs can be thought of as a transition for women who go out to work for the first time, since the tasks are familiar and the usual conceptions of "femininity" can be maintained. On the other hand, however, the traditional conceptions of the subordinated, supportive, helping function of women are reproduced in the new field of work.

This outcome of the division of labor between the sexes has led to a discussion of whether such forms of work actually do extend women's horizons. For example, monotonous work on an assembly line is unfavorably compared with the variety of chores in the household and, above all, with the rearing of children. However, when the emancipatory effect of many current jobs is questioned, the alternative given is seldom a return to the traditional female duties in the home and the family. Many women reject the alternative of returning to the life of the so-called "mere" housewife--and not only for economic reasons--although a large number of them do see immediate relief from the "double burden" in the temporary interruption of work.[8]

On a long-term basis, the contradictions within the division of labor between the sexes can be solved only with the reduction of unqualified, one-sided, monotonous work, i.e., by enriching the labor functions. Overcoming the division of labor between the sexes is a concrete form of the attempt to decrease social differences under socialism. The speed and course of this process are determined above all by the corresponding material and technical basis,[9] and by subjective factors. These latter include, for example, the positive experiences of women when they break out of their narrow family lives, but also their experiencing of the limits to their emancipation set by the division of labor between the sexes in industry, which causes dissatisfaction with what has been achieved and can give rise to demands for more interesting work.

It can thus be stated that while work outside the home alone does not bring about the emancipation of women, and certainly not under the present circumstances of the division of labor between the sexes, women would have no basis upon which to build without work. For this reason, the government is intent upon helping women make better use of their vocational training. This means creating conditions in which women can fully use their qualifications, without impairing their possibilities for motherhood.[10] It also entails increasing women's flexibility by giving them more opportunities--they now have fewer than men--for further training in their professions.[11]

2. Is there a "new motherliness" in reaction to the "double burden"?

That women see the compatibility of work and family as essential for their identity is, on the one hand, an expression of a basic change in their lives; on the other, it points to the fact that their traditional feeling of family responsibility continues unabated. Women still do two-thirds to three-quarters of the housework. They are usually responsible for both the household and for bringing up the children.[12] The present stage of development in the productive forces, which necessitates the division of labor between the sexes in industry, also causes a discrepancy between the progress being made in the "private" and the social reproduction spheres. As a result, the traditional roles of men and women within the family and the corresponding norms of "typically" female and male behavior continue to function and be reproduced. This also means that changes in the sex "roles" do not take place as a radical break with the past but as modifications of the normal division of labor in the family, and very often they are so gradual that individuals involved hardly notice them. That young men now look after their children, take them to kindergarten or to the doctor is still not completely "normal," but it no longer causes a sensation.[13] To do this would have been unthinkable for their grandfathers. Despite these tendencies, however, most women still bear a "double burden," have little time for themselves, and are very often overtaxed.

In the early 1970s several socio-political measures were introduced with the aim of improving the situation of working women with children: shorter daily working hours and longer holidays, increased prenatal and postnatal leave (to 26 weeks), a fully paid "maternity year" after the birth of a second child, and 18 months paid leave after the birth of each subsequent child, for example. These measures help balance the unequal conditions between men and women, but they cannot eliminate the inequality. In fact, in some respects they consolidate the traditional division of labor in the home.

In the years ahead, women's lives will continue to be determined by a typical contradiction: they must develop skills and needs in two very different spheres and make these--relatively--compatible in their self-conception. Feeling responsible for the functioning of the household and for a harmonious family atmosphere conflicts, to varying degrees, with the demands made by a job and by interests oriented toward career and self-development. In her story "Selbstversuch," Christa Wolf describes the dilemma of many women: "zwischen Mann und Arbeitsdrang, Liebesglück und Schöpfungswillen, Kinderwunsch und Ehrgeiz ein Leben lang zickzack laufen wie eine falsch programmierte kybernetische Maus."[14]

These contradictions are reflected in decisions women are making today in regard to their professional life: part-time work, temporary retirement from work while the children are small, accepting jobs for which they are overqualified because the work place is near home and they aren't required to work shift, and sacrificing their own job development for that of their husbands. The higher the qualification, however, the fewer the women seeking such solutions; women with higher levels of education and training tend instead to search for ways in which they can use their professional skills in the same way as men. And they are being encouraged to do so-- with social encouragement plans and individualized working time, for example.[15] But these women, too, have a "double burden."

3. <u>Is there an "unbroken conservatism" in sex relations and norms?</u>

The solutions discussed show that women are trying to cope with conditions in which they are at a real disadvantage. The solutions they find should not

be seen only in a negative light, however. The women
of the first generation were faced with a situation
in which they were forced to work in order to feed
themselves and their children; they had neither kin-
dergartens nor creches to help them. In the 1950s the
women often organized such facilities at their place
of work, through the factory women's committee. The
system of day-care centers known today became a comprehensive system only in the 1960s. Today women have
little difficulty finding a spot for their children
and know that the children are well looked after
while they are working. This improved situation has
caused many women to reconsider the significance of
having children for their own happiness and self-
fulfillment, and the importance of the family for
providing the emotional security that is the basis
for the harmonious development of children. In contrast to their mothers, women today can see that going out to work is not enough for their emancipatory
needs and their identity. Emancipation also includes
the ability to bring up children and to develop and
maintain harmonious human relations--and having the
time to do these things. When women today insist on
their motherliness and caring for others, they are
not merely adhering to traditional functions. It is
instead a matter of the harmonious development of individual needs and skills in a human totality. This
conception includes men as well as women, and overcomes the one-sidedness of traditional female and
male "roles" and the apparent or real privileges
these involve. With such a conception the current
achievements are seen critically. The prerequisite
for such a view is the refusal to live in accordance
with imposed norms--to be a "vorzeigbares Beispiel
für gehorsame Gleichberechtigung" (p. 207), as Christine Wolter puts it in her novel; that is, the insistence on being oneself. Many women today share
this critical view and will not give it up, because
they are not willing to give themselves up.

   The changes in the lives and self-conception of
women are taking place largely within the framework
of the traditional functional divisions between men
and women, and within sex stereotypes. However, they
have caused the practices and norms in relations
between the sexes to crack and become more equivocal.
The fact that women are emphasizing the value of
motherhood, that they are refusing to take on manage-
rial positions, can be the conscious rejection of a

life that they consider unacceptably one-sided. However, it can also be understood as exploiting advantages given to women by patriarchal traditions: "zum Beispiel Rückzugsmöglichkeiten bei Bequemlichkeit, Angst vor Verantwortung oder der Last von Entscheidungszwängen."[16] When women emphasize their femininity in their clothes and their behavior, this can be a sign of the more or less "blind" acceptance of the "feminine mystique." However, it can also be a consciously chosen protection against the insecurities and uncertainties of their female identity experienced by many women who have stepped into what have hitherto been purely male domains. Today, the usual motivation of women for working is the extension of their social contacts and interests, not the amount of money they earn. This may reflect the conception still widespread among many men that they are the "family provider." And this can definitely contradict women's real feelings of economic independence--evidence for this is the number of divorces initiated by women. The fact that men and women in all age groups place marriage and family high up on their list of values (next to profession) says nothing about the changed conceptions and practices of the division of labor within the family, the relations between men and women, adults and children, that lie behind the apparently unbroken "conservatism," nor does it say anything about the experiences and problems of single-parent families and, above all, the problems resulting for the children.

In a recent interview, Irmtraud Morgner reflected on the currently contradictory situation of women, and I would like to close with a quotation therefrom:

> Kurzum: Emanzipation (nicht nur der Frau) ist kein Kampagnethema, sondern--nach Marx --ein Epochenproblem. [Dabei]. . . kann es sich nicht um irgendeinen kleinen Nebenwiderspruch handeln. Oder gar um eine Mode, heute "in" und morgen passé.[17]

Notes

¹ Erich Honecker, *Bericht an den VIII. Parteitag der SED* (Berlin: Dietz, 1971), p. 62.

² See, for example, the experiences reported by the Science Trade Union about the situation of women at GDR universities and colleges in *Informationen des wissenschaftlichen Rates "Die Frau in der sozialistischen Gesellschaft,"* No. 2 (1982), pp. 6-29.

³ Literature is useful here for two reasons: first, because art reflects social processes from an individual point of view and shows the effects these processes have on individual action and conflicts; secondly, because the changes in people's way of life and the conflicts in human relations which result from these changes are often expressed in the arts before they are documented by scientific investigations.

⁴ Christine Wolter, *Die Alleinseglerin*, 2nd ed. (Berlin: Aufbau, 1984), pp. 208-09.

⁵ Rolf Borrmann and Hans-Joachim Schille, *Vorbereitung der Jugend auf Liebe, Ehe und Familie* (Berlin: Deutscher Verlag der Wissenschaften, 1980), pp. 91ff.

⁶ Brigitte Weichert, "Zur Weiterentwicklung der gesellschaftlichen Stellung der Frau in den 80er Jahren," in *Informationen des wissenschaftlichen Rates "Die Frau in der sozialistischen Gesellschaft,"* No. 5 (1982), p. 6.

⁷ Helga Königsdorf, "Hochzeitstag in Pizunda," in her *Meine ungehörigen Träume* (Berlin/Weimar: Aufbau, 1978), p. 129.

⁸ I do not consider the term "double burden" appropriate and use it here only because it has become customary and therefore generally understandable. It corresponds to daily experience insomuch as women still typically bear the responsibility for the household and family. However, it also suggests that working is an (additional) burden and thus, in my opinion, veils over the fundamental importance of work outside the home for women's emancipation.

[9] Changes in the material and technological basis are themselves very contradictory. The introduction of new technologies in the next few years will not automatically lead to a reduction in the division of labor between the sexes in industry; it will instead first be linked to forms of reproduction and the reconstitution of this division.

[10] Weichert, pp. 10ff.

[11] "In der Industrie ist der Anteil von ausgebildeten männlichen Facharbeitern mit Zusatzqualifikation zwei- bis dreimal so hoch wie bei Frauen... Neben der Berücksichtigung der Bildungserfordernisse durch das immer schnellere Voranschreiten des wissenschaftlich-technischen Fortschritts geht es heute darum, ungerechtfertigte Differenzierungen im Qualifikationsniveau, im beruflichen Einsatz für verschiedene Bereiche oder Berufe aufzudecken und im Sinne der weiteren Förderung der gesellschaftlichen Stellung der Frau abzubauen." ("Die berufliche Qualifizierung der werktätigen Frauen als Beitrag zur weiteren Förderung der gesellschaftlichen Stellung der Frau im Prozeß der Gestaltung der entwickelten sozialistischen Gesellschaft," in Informationen des wissenschaftlichen Rates "Die Frau in der sozialistischen Gesellschaft," No. 5 [1983], p. 10).

[12] "Die Doppelbelastung der Frau in Beruf und Haushalt wird durch die zurückhaltende Beteiligung der Ehemänner an der Hausarbeit nur sehr langsam gemindert. Untersuchungen ergaben, daß in den Familien der DDR 1965 47,5 Stunden und 1970 47,1 Stunden für Hausarbeit geleistet wurden. Davon leisteten:

	1965	1970
Männer	11,6%	13,0%
Frauen	79,4%	78,7%

Die Veränderungen sind sehr geringfügig und deuten auf einen 'Jahrhundertprozeß' hin." (Alice Kahl, Steffen H. Wilsdorf, and Herbert F. Wolf, Kollektivbeziehungen und Lebensweise [Berlin: Dietz, 1984], pp. 99-101). This corresponds to the fact that men define themselves largely through their work and their public activities. Although most men, when planning their lives, place great value on having a family, their functions as husband and father are of secondary significance for their self-conception.

[13] At the moment, the greatest changes in the traditional division of labor within the family can be seen in families in which both husband and wife either are highly qualified or work shift. Working in different shifts means that the husband not only <u>helps</u> in the household, but, at definite set times, is <u>responsible</u> for it and for looking after the children. Joan Ecklein has shown that there is a discrepancy between men's verbal acceptance of equality and their actual, practical behavior within the family (Joan Ecklein, "Die sich verändernde Rolle der Männer in der Deutschen Demokratischen Republik," in <u>Informationen des wissenschaftlichen Rates "Die Frau in der sozialistischen Gesellschaft,"</u> No. 3 [1984]).

[14] Christa Wolf, "Selbstversuch," in her <u>Unter den Linden</u>, 3rd ed. (Berlin/Weimar: Aufbau, 1976), p. 112.

[15] For example, factory management is obliged to set up special plans for female university and college graduates which contain concrete steps toward their professional development and eliminate conflicts between the assuming of a responsible position and their personal situation, e.g., birth of a child or caring for children already born.

[16] Quotation from Irmtraud Morgner, in Eva Kaufmann, "Interview mit Irmtraud Morgner," <u>Weimarer Beiträge</u>, 30, No. 5 (1984), 1501.

[17] Kaufmann, p. 1502.

Changing Patterns of Male and Female Identity
in Recent GDR Prose

Christiane Zehl Romero

When considering changing patterns of male and female identity in GDR literature in an interdisciplinary context, it may be useful to recall the beginning of Tolstoy's <u>Anna Karenina</u>: "All happy families resemble one another, but each unhappy family is unhappy in its own way."[1] Among other things this sentence reminds us that literature can never be seen as a direct mirror of everyday life and social conditions since it has always been more interesting to write about the specificities of unhappiness than the sameness of contentment.

In regard to the relations between men and women and what they tell us about individuals in a society however, another literary tradition is at least equally important: the use of happy endings in the form of supposedly mutually satisfying unions between men and women to signify successful integration of the individual into a given society. These endings symbolize the fusion of the most private needs of the sexes with societal expectations of them.

Both literary traditions bear directly on what I will discuss in this essay, the bleak picture--on first impression at least--of the relations between men and women in recent GDR prose and its presumable cause, changing patterns of male and female identity--or the lack thereof. While one tradition reminds us to see such bleakness in perspective and not to draw simplistic conclusions for everyday reality, the other suggests far-reaching social implications in the authors' reluctance to provide their readers with satisfactory relationships between men and women, implications which literary discourse, with its interpenetration of what is with what we fear or hope for, has made its special province to explore.

Bleakness concerning the possibilities of love is anything but new. Much of the fiction of the 19th and 20th centuries deals with it. Usually this bleakness is seen as an indictment of the existing society, which alienates the individual and corrupts all human desire and human relations. Marxist interpretations fault the capitalist system and its attendant woes, including patriarchy; feminists criticize patriarchy and often capitalism as well.

In this context the quick and easy happy endings of early GDR literature appear logical. Since socialism did away with capitalism and patriarchy, the new man and the new woman who emerged would live happily ever after--in marriage, that is. Previous socialist thinking on free love was never even entertained because it had already been discarded as inefficient in Soviet Russia and would not do for a country in dire need of reconstruction.[2] The writers of the <u>Aufbau</u> period in the GDR considered it their task to support the all-out effort by helping to define the socialist personality, which would not only reconstruct the old but build something new, and they liberally used happy endings as rewards and indicators of successful transformation. The ethos of the time was rigorously productivist and--this was new--applied to women as well as men. The former were not only badly needed in the labor force; their right to work outside the home was also considered a basic first step towards the emancipation promised them by socialism. This ethos implied the most profound changes for women. While female characters in literature--more even than women in real life--had traditionally been defined in terms of their domestic and romantic relationships, authors now argued for their right and their duty to participate in production and the public sphere. These changes were so new to the imagination and resulted in so many conflicts, due mostly to societal and particularly male resistance, that the authors--the large majority of them men, but the few women writers of the time, e.g., Elfriede Brüning and, to a certain degree, even Anna Seghers, were no exceptions--failed to realize the inherent and fully antagonistic contradiction between this productivist ethos and traditional feminine identity centered on reproduction.

They simply expected the latter to survive undamaged.

In addition, their eagerness to create positive role models for women prompted the authors to continue the old literary and cultural tradition of using women as "the other," as incorporations of ideas which men project upon them. The most readily available models came from German Classicism. Goethe's famous lines from <u>Torquato Tasso</u>, "Willst du genau erfahren, was sich ziemt / so frage nur bei edlen Frauen an,"[3] applied, albeit in proletarian settings. Positive women characters were often drawn to be particularly unselfish and strong in their dedication to the new ideals, and functioned as educators for their men. Whatever changes the latter had to make to become socialist personalities did not touch their identities as men. All they had to do was accept that their women, in addition to fulfilling the traditional roles, would assume new ones as well.

Over the years not much appears to have changed in this image created by men. The same expectations still confront women. In "Das heutige Weibliche," first published in 1980, Daniela Dahn, who belongs to the generation of younger GDR writers born after the war, draws up a catalogue:

> Allein durch das Mütterliche ist man derzeit noch lange keine gemachte Frau. Von den drei K "Kinder, Küche, Kirche" ist letzteres durch "Kulturobmann" ersetzt worden. Im Beruf werden gleiche Ansprüche gestellt, Maßstab sind männliche Leistungsnormen. Da gibt es keine getrennten Staffeln, auch wenn für die Frauen ein anderer Wind weht. Bis auf den Haushaltstag, großzügig von Männern erlassen, denn er manifestiert: ihr Gebiet.
>
> Als Ehefrau hat man heutzutage schön, klug und begehrenswert zu sein, bei allem sanft und nie aggressiv. Zu kulturellen Höhepunkten erweist man sich als gesellschaftsfähig, belesen, geistreich und stets über das Neueste informiert. Als Gastgeberin bewirtet man mit hausfraulichem Können, zeigt pädagogisches Geschick beim Vorführen der Kinder und im Gespräch charmanten Unterhaltungswert. Im Urlaub stellt sich heraus, daß man unternehmungslustig, sport-

> lich und obendrein in bester Kondition ist.
> Kuren sind eigentlich überflüssig, denn
> gesund möchte man zu alldem schon sein!
> Kurz und schlecht, die Emanzipation hat
> das Gleichgewicht ziemlich einseitig ver-
> schoben, in Richtung höhere Leistung, also
> Belastung, <u>Stärke</u>.[4]

Daniela Dahn continues by arguing for the chance to be weak occasionally--"ohne daß dann gleich alles zusammenbricht" (p. 347)--for women and for men as well. In fact, as we will see, this question of strength and weakness, its definitions and redefinitions in relation to men and women, are an important aspect of GDR discussions of changing male and female identity in literature and elsewhere, albeit often in the subtext.

But to go back and proceed chronologically: with the changes of the 1960s, the emphasis on scientific and technological development and women's participation in these processes through higher training and better qualifications, the demands made upon women in literature and in life only increase. Although the <u>Ankunftsliteratur</u> is considerably more sophisticated in dealing with the problems faced by women and men, and happy endings become much more of a rarity, belief in the strength of women to handle problems and be capable and ready to renounce personal happiness for the sake of society has, if anything, increased. Not only do women continue to be responsible for the area of feeling; as Patricia Herminghouse has pointed out,[5] they are also expected to exert moral leadership through this domain, which has become more important and thus more of a source for conflict. While men tend to hold the socially and professionally stronger positions, women are seen as morally and emotionally superior, surer, more courageous, more uncompromising. The range runs from such unreflected stereotypes as Vera in Kant's <u>Aula</u> to Katrin in Neutsch's <u>Spur der Steine</u> and Fräulein Broder in de Bruyn's <u>Buridans Esel</u>. While such images may be flattering to women, their ultimate purpose is to serve the needs of men and the world men created. Female strength does not involve power; it is nurturing, supporting, capable of sacrifice. The identity proposed to women has an added dimension, that of production, but it has not really changed. Still, there has been some gain: "Sie [die Frau] arbeitet wie ein Mann, das ist der Fortschritt. Und es <u>ist</u> ein Fortschritt."[6] These are the words Christa Wolf uses in her "Büchner-Preis-Rede" to characterize what has been achieved. At the same time and more importantly, she signals the starting point at which women begin to enter the scene as writers who use what self-confidence this progress has given them to articulate the need to find their own voices and create their own identities.

Christa Wolf began to do so before the others and much earlier than is generally assumed, namely with <u>Der geteilte Himmel</u> (1963). Seemingly staying within the general framework of the <u>Ankunftsromane</u> and their portrayal of "strong, new" women, she raises serious questions concerning that image. Her heroine, Rita, is capable of sacrifice and is in that sense strong: when she cannot hold and suppport her lover, Manfred, enough to keep him from despairing and leaving the country, she gives up her love and returns to the GDR. Rita makes the morally right, but--Wolf emphasizes--extremely painful, choice. At that point she defines her identity, fragile as that may still be, through her involvement with her work and her society, the very sources which have always given men their sense of self and which are now being offered women as an additional dimension. With Rita's choice, Christa Wolf gives this dimension priority and suggests that the hope embodied in her East is also based upon the emancipatory and egalitarian possibilities which were opened to women by their inclusion in production. At the same time, however, she forces Rita to choose. With the renunciation of her lover, the girl gives up the chance--for the duration of the novel at least[7]--to define herself in the traditionally feminine way. What is important, is the fact that there is no easy confluence, but a split between the old and the new, and that this nearly kills her. Indeed, Christa Wolf describes Rita's suicide attempt in terms of two trains inexorably rolling towards her from opposite directions, a symbol of the heroine's predicament, her conflicting needs as a woman. The nearly tragic love story can be seen as a tentative and still in many ways unsatisfactory attempt at exposing the central contradictions contained in the emancipation of women conceived by men. It is here that Christa Wolf begins to embark upon the enterprise which will continue to occupy her and lead her to ever more probing and demanding questions concerning woman's role, identity, and self-expression. "Als Frau ich sagen,"[8] what does it mean, what might it involve?

I have dealt with these earlier developments at some length because they are important to what happens in the 1970s and the first half of the 1980s. The images of women created in the beginning phase of GDR literary and cultural development, and refined in the subsequent period, still hold sway, if sometimes only as impossible constructs in need of deconstruction. For by 1974 women in large numbers have begun to join the writers' ranks and have started to work alongside Christa Wolf in trying to speak for themselves and to define their own identities.[9] Do they at the same time attempt to project <u>their</u> images of men, the men they see or would like to see? And how have men responded, have they made substantial revisions?

The "veränderte Literaturlandschaft" of the last decade has often been described;[10] suffice it to say that the changes have to do with increased openness and experimentation in form, style, and subject matter, and with a turn to the private and everyday spheres, while maintaining that the private is also the political and often enriching the everyday with substantial doses of the fantastic. The emphasis is on the concrete for reasons expressed by Franz Fühmann in his collection of stories <u>Saiäns-Fiktschen</u>:

> Denn das Konkrete ist schon dadurch, daß es konkret ist, das Andere zu einem Abstrakten, das Anschauliche das Andere zum Unanschaubaren, und wo Geschichte als ein Andres sich zeigt, wird sie schon in ihrer äußeren Erscheinung das, was sie ihrem Wesen nach ist: die Daseinsform von Alternative.[11]

What Fühmann says applies to male and female writers alike but is especially significant for the female authors with their close look at the everyday realities of individual women's lives as well as the larger historical visions undertaken by writers such as Morgner and Wolf. In fact, the most striking change in the "veränderte Literaturlandschaft" may be the large role played by women. It would be tempting to say, but hard to prove, that women writers not only contributed substantially to the developments but actually initiated them. The sheer number of women involved, and the stature of some, particularly of Christa Wolf, might point in this direction. It is also important to note that these changes occurred against the background of diminishing expectations in terms of careers (even though the specter of unemployment does not loom large in the GDR--as it does in Western countries--there too interesting and leading positions are occupied by relatively young people, leaving little chance for the younger generation to move into them) and a darkening global horizon with the threat of environmental destruction[12] and nuclear holocaust.

Under these circumstances both male and female writers and their protagonists have come closer together and jointly moved away from the productivist ethos of the 1950s and 1960s.[13] A woman, again Christa Wolf, was a pioneer. Nachdenken über Christa T. deals with individual failure--to assimilate and perform as expected in work and the public sphere--as something potentially positive because it could indicate a deeper commitment to life and society than ready and easy adaptation. In the 1970s and beyond, many authors have followed her lead and created protagonists, men and women, whose failures, partial or complete, are presented sympathetically or positively as refusals to participate in a work world and social environment which they perceive as alienating, destructive, or simply unresponsive. For male protagonists this refusal also involves a shift away from such aspects of traditionally masculine identity as goal orientation, instrumental rationality, repression of emotion, and self-assurance, towards a more androgynous kind of personality. One thinks of such different characters as Plenzdorf's Edgar and Paul, Braun's Frank, Loest's Wolfgang Wülff, Becker's Simrock, and Paul Gratzik's Kohlenkutte.[14]

An effective ironic perversion of such trends is Günter de Bruyn's Neue Herrlichkeit.[15] The title ostensibly refers to the setting, an old manor house, but the novel plays with both the sexual and social implications of "neu" and "Herr." Viktor, the protagonist, is a weak man, without ambition and without traditional male assertiveness. Yet, because of his "high birth" he is not a failure in social terms, and he is perfectly capable of using his social and attendant sexual status to "seduce" and "abandon" a girl to whom his important father refers as "the maid." Viktor has rid himself of the more strenuous aspects of traditional bourgeois masculinity in order to enjoy the more comfortable and more exploitative ones to the full. It is probably no coincidence that the 18th century aristocratic seducer à la Lovelace, Valmont, and Mellefont comes to mind,[16] with the implication that social and sexual relationships and their interplay have not changed for the better since bourgeois times, but for the worse: men are taking advantage of the new responsibilities given women by "emancipation" to escape demands made upon the male by the bourgeoisie; they are reverting to feudal attitudes of self-indulgence.

In the process, de Bruyn, ever the ironic observer of GDR manners and morals, puts his finger on something which has recently received more, and more explicit, attention, namely men's identities as males and their sexual behavior. Gratzik's <u>Kohlenkutte</u> and Brasch's <u>Vor den Vätern sterben die Söhne</u>,[17] albeit works published only in the West, but also Fries's <u>Alexanders neue Welten</u>[18] are quite graphic in their descriptions of sexual, even homosexual, intercourse and thus reveal more clearly that old instrumental attitudes towards sex still operate. Women's equality comes across as fantasies of women who complement the male "Wham bam, thank you, ma'am" with "Wham bam, thank you, mister."

What also emerges, for the first time in GDR letters, I believe, is the exploration and/or expression of male ambivalence towards women. An extreme and ironic example is Fries's "Frauentags Anfang oder das Ende von Arlequ und Paasch."[19] The two men have killed the women they had married in Fries's earlier novel <u>Der Weg nach Oobliadooh</u>[20] and, in an orgy of drinking and fast driving, they reach the coast, from which there is no escape. While they self-destruct, the country celebrates the "Frauentag."

This story is of course extreme, but whether women are seen positively and often consciously or unconsciously exploited, or negatively, as a force to be feared and avoided, they are perceived by male writers as very strong indeed. And it is difficult for the men, both as writers and protagonists, to come to terms with their perception. In addition, female strength which is primarily derived from traditional male sources, professional achievement and/or lack of emotionality, has recently been seriously called into question by Christoph Hein's <u>Der fremde Freund</u>.[21] This is not, I believe, a revisionist gesture, but an effort at exposing the poverty in the heroine's life--a poverty which becomes still more readily apparent in a woman--and thereby criticizing a general way of life which has always--and wrongly-- been quite acceptable for men.[22]

Women, especially women writers, largely share the men's belief in their strength, but with considerable differentiation and some misgivings. One vital reason for self-confidence on the part of women authors is best expressed by the following statement made in the context of Western feminist criticism but also, and even better, applicable to the women writers of the GDR:

> The son of many fathers, today's male writer feels hopelessly belated, the daughter of too few mothers, today's female writer feels that she is helping to create a viable tradition which is at last definitely emerging.[23]

Even the most dejected voices on the women's situation--one thinks of Doris Paschiller or Rosemarie Zeplin[24]--gain strength from their sense of contributing to that tradition. There are many instances of women writers supporting each other and referring directly or indirectly to each other's works. In Karin Simon's story "Der Bogen," for example, a young woman reads <u>Nachdenken über Christa T.</u> and cannot put it aside until she has finished it.[25] There is a strong sense among women writers of creating an alternative public sphere where issues and concerns important to women and thus to society at large can be discussed. Christa Wolf uses the term "Berührung" to express a feeling of "Schwesterlichkeit"[26] which is emerging from the combined efforts of women to define who they are and what they want.

In the process, they necessarily go beyond men in exploring the problems of the productivist ethos, because they experience its conflicts with their reproductive duties and urges most immediately. And they cannot be blind to the fact that in terms of life expectancy, which in the GDR in spite of the country's health-care system is relatively low precisely because of the heavy emphasis on production, GDR women compare less well with women in other industrialized countries than do GDR men with men elsewhere. Their double responsibility, to production and reproduction, is taking its toll on their health. From their difficult vantage point à cheval in two worlds, women are taking a critical look at the productivist ethos and reevaluating traditional feminine identity for its potential to create something altogether new, something that is yet to be realized. One thinks of the sensitive portraits of mother-child relationships (and the hopes put in them),[27] of old people and of relationships to the old, of support and friendship among women, and the explicit or implicit demand that the qualities of nurture and caring needed in these private associations be transferred to the public and political sphere as well.[28]

Such a general picture may sound overly optimistic in the face of the large body of writing by women about women where the actual conditions under which women live are anything but rosy. Yet one of Helga Königsdorf's "Ungehörige Träume" may serve as a paradigm for the paradoxical situation. The heroine has tried to fly, a symbol of her longing for liberation from everyday contradictions and pressures. When she wants to end what is obviously merely an escapist dream, she can only let herself fall: "Meiner Mentalität entspricht es jedenfalls, erst einmal abzustürzen, sich ein paar Schrammen zu holen, damit man das Leben durch die Haut pulsieren sieht."[29] While this could be interpreted as a kind of masochism, it more readily suggests a need for reality and life, which also involve pain. Such a view is corroborated by the protagonist's own dream interpretation of her flying and falling:

> Plötzlich wird mir die ganze Tragweite bewußt. Es ist etwas geschehen. Ich bin ausgebrochen. Ich habe soeben ein Bild von mir zerschlagen. Ich kann mich um ein neues Bild bewerben. Ich gehe in meinen Tag hinein und weiß, daß ich diesen Tag ändern muß, will ich der Nacht das Glück zurückgewinnen.[30]

The need for change is as unquestionable as is the

necessity for effecting it through a new identity gained in living and changing every day with its problems and sufferings.

In Helga Königsdorf's "dream" the ultimate goal is "der Nacht das Glück zurückgewinnen." Whatever this figure of speech may suggest in terms of emotional and sexual fulfillment and the involvement of men in that, Königsdorf does not follow up on its implications. The striking thing about much of the recent fiction by women is in fact the relative paucity and insignificance of men. I have discussed this elsewhere.[31] In spite of their heroines' often freely expressed longing for love, women writers have had limited interest in describing and defining men as they are. Christa Wolf has spoken of men's inability to love as an individual and cultural-historical problem from which the men, and indeed the world, suffer as much as women.[32] Without that capacity, however men hold little interest for women who otherwise can fend for themselves. With rare exceptions--Aeneas in Kassandra is one[33]--female authors have also hesitated to create a new identity for men, to imagine what men might or should be like in order to become desirable partners. But since such projections can be seen as gestures of dominance, women writers have good reason to refrain from making them. They would be doing to men what has been done to women for centuries and would only reverse the pattern, not alter it. The expectation may be for men to eventually respond adequately and positively to the changing identities of women.

In the meantime, one must accept the absence of "happy marriages" which I mentioned initially. In contrast to much fiction of the 19th and early 20th century, however, such absence contains positive aspects: there is a clear rejection of the old, mutually destructive relationships, including the refusal to look for individual fulfillment outside society, in the grand, if tragic, tales of asocial or antisocial passion. One thinks of the large role adultery has played in the literature of the past, or of the expectations brother and sister in Musil's Mann ohne Eigenschaften place in their incest, and compares these works to a story such as Helga Königsdorf's mocking "Bolero" or, in a different vein, Wolf's Kassandra, where the love between the seer and Aeneas cannot have any future because it would be outside of history.[34] The hope is for something really new which would transform society and history, and for which the bonds between women, which are occasionally possible, might be models: Christa Wolf speaks of a "Gemeinschaft, deren Gesetze Anteilnahme, Selbstachtung, Vertrauen und Freundlichkeit wären."[35] This is an appealing utopian vision, even if we realize full well that for many GDR heroines, authors, and of course women, as for the rest of us, such utopian hopes are small solace for a present in which rising but still largely unsatisfied expectations, certainly on the part of women, and some confusion and searching as to their identities among men as well, are still the only signs of real changes yet to come.

Notes

[1] Leo Tolstoy, *Anna Karenina*, ed. George Gibian (New York: Norton, 1970), p. 1. As I was reminded by Jeanette Clausen, Christa Wolf in *Nachdenken über Christa T.* (Neuwied/Berlin: Luchterhand, 1971), p. 155, contradicts Tolstoy (without mentioning him or referring to marriage in particular). This is important for the content of my paper because it indicates that Christa Wolf certainly is aware of the literary traditions I mention and is consciously writing within and against them. (She refers directly to Flaubert's *Madame Bovary* in *Christa T.*)

[2] Cf. Liliane Crips, "Une Tragédie optimiste. L'image de la femme et la conception de la morale dans le roman de la R.D.A. (1949-1964)," *Recherches Germaniques*, No. 8 (1978), pp. 114f.

[3] Johann Wolfgang von Goethe, *Torquato Tasso*, lines 1013-14.

[4] Quoted from *Angst vor der Liebe und andere Geschichten über Frauen*, ed. Meta Borst (Halle/Leipzig: Mitteldeutscher Verlag, 1984), pp. 346-47. Originally published in Daniela Dahn, *Spitzenzeit* (Halle/Leipzig: Mitteldeutscher Verlag, 1980).

[5] Patricia Herminghouse, "Wunschbild, Vorbild oder Porträt? Zur Darstellung der Frau im Roman der

DDR," in Literatur und Literaturtheorie in der DDR, ed. Peter Uwe Hohendahl and Patricia Herminghouse (Frankfurt: Suhrkamp, 1976), pp. 302-12. Cf. also Liliane Crips, "Une Tragédie optimiste" and "Metamorphoses. L'image de la femme et la conception de la morale dans le roman de la R.D.A. (1964-1976)," Recherches Germaniques, No. 9 (1979), pp. 187-203.

[6] Christa Wolf, "Büchner-Preis-Rede," in Lesen und Schreiben. Neue Sammlung (Darmstadt: Luchterhand, 1981), p. 326. On the question of women's work in relation to family obligations in literature, cf. also Dorothy Rosenberg, "On beyond Superwomen: The Conflict between Work and Family Roles in GDR Literature," in Studies in GDR Culture and Society 3, ed. Margy Gerber (Lanham/New York/London: University Press of America, 1983), pp. 87-100.

[7] How well Christa Wolf is aware of her contemporary readers' expectations and how hesitant she is to disappoint them totally is shown in the figure of Ernst Wendland: the possibility that his interest in Rita might go beyond that of a Werkleiter is never completely discounted.

[8] Christa Wolf, Voraussetzungen einer Erzählung. Kassandra (Darmstadt/Neuwied: Luchterhand, 1983), p. 148.

[9] Cf. the overview by Sara Lennox, "'Nun ja! Das nächste Leben geht aber heute an,' Prosa von Frauen und Frauenbefreiung in der DDR," in Literatur der DDR in den siebziger Jahren, ed. Peter Uwe Hohendahl and Patricia Herminghouse (Frankfurt: Suhrkamp, 1983), pp. 224-58.

[10] Cf. Hans Kaufmann, ed., Tendenzen und Beispiele. Zur DDR-Literatur in den siebziger Jahren (Leipzig: Reclam, 1981); Klaus Jarmatz, "Erkundungen, Erfahrungen, Erwartungen, I, II, III," Neue Deutsche Literatur, 31, Nos. 3, 4, 5 (1983), 124-35, 127-48, 104-13; Hans Richter, "Gegenwartsprosa der Deutschen Demokratischen Republik in gattungs- und stiltheoretischer Sicht," Sinn und Form, 36, No. 3 (1984), 563-75.

[11] Franz Fühmann, Saiäns-Fiktschen (Rostock: Hinstorff, 1983), p. 98.

¹² Because of its industrial structure the GDR is among the countries where this global problem is particularly serious. Thus life expectancy is relatively low--28th among developed countries--in spite of a good health-care system.

¹³ It may be relevant to note that the GDR economy has recently undergone structural changes which respond to the environmental problems and relate to the changes in attitude: while still emphasizing production, it has shifted priorities from quantity to quality in order to save precious energy and raw materials and to, at least, slow damage to the environment.

¹⁴ In Ulrich Plenzdorf's *Die neuen Leiden des jungen W.* (1972) and *Legende vom Glück ohne Ende* (1979), Volker Braun's *Unvollendete Geschichte* (1975), Erich Loest's *Es geht seinen Gang* (1978), Jurek Becker's *Schlaflose Tage* (1978), and Gratzik's *Kohlenkutte* (1982).

¹⁵ Günter de Bruyn, *Neue Herrlichkeit* (Frankfurt: Fischer, 1984). The GDR edition appeared a year later: *Neue Herrlichkeit* (Halle: Mitteldeutscher Verlag, 1985). However, the novel had been announced much earlier when sections were published in *Sinn und Form*, 34, No. 6 (1982) and *Neue Deutsche Literatur*, 31, No. 3 (1983). On the latter occasion it was referred to as a *Neuerscheinung*. For information on the pre-publication problems, cf. *Frankfurter Allgemeine Zeitung*, 24 July 1984, p. 21, and 9 March 1985, p. 25.

¹⁶ Lovelace in Samuel Richardson's *Clarissa Harlowe*, Valmont in Choderlos de Laclos' *Les Liaisons dangereuses* and Mellefont in Lessing's *Miss Sara Sampson*.

¹⁷ Paul Gratzik, *Kohlenkutte* (Berlin: Rotbuch, 1982); Thomas Brasch, *Vor den Vätern sterben die Söhne* (Berlin: Rotbuch, 1977).

¹⁸ Fritz Rudolf Fries, *Alexanders neue Welten* (Berlin/Weimar: Aufbau, 1982).

¹⁹ Fritz Rudolf Fries, "Frauentags Anfang oder das Ende von Arlequ und Paasch," *Sinn und Form*, 34, No. 2 (1982), 359-72.

[20] Fritz Rudolf Fries, *Der Weg nach Oobliadooh* (Frankfurt: Suhrkamp, 1966).

[21] Christoph Hein, *Der fremde Freund* (Berlin/Weimar: Aufbau, 1984). West German edition: *Drachenblut* (Neuwied/Berlin: Luchterhand, 1985).

[22] Another recent novel to deal with the theme of emotional poverty is Günter Görlich's popular and much-discussed *Die Chance des Mannes* (1982). Here it is indeed a man, decent, hardworking, successful, whose emotional impoverishment causes his marriage to collapse. Dorothea Kleine's *Jahre mit Christine* (Rostock: Hinstorff, 1980), now in its third edition, is an unusually negative portrait by a woman writer of a career-oriented woman who loses touch with her feelings and her family.

[23] Sandra M. Gilbert and Susan Gubar, *The Madwoman in the Attic* (New Haven/London: Yale Univ. Press, 1979), p. 50.

[24] Rosemarie Zeplin, *Schattenriß eines Liebhabers* (Berlin/Weimar: Aufbau, 1980) and *Alpträume aus der Provinz* (Berlin/Weimar: Aufbau, 1984); Doris Paschiller, *Die Würde* (Berlin: Buchverlag Der Morgen, 1980).

[25] Cf. an unpublished paper by Gertraud Gutzmann, "Arbeit, Umwelt und Natur in der Perspektive einiger DDR Schriftstellerinnen." The paper was prepared for the Northeast Modern Language Association Conference in Philadelphia, 1984. For other examples, see my paper "'Remembrance of Things Future'-- On Establishing a Female Tradition," to appear in Marilyn Fries, ed., *Critical Essays on Christa Wolf* (Detroit: Wayne State Press).

[26] Christa Wolf, "Berührung," in *Lesen und Schreiben*, pp. 209-21.

[27] Cf. my essay "Vertreibung aus dem Paradies: Zur neuen Frauenliteratur in der DDR," in *Studies in GDR Culture and Society* 3, pp. 71-85. Besides the works discussed there, many others could be mentioned, most importantly perhaps Christa Wolf, *Kindheitsmuster* (Berlin/Weimar: Aufbau, 1976), and Irmtraud Morgner, *Amanda. Ein Hexenroman* (Berlin/Weimar: Aufbau, 1983).

28 The last point is made most emphatically in Morgner's Amanda. Support and friendship among women plays a central role in Christa Wolf's interest in and essays on Bettine von Brentano and Karoline von Günderrode (in Lesen und Schreiben), in Morgner's Leben und Abenteuer der Trobadora Beatriz nach Zeugnissen ihrer Spielfrau Laura (Berlin/Weimar: Aufbau, 1974) and Amanda. Some other examples are Christine Wolter, "Ich habe wieder geheiratet," in her Ich habe wieder geheiratet (Berlin/Weimar: Aufbau, 1976); Doris Paschiller, Die Würde; and Angela Krauß, Das Vergnügen (Berlin/Weimar: Aufbau, 1984). Stories about old people include, e.g., Sylvia Kabus, "Das alte Weibchen," Temperamente, No. 4 (1979), pp. 84-89; Beate Morgenstern, "Gemüse-Erna," in her Jenseits der Allee (Berlin/Weimar: Aufbau, 1979); Monika Helmecke, "Klara, mach das Fenster zu," in her Klopfzeichen (Berlin: Verlag Neues Leben, 1979); Rosemarie Fret, "Windstill," in her Hoffnung auf Schneewittchen (Halle/Leipzig: Mitteldeutscher Verlag, 1981); Maria Seidemann, "Klara und die Tauben," in her Nasenflöte (Berlin: Eulenspiegel Verlag, 1983).

29 Helga Königsdorf, "Die Nacht beginnt am Tag," in her Meine ungehörigen Träume, 4th ed. (Berlin/Weimar: Aufbau, 1984), p. 100. Cf. also Antonia Grunenberg's interpretation in "Träumen und Fliegen. Neue Identitätsbilder in der Frauenliteratur der DDR," in Jahrbuch zur Literatur in der DDR, III, ed. Paul Gerhard Klussmann and Heinrich Mohr (Bonn: Bouvier, 1984), pp. 157-84.

30 Königsdorf, p. 102.

31 Cf. my essay "Vertreibung aus dem Paradies."

32 Especially in the "Büchner-Preis-Rede," pp. 382f.

33 As Dorothy Rosenberg reminded me, another would be Benno Pakulat, Laura's second husband in Morgner's Leben und Abenteuer der Trobadora Beatriz. It is significant, though, that Morgner has him die in the sequel Amanda. Ein Hexenroman. In the darkening world she describes here, there is no possibility for a positive relationship.

34 Cf. Notes 33 and 1.

35 Christa Wolf, "Berührung," p. 209.

Official Policy and the Attitudes of GDR Youth towards Marriage and the Opposite Sex as Reflected in the Column "Unter vier Augen"

Rüdiger Pieper

In the West, large numbers of young people have been discussing and practicing alternatives to marriage for fifteen years or more. This appears to be much less the case in the GDR. And while this social behavior is at least tolerated officially in the West, it is renounced in the GDR. In the GDR's official policy, marriage is regarded as having no alternative. As Rolf Borrmann and Hans-Joachim Schille wrote in 1984: "Currently there is not even a hint of any kind of relationship that could replace marriage based on the norms of socialist morals, or that could question its right to exist."[1] Alternatives such as communes are termed decadent and held up as evidence of the crisis of capitalist society.[2]

Official views such as these do not necessarily represent the views of the population, however. Often they reflect policy goals rather than reality. Are young people in the GDR really living according to the official norms? How would they like to live? What kind of problems do they have and discuss?

There are different ways of trying to find answers to questions such as these. One method is the conducting of surveys. Taking surveys in the GDR is, however, not possible for Western scientists, who are thus dependent on surveys done by GDR colleagues and who, generally speaking, have access only to those surveys officially sanctioned through publication. A second possibility is the study of documentary literature, of collections of interviews--such as Maxie Wander's <u>Guten Morgen, du Schöne</u>, or the more recent

Männerprotokolle.[3] To this second source of information belong Leserbriefe, letters written by GDR citizens to newspapers and magazines, in which they comment on matters of daily life. Here, too, of course, one must keep in mind that the sources are edited for publication. In regard to Leserbriefe, one has no way of determining the authenticity of the letters or the criteria used to select them. Still, Leserbriefe provide direct information and reflect public opinion as well as official policy.

In answering the questions formulated above, I will mainly use the latter approach. My source of public opinion will be the column "Unter vier Augen," which appears every Wednesday in the Junge Welt, the daily newspaper of the FDJ. I examined this column for the two-year period 1983 to 1984. To complete the picture, I will also discuss official GDR surveys dealing with the attitudes of young people.

First, however, I would like to set down in broad terms the socialist concept of marriage. According to Marxist theory, marriage in socialist society differs from marriage in capitalist society since in socialism there is no economic--or any other --compulsion to marry: marriage is founded exclusively on love and on the equality of men and women.[4] Only socialist society is able to create the conditions that make marriage a stable institution that benefits both the individual and society as a whole. Preparation for marriage and family life is part of the program for the development of the socialist personality, the goal of education. The socialist norms on which marriage is based include the ability to love, the knowledge of how to care for and educate children, and "knowledge and ability in matters of housekeeping."[5] In socialist marriage, the traditional division of labor between the sexes--the wife being responsible for the household, the husband being the breadwinner--should no longer exist: both are to share in the housework and the wife should be financially independent of her husband. There is to be no "double standard"--the wife is to have the same rights and freedoms as the husband. So--in short-- goes the theory.[6]

Information about the praxis of socialist marriage, especially the attitudes of young people toward marriage and family, can be found in surveys published in the GDR in recent years, for example, in Rolf Borrmann and Hans-Joachim Schille's book <u>Vorbereitung der Jugend auf Liebe, Ehe und Familie</u> (1980), or Kurt Starke and Walter Friedrich's <u>Liebe und Sexualität bis 30</u> (1984).[7]

Of the young people questioned by Borrmann and Schille, 85% said they wanted to marry; 11% said maybe; and less than 3% said no. About half of the teenagers canvassed thought that 20 was the ideal age for getting married; 33% preferred age 18 or 19; and only 2% favored age 25 or older. Young academics distinctly favored marrying later; one-third preferred ages between 21 and 24. According to Borrmann and Schille's survey, 74% of the young people (both sexes) wanted to have two children; 8%, more than three children; only 1% wanted no children at all. Of the girls responding, 14% indicated that they would rather not work when their children were small; 25% of the boys said that they would like their wife to stay at home during that period. Of the girls, 28% wanted to continue working under all circumstances, while only 20% of the boys supported this attitude. It is interesting to note that only the girls were asked whether they wanted to reduce their work hours or stop working after having had children. The boys were only asked about their expectations in regard to their wives, not whether they--as fathers-- would prefer to stop working and care for their child(ren) instead of the mother. The same survey also asked about the amount of time spent on housework: women worked an average 37.7 hours per week in the home, as compared with only 5.5 hours for men, and 4.3 hours for children.

Neither this survey nor surveys done by Kurt Starke and Walter Friedrich give information about the attitudes of young people toward alternative ways of living, such as communes, or about their views on living singly or as an unmarried couple. Starke and Friedrich do however mention that a growing number of young people between the ages of 18 and 30 are living alone (p. 259).

The column "Unter vier Augen"--the title translates as something like "Strictly Personal"--consists of letters written by readers and answers and comments given by the psychologist Jutta Resch-Treuwerth. The letters deal with problems shared by a large segment of GDR youth and/or questions which the policymakers regard as being problematic. The responses of Resch-Treuwerth clearly represent current policy.

A statistical overview with information about the contributors to the column and the types of problems raised is published at the end of each year. In 1983 and 1984, the years I am investigating here, the overwhelming majority of letters were written by girls and young women. Only about 30% of the letters were sent by males. Most letters came from teenagers between 16 and 18 years of age. This group was followed by youngsters aged 15 and under. In third place was the age group 19-20; in fourth, 20 and older.

In regard to the issues raised, it is interesting to note that more than half of the questions concerned with sexuality were asked by male writers (in spite of their relatively low rate of letter writing), while their share of questions about love problems and parental conflicts amounted to only 10%. The questions coming from the youngest age group (14-15 year olds) were mainly concerned with problems of love; those of the age group 16-18 dealt mainly with relationship problems and parental conflicts.

In the following, I will focus on three subjects discussed in the column during 1983 and 1984: marriage and possible alternatives; relationships with the opposite sex and patterns of male and female identity; and sexual minorities.

Marriage and Possible Alternatives

In 1983 there was an increase in the number of letters concerning early marriage. Noting this, Resch-Treuwerth comments: "This clearly shows the fragility of marriages that are contracted too early, that is, when both partners were 18 or 19."[8] In her statistical overview for 1984, Resch-Treuwerth points out that letters from young married couples and individuals were ordinarily written after the initial decision to seek a divorce had already been made. "This happens very quickly today, too quickly, often before any serious effort has been undertaken to solve the conflict."[9] She finds the reasons for divorce mainly within the individuals themselves: insufficient maturity of one or both of the partners, turning to another partner rather than trying to work things out. The high rate of divorce among GDR young people does not cause Resch-Treuwerth to question marriage, however.

The incontestability of marriage becomes even clearer when possible alternatives are discussed. In response to a letter asking about living together before marriage as a means of testing the relationship, Resch-Treuwerth argues that couples getting to know each other need to have a certain distance from one another, need to maintain their independence. She notes: "In practice it is not possible to create --so to speak--special laboratory conditions for a trial marriage that enable one to stop the experiment at any time."[10] Although she concedes that such experiments are almost the same as marriage and that the separation is like divorce, she strongly defends the exclusive furtherance of marriage in GDR society: "Flats suitable for families should be given first of all to those who have officially professed family life. The fact that in young marriages, too, some things are regarded too much as experimental and many things still go wrong seems to me to be a weak argument against the special societal support of young marriage." If we consider that these statements go well beyond the question raised in the letter, it seems justified to assume that Resch-Treuwerth took advantage of the opportunity to defend the State's support of marriage--as opposed to support of communes or other alternate forms of marriage, that she anticipated arguments against this policy from her readers.[11]

A similar defense appeared in June 1984 when an unmarried couple asked why only married couples can get double rooms in university dormitories.[12] Resch-Treuwerth begins her answer with a statement praising the support system for students in the GDR: that 75% of all university students are accommodated in dormitories. She goes on to say that there is nevertheless not enough space to give each couple or all those people who want to live together their own room--the missing logical link, namely, that students sometimes live three and more in a room is not mentioned--and that in any case there must be a difference in the support of married and unmarried couples. At the same time, Resch-Treuwerth strongly criticizes young people who look for ways of gaining these advantages without genuine motivation, i.e., who marry just to get their own room or flat.

A month later Resch-Treuwerth presents an ideal married couple to her readers: Gerlinde, a 23-year-old <u>Diplomingenieurökonom</u>, and Andreas, 25-year-old <u>Diplomökonom</u>--the one-thousandth couple to wed in the special marriage room of East Berlin's town hall. Their answers to Resch-Treuwerth's questions mirror the expectation of GDR society for young people: "We want to have children, first of all, at least two."[13]

Communes were not discussed in "Unter vier Augen" during 1983-84. Questions about single parents were raised, but none about individuals who want to live alone. Even the problems of singles were only discussed in connection with marriage, as the following examples show:

In August 1984 a 20-year-old girl writes about her difficulties as a single mother. She has a boyfriend who does not want to marry her because her son is not his. Resch-Treuwerth indicates in her answer that such attitudes are rare in GDR society: "Public opinion is free of all discrimination against single mothers. This is reflected in the fact that in 1981 every fourth child was born out of wedlock. Today it is nearly every third."[14] She concedes that a certain percentage of the population is not willing to marry someone with children; she places the blame for this attitude on parents who discourage their children from taking on "such a burden," as they see it.

In a letter published in September 1983 another 20-year-old single mother describes her problems with her friend who, in this case, is the father of her recently born child. She wants to marry him, but he isn't willing to get married, maintaining that he first wants to do his military service and work abroad for awhile. He suggests that they live together instead. Resch-Treuwerth's answer is quite interesting: she defends both the institution of marriage and the decision of the young man, which in her view is understandable. A child is insufficient reason for getting married; she even blames the girl for not having used contraceptives, which she calls irresponsible and typical of many girls who try in this way to bind their friend. (She also criticizes men who think that contraception is the exclusive responsibility of the girl.) Resch-Treuwerth proposes to the girl that she live alone with the child for a time and learn to be independent, rather than moving in with a man who still has to learn to think in terms of another person.[15] This reply shows that the norm of marriage is differentiated in actual practice: to marry is the official goal, but marriage is not the best solution under all circumstances.

Partnership Problems and Patterns of Female and Male Identity

The most common topic treated in the column concerns relationships between the sexes. Jealousy, for example, was treated a total of five times in the two-year period, an average of 5%.

In a letter that appeared in March 1984 a mother of two children describes her problems with her husband, who does not want her to go to the parties of her brigade alone. Again the reply is a kind of compromise: Resch-Treuwerth maintains that the social activities of the brigades are important and necessary, at the same time noting a contradiction in the attitudes of husbands and male colleagues who expect their female colleagues to participate in the social life of their brigade, but whose own wives are to come home promptly after work. Resch-Treuwerth reaffirms the socialist position that men and women must have the same rights and freedoms. Her practical solution to the problem is that brigades should--at least from time to time--invite the partners of their members to attend their social events, in the hope of increasing the acceptance of brigade activities.[16]

Maybe it is a coincidence, but all of the letters dealing with jealousy were written by women: either the man is--in the eyes of the woman writer--too friendly with other women or he does not want her to do something without him. In my opinion, this is an indication that traditional role behavior can still be found in the GDR: men continue to have more sexual freedom while women have a stronger orientation toward the family.

The second half of this thesis is strengthened by a discussion about housework that was published in a series entitled "Family Life - Burden or Pleasure?" in the summer of 1984:[17] in addition to questions on leisure time and shift work, which I will not go into here, the newspaper wanted to know whether its readers thought that the sharing of housework in their family was fair, and, more specifically, whether sons and daughters have the same duties. In the course of the discussion, which extended over five issues of the paper, 34 letters were--at least partly--published. Among them were several examples of families in which the father or husband does almost nothing around the home. An 18-year-old student, for example, wrote: "The sharing of housework in our family is not as it should be. Mom has to do everything herself. When Dad dries the dishes he's in a bad mood for days afterwards."[18] This letter and similar ones indicate that the desired norm, i.e., the equal sharing of housework, is not reality in many families. The fact that Junge Welt gave so much space to this question shows too however that official efforts are being made to change this situation. Young people are to be taught that the household is the responsibility of both partners and all other family members as well. It was interesting to note that the negative letters published as a part of this discussion came at the beginning; later issues tended toward the positive: praise for men who do their fair share.

Another discussion spread over various issues of Junge Welt in 1983 and 1984 dealt with the problems of young couples who are separated for a long period of time, as happens, for example, when the husband is called up for military service. Given the high rate of early marriage in the GDR, this is a frequent occurrence. Most questions concerning this issue were raised by women, who often asked for advice on how to live during this period. "How can I survive our separation normally?" a young mother asks in October 1984.[19] Resch-Treuwerth's advice is to be active: to learn to do things in the household (painting, paperlaying, upholstering) that she hasn't done before, to do community work, visit her parents and her inlaws, occasionally take care of another child from the neighborhood, etc. "I think that courage and the development of responsibility on the part of the women is their equivalent [Gegenleistung] to the military service of the men."

A month later several letters commenting on this letter and Resch-Treuwerth's answer were published.[20] Some of the women complain that society does not do enough for women in this situation. Another writer shows little sympathy for the young mother: "Nothing happened to her that she couldn't anticipate. If you marry someone who has not yet done his military service you have to expect that this test will come." One letter even criticizes Resch-Treuwerth's advice: "The suggestions on how to spend the evening can't help to overcome her longing. She's still alone. . . . The idea of taking care of other children is absurd considering that this is her first child."

In a letter published in May 1984 a young wife expresses her anxiety about living with her husband again after the 18-month separation. Although the woman gives no reasons for her fears, Resch-Treuwerth explains them so: ". . . you have developed independence and the ability to make decisions, which you are afraid you'll lose now that he's back. . . ."[21] She suggests talking with her husband in the first days after his return to clearly determine each partner's responsibilities in the home.

Two letters published at the end of 1983 show that not only women have problems during such times of separation but men as well--although their problems are somewhat different. The men often find girl friends during their period of service in the army: the girl friend for weekdays, the wife for the weekend, as Resch-Treuwerth puts it.[22] She strongly criticizes these men and urges the wives to give their husbands an ultimatum, either one or the other. The only letter written by a man concerning the question of separation during the husband's military service deals with the question of such a triangle and the role of the collective in this situation. The soldier asks whether he or the collective should interfere. Resch-Treuwerth responds that the collective not only should, but must interfere: "A direct opinion, even a dressing down is in my opinion essential whenever the respect and dignity of another person are being clearly violated and his or her physical and mental well-being and ability to function are being affected by a partnership problem."[23] That reality is different is indicated not only by the question of the reader, but also by Resch-Treuwerth's remark: "It often happens that everyone is keenly interested in the developments of such a delicate story, that the unfaithful husband is celebrated as a 'devil of a fellow,' and others are even willing to help hush up the resulting complications."

Sexual Minorities

Finally, I come to an issue that is no less critical in the GDR than elsewhere: sexual minorities. Given the social norms of marriage and children, homosexual men and women live under special pressures in the GDR, in spite of the fact that legal discrimination was abolished relatively early, in 1968.

The only time homosexuality was a subject in "Unter vier Augen" was in October 1984 when a mother of a 16-year-old boy wrote that one of the boys in her son's class was gay.[24] She was worried that he could seduce others to homosexuality, but she also wanted to know how to help him. Resch-Treuwerth's answer is free of any discrimination, as can be seen already in the subtitle of the column, "Reacting with Understanding." In response to the letter, Resch-Treuwerth interviews an educator, Kurt R. Bach, who has written books on sex education and sexuality in general. Bach, too, affirms that "homosexuals are and remain precious members of the collective. They are colleagues and friends like all the others." (This in spite of the fact that just ten years earlier he had called homosexuality a "defect" and advised against friendships with homosexuals[25]--a change of view that indicates that social norms are not fixed and can and do evolve with time.) Resch-Treuwerth's interview with Bach deals primarily with remaining prejudice against homosexuals. Collectives are urged not to isolate homosexual pupils, but to help them.

No letters written by homosexuals themselves appeared in the column. Advice was thus given to straight readers on how to treat homosexuals, but no advice was given to gays on how to cope with the myriad social and psychological problems they face. This in itself is of course a form of discrimination.

Assessment

Summing up the tone of the questions and answers discussed above, one can say that the way of life in the GDR is more or less traditional, sometimes even more traditional than the socialist norms would like, for example, when it comes to the division of labor within the family. Nevertheless, certain changes have clearly taken place: women are more self-confident and make more demands on their partners. Divorce seems to be less of a problem for the people concerned than for the State and the official morals. Economic questions do not play a role in marriage and divorce--except that the chances of getting one's own apartment increase when the couple is married.

Different life styles are not officially accepted in the GDR. Unmarried people--with the exception of unmarried mothers--encounter a number of bureaucratic problems. Discussions about alternative ways of life are not openly held; communes are strongly attacked by the representatives of the official morals.

A look at the column "Unter vier Augen" cannot pretend to give adequate answers to the questions raised at the beginning of this paper, but it can give some additional information and complement findings from other, more scholarly, sources, thus broadening our knowledge of these aspects of everyday life in the GDR.

Notes

[1] Rolf Borrmann and Hans-Joachim Schille, Eltern als Sexualerzieher (Berlin: Volk und Wissen, 1984), p. 85. My translation, as will be the case throughout.

[2] See, for example, Rolf Borrmann and Hans-Joachim Schille, Vorbereitung der Jugend auf Liebe, Ehe und Familie (Berlin: Deutscher Verlag der Wissenschaften, 1980), pp. 123-32.

[3] Maxie Wander, Guten Morgen, du Schöne (Darmstadt/Neuwied: Luchterhand, 1978); Christine Müller, Männerprotokolle (Berlin: Verlag der Morgen, 1985).

[4] Cf., e.g., Herta Kuhrig, "Familie und Familienglück," Einheit, 40, No. 12 (1985), 1099-1105.

[5] Borrmann/Schille, Eltern als Sexualerzieher, p. 89.

[6] For more information on the official views on marriage in the GDR, see Anita Grandke, <u>Junge Leute in der Ehe</u> (Berlin: Staatsverlag der DDR, 1982) and her <u>Familienförderung als gesellschaftliche und staatliche Aufgabe</u> (Berlin: Staatsverlag der DDR, 1981).

[7] Kurt Starke and Walter Friedrich, <u>Liebe und Sexualität bis 30</u> (Berlin: Deutscher Verlag der Wissenschaften, 1984).

[8] "Unter vier Augen," 28 December 1983. In the following only the dates of the columns will be noted, since the title of the column is always the same.

[9] Column from 2 January 1985.

[10] Column from 15 February 1984.

[11] As an example of state support of marriage, married couples under the age of 26 receive interest-free loans of 5000 Marks to be used for establishing their household (<u>Familiengründungskredit</u>). The loans, which are to be paid back within 8 years, are reduced with the birth of children: by 1,000 Marks, first child; 1,500 Marks, second child; 2,500 Marks, third child. Unmarried couples, singles, etc. are not eligible for this support.

[12] Column from 13 June 1984.

[13] Column from 4 July 1984.

[14] Column from 11 April 1984.

[15] Column from 16 November 1983.

[16] Column from 14 March 1984.

[17] "Familienalltag - Last oder Lust," five columns: 18 July, 1 August, 29 August, 12 September, 26 September 1984.

[18] Column from 1 August 1984

[19] Column from 31 October 1984.

[20] Column from 21 November 1984.

[21] Column from 2 May 1984.

[22] Columns from 23 November and 7 December 1983.

[23] Column from 11 January 1984.

[24] Column from 24 October 1984.

[25] Kurt R. Bach, *Geschlechtserziehung in der sozialistischen Oberschule* (Berlin: Deutscher Verlag der Wissenschaften, 1974), p. 256.

Illness and the Socialist Personality:
Philosophical Debates and Literary Images in the GDR

Carol Poore

> "Dringender als der Technik
> bedürfen wir der Mensch-
> lichkeit."[1]

In the past fifteen years or so, a widening discussion has developed in GDR philosophy and medical ethics about such questions as a Marxist perspective on death, the normative concept of the "socialist personality," and the relativizing of the value attached to performance in a society which officially places the greatest emphasis on "scientific-technical" progress. Many of the factors contributing to these discussions are international and not specific to the GDR, such as recent developments in life-saving technology, the United Nations Year for the Disabled in 1981, which led to a heightened awareness of many issues, and a general rise in the standard of living, which has made more funds available for improving the health-care system. However, the discussion of the integration of people with illnesses and disabilities into society and of the relevance of the concept of the "socialist personality" for this has taken on a special cast in the GDR.

As Hahn and Thom point out in the most important book on recent debates, if adequate solutions have yet to be found for problems of integration and care, this is only partially due to a lack of funds and technical progress.[2] Rather, as they assert, it is also due to ways of life and traditional attitudes or prejudices. They enumerate these as the unavailability of the working population for primary care, the difficulty of integrating many people into demanding work processes, the tendency to delegate responsibility to institutions, and outright rejection of those who are "different." With respect to this last point, the authors observe that, in addition to prejudices and defensive reactions continuing from earlier times, it can be assumed that a one-sided orientation towards the ideal of the socialist personality has also created barriers and a lack of understanding for those who can hardly develop in this way. Here, the ideal of the socialist personality is defined as manifesting those qualities which are considered important for the further "progressive" development of society: "Bewußtheit, Aktivität, Kollektivität, Parteilichkeit."[3] In this connection, another standard work asserts that the moral and social legitimation for rehabilitation depends on the extent to which this concept of the "personality" can be applied to people who are physically or mentally disabled, as well as on the degree of importance attached to performance for those who are unable to work.[4]

Both discussions criticize an exclusive orientation towards performance as a holdover from capitalism, emphasize that there is no objective way to measure the "value" of a life, and, with respect to the issue of suicide, assert that it is also a continuation of bourgeois ethics simply to pass a moral judgment on those who find their lives unbearable and meaningless, rather than trying to understand and change the conditions which lead them to such a desperate act. Thus one of the most significant things about these discussions is that they are beginning to develop a materialist rather than idealist concept of the socialist personality. In this context, Hahn and Thom quote Irene Dölling on personality development:

> Das Ideal der allseitig entwickelten sozialistischen Persönlichkeit ist keine abstrakte Summierung aller denkbaren positiven Verhaltensweisen, wonach die wirklichen Menschen sich um jeden Preis zu richten haben. Es ist vielmehr umgekehrt; unter Berücksichtigung der Bedingungen und Gesetzmäßigkeiten der individuellen Entwicklung, zu denen auch die "körperliche Organisation" der Individuen in ihrer historischen Konkretheit gehört, werden im Persönlichkeitsideal soziale Bedingungen und Prozesse daraufhin bewertet, wie sie die

Ausbildung des "subjektiven Vermögens" der Individuen fördern.5

These discussions in philosophy and medical ethics in the GDR are carried out among small circles of experts, rather than in larger public forums. In fact, authorities such as Hahn and Thom criticize the discussion of difficult problems of medical ethics in the Western media as "sensationalistic" and view it as the experts' "responsibility" first to consider all these issues carefully and then to acquaint the public gradually with them. This lack of public discussion has important implications for the function of literary works which thematize these problems. For one thing, since the theoretical discussion aims towards arriving at a "correct" perspective rather than investigating actual conditions, there are, as these sources themselves point out, no reliable sociological studies in the GDR on attitudes towards people with illnesses and disabilities. Thus, as with other areas of life, literary depictions--whether in documentary reports or fiction--take over some of the functions of sociology by presenting otherwise unavailable information on daily life. In this sense, such works provide a certain voice to other sectors of the population besides the "experts," thus serving a function not performed by the media.

Since the late 1970s, more than half a dozen documentary reports on the lives of people with illnesses and disabilities have appeared in the GDR, whereby the major accent lies on developmental or psychic problems.6 All these accounts take for granted the level of medical care available to all, and report extensively on its inadequacies and the difficulties of daily life for people who fall outside the mainstream. These books provide information not available elsewhere about the experiences of people who are made to feel singled out, different, or isolated. There are numerous indications of pervasive pressures to conform and tendencies to segregate those who cannot adjust, be it to standards of behavior and appearance, or to social expectations concerning work and performance. These writers often mention the fear of being "conspicuous" as the most unbearable new experience of all which they must learn to face, an experience far more difficult to deal with than the actual disability. Other examples show the extreme feelings of social devaluation accompanying a decreased ability to work, which point not only to the continuing need for self-realization through productive activity, but also to deeply anchored beliefs about the "value" of individuals to a society oriented towards performance. Written with the aim of bringing such problems into public consciousness, these reports hope to further sensitivity and tolerance towards a wider range of ways of living a satisfying life, ways in which individual development would not be measured according to impossible ideals of achievement and personality development.

Along with these documentary reports, fictional depictions of illness and disability in GDR literature also bring to the fore social processes and forms of consciousness that are hardly dealt with elsewhere. Thus, as part of the broader debate about performance, the socialist personality, and the quality of life, it is useful to trace images of illness in GDR fiction, not so much for their informative value about daily life as for insight into what they signify in cultural discourse.

> "Sie hat promoviert und ist verrückt geworden."[7]

Such a sentence, written about a young Party member who finished her doctoral work with honors, would hardly be found in early works of socialist realism. Rather, the "positive heroes" there possessed disciplined, strong bodies and minds which they devoted to furthering historical progress. However, these "saubere Mädel" and "starke Genossen"[8] of socialist realist tradition who exuded healthiness, vitality, and the undiminished capacity to act have long since made way for other, much more complex depictions of characters living under the conditions of "real socialism." In such works of GDR literature, the sort of "health" which was equated earlier with self-control appears much more difficult to maintain. Characters suddenly cannot go on any more in the old ways--whether politically, at work, or in their personal relationships--and often the only way out is to fall ill or die. Thus, the questions to keep in mind here in discussing these works would include the following: What is it that these characters are really suffering from? If the "old ways" of working and living with others are somehow no longer adequate, is the presentation of illness linked at all to another way of living or hoping? Do we find any indications of what could make these characters feel more alive and integrated into their world?

A work in which the metaphor of illness could be characterized as transitional is Stefan Heym's Collin (1979). Here, the heart problems of the main character, caused by stress, are related to his inability to break through his writer's block and write authentically. Once he decides to include in his memoirs the truth about conflicts within the Party, he no longer needs to be in the hospital. This conviction that a productive solution to Collin's problems is possible is underscored by the fact that Comrade Urack, the head of the secret service and Collin's adversary, is a patient in the same hospital. Urack has also suffered a heart attack, and the two are competing, in a manner of speaking, to determine who will outlive the other, whose perspective will prevail. Thus, illness here indicates wornout ideas in the case of Urack, and interruption in the creative process for Collin, but the possibility of finding a productive solution within Collin's profession as a writer, in the eventual service of social progress, is not fundamentally doubted.

A different, more radicalized situation exists in other recent works portraying stressful situations or outsider figures whose alienation may be so extreme that it leads to suicide.[9] In these works, characters experience severe difficulties in finding their appropriate "place" in the socialist community, in adjusting to pre-established norms which they find alien to themselves, in resolving conflicts between emotional needs and social expectations. In this connection, Brigitte Martin's novel Nach Freude anstehen (1981) illustrates the increasing interest in portraying psychological disorders in GDR literature.[10] This novel depicts the life of a divorced woman, Edith, who is a computer scientist with two young daughters. Because of her efforts to accomplish everything--to advance professionally, maintain a satisfying relationship with a man, and be a good mother--she begins to suffer psychosomatic symptoms of stress and becomes increasingly depressed and dissatisfied with herself and other people. Growing up in such a tense atmosphere and feeling neglected, her daughters also become more and more disturbed, withdrawn, aggressive, and fearful, until one is briefly committed to the Charité. For Edith, conflicts between work and emotional needs lead to physical and mental breakdowns. The source of her deep dissatisfaction is that so much emphasis is put on working for goals, for an idea of what she should achieve in life, that she finds it extremely difficult, if not impossible, to enjoy processes of living which are not necessarily directed towards a purpose. Edith knows that she wants more out of life; she says: "Das Tägliche nicht als Summe aus Arbeit und Wohnen, nicht als Aktivitäten zur Aufrechterhaltung auffassen" (p. 11). However, she cannot find the meaning and intensity she would like in political commitment, work, family, or intimate relationships.

In Jurek Becker's <u>Schlaflose Tage</u> (1978), fear of a heart attack and imminent death leads the teacher Simrock to re-evaluate his previous life and to strike out in totally new directions, in contrast to Collin.[11] He gives up his teaching position, which now seems full of unbearable compromises and dissimulation towards pupils, and takes a job driving a bread truck--a new experience for a teacher who has no first-hand knowledge of manual labor. He also makes drastic changes in his personal life, leaving his "boring" marriage and seeking more intense, less restrictive relationships. Yet the novel does not romanticize this sort of "life on the margins." Rather, the undertones are more serious. Simrock escapes what has become a stressful, unbearable situation for him, and his heart problem (perhaps imaginary in the first place) disappears, but his new life does not seem fundamentally satisfying, either. It may be more peaceful and honest, but one also has the sense that he is merely passing time.

In contrast to Simrock, who gives up a socially accepted position, the young boy in Ulrich Plenzdorf's short story "kein runter kein fern" (1980) has always been isolated from the mainstream; as a child with dyslexia he has been sent to a "Hilfsschule." The boy's learning disability enters into the form of the story, which is narrated from his point of view. His difficulty in spelling, forming complete sentences, and thinking in a connected way is reflected in the three levels of language in the story: the pathos of official slogans, his father's words, and his own thoughts. These three levels are jumbled together in his mind, existing alongside each other, unconnected. The emphasis in the official speeches on decisiveness, competence, cheerful resolve (a parody of Neues Deutschland) complements his father's rigidity and strictness (a parody of authoritarian narrow-mindedness, as when the boy remembers his father's saying: "Schwachsinn ist doch nur eine Folge kapita warte mal also kapita wo soll im Sozialismus der Nährboden für Schwachsinn! Wo ist im Sozialismus der Nährboden für Krebs? Krebs ist eine Krank. Schwachsinn ist auch eine Krank").[12] The boy cannot perform as required by the political and educational system or by his father and policeman brother, and is therefore isolated and harrassed. At the same time, his own fantasies remain unattainable--whether of taking infantile, violent revenge against the "cops," of hearing the Rolling Stones, of becoming a carpenter rather than attending school, or of finding security again with his mother, who has gone to the West. The boy's inability to bring together the spheres of politics and family with his own needs is clearly not due primarily to his own inadequacy, but to the inflexibility of a society which defines "normality" in a narrow way and makes little provision for those like him who fall "outside."

More unfamiliar in the West, Winfried Völlger's novel Das Windhahnsyndrom appeared in 1983, with a second printing in 1985. It depicts the case of Claudia, a young woman philologist, who is allowed to travel to the Himalayas to study languages spoken there. Upon her return to the GDR, she has contracted a strange disease which makes her laugh uncontrollably at times; she is under psychiatric care. The narrator is the doctor in the psychiatric clinic who was her childhood friend and later her lover, and who now wants to try to understand and help her. The book is divided into four sections corresponding to the structure of a case history. In the first, "Versuch einer Anamnese," the narrator reviews the days of their childhood and youth, whereby the most significant event for later developments is that Claudia joined the Party without real inner conviction. The second part, entitled "Peristase," traces her daily life with friends and lovers up to the point when she receives her doctor's degree and is ready to set off on the Himalayan expedition. In the third section, "Das Leiden," the narrator tries to get to the bottom of Claudia's strange illness, and it becomes clear that the attacks of laughter started after her confrontation with the world outside. (Her filmmaker friend who accompanied her, in contrast, did not return but used the trip as a "Chance zur Welt," which her professor comments on by saying: "er hat das einzig Richtige getan," p. 258.)

The situations in which she begins to laugh uncontrollably are varied, but most have to do with traveling--she laughs, for example, when she remembers playing a childhood game of journeying to the North Pole, or when she receives a card from her niece in Crete--or with hypocritical or defensive reactions to life in the GDR. Thus, she cannot restrain herself at the funeral of an old professor, described earlier in the novel as giving extremely abstract lectures on Marxism, when she sees the red flag on his coffin. Or, she has to laugh when, upon her parents' visit from the West, her GDR doctors express their fear that the former will defame GDR psychiatric care in the Western media.

Finally, in the last section, "Die wunderbare Heilung," Claudia meets a man who was her boyfriend in school and who had broken up with her because of his religious beliefs and her sudden joining of the Party. He is now living in the West, and discusses with her his travels in Israel and his upcoming trip to Auschwitz, saying that as a GDR citizen he had never felt a need to go there and that he is now ashamed of this. After these talks, and also as a result of the narrator's ongoing care, Claudia is no longer plagued by laughter, but is able to smile a "good smile." Her laughter had been rooted in sadness and mourning over deceit, hypocrisy, missed opportunities, a life not yet lived. She has indeed changed, for she now wants to visit relatives in the West, which she had always avoided before. Furthermore, she has become much less pedantic about her work as a translator, believing now that certain texts from other cultures can only be roughly approximated in German and deserve to be approached on their own terms. In other words, she is taking the first steps away from being a person with the "beschränkter Blick des Inselbewohners" (p. 296) who has shut herself up in abstraction out of the inability to deal with reality, out of desperation, or simply out of convenience and thoughtlessness.

This novel does not only trace Claudia's illness; it is also the story of the narrator, the physician, who realizes that "healing" may change a person significantly. He learns that his task is to facilitate such a transformation rather than to try to force his patient back into old molds. In other words, the fact that Claudia is someone he cares for as a unique individual leads him to become conscious of the disparity between the person she really is and what is best for her, on the one hand, and, on the other, the "Bild der unversehrten Persönlichkeit" (p. 316), which functions as a model in psychiatry. His effort not to do violence to her feelings and her needs leads him to question accepted views of what "health" is and to abandon "alle gängigen Wege der Therapie" (p. 316). Thus, the optimism of the ending, the "miraculous cure," lies less in resuming political activity or professional goals (which remain very much in the background) than in consciously developing the ability to tolerate complexity and avoid thinking and acting according to absolute dualities. These, in the context of the novel, could be expressed as: West/East, the bad Germany/the good Germany, sickness/health, other/self.

In a 1984 interview Christa Wolf was asked whether she saw a connection between illness and hope. She replied that she did see such a connection at times, though more in the sense of illness "als Ausdruck einer inneren Verfassung einer Person," of a signal for the "Unbewältigbarkeit der Probleme."[13] The theme of illness in Wolf's works would warrant a separate study--one thinks of Rita's recovery from her suicide attempt, of Nelly's "Genesung," of Günderrode's and Kleist's precariously balanced lives. In the present context, Christa T.'s fatigue and illness are paradigmatic. The narrator ponders the cause of her death, saying: "Und die Frage, woran Christa T. gestorben ist, werde ich selbst stellen, zu ihrer Zeit, ohne in Zweifel zu ziehen, daß es die Krankheit war, Leukämie, mit der sie nicht fertig werden konnte."[14] Christa T.'s leukemia is the metaphor for the psychic exhaustion and emptiness that she feels in her thwarted attempts to live authentically--whether in her work as a teacher with pupils who are all too ready to conform or in her marriage, which is lacking in intensity. The narrator comments: "Niemals kann man durch das, was man tut, so müde werden wie durch das, was man nicht tut oder nicht tun kann. Das war ihr Fall" (pp. 175-76). Her illness and death signify both that she is living through the contradictions of her time without accepting false solutions, and, devastatingly, that there is "no place" in her world where she can live authentically.

In this work and others discussed here, the metaphor of illness signals the difficulty, if not impossibility, of defining one's own work and life as a subject. Thus, the distance of these characters from the ideal of the "socialist personality" calls into question the concept of progress implied in this ideal which has no room for their needs and experiences. Of course, the alternative to such exclusions points beyond the literary texts. It would have to do with respect for otherness, for different modes of perception and living, which would entail integrating these differences into work and personal life without destroying them.

Common to all these presentations--whether theory, documentary reports, or fiction--is a problematizing of the concept of performance and its implications thus far for the "value" of individuals to scientific and technical progress. To be sure, in all of these works, the economic and social achievements of socialism exist as given. However, the works rarely give the impression that economic transformations have effected fundamental changes in values, interpersonal relationships, or the lives of people who do not fit smoothly into the usual order of things. In this regard, these portrayals of illness, disability, and the experiences of such outsider groups are part of a growing <u>Zivilisationskritik</u> in the GDR. In particular, awareness of the need for a "revolution in feelings" to accompany the "scientific-technical revolution" has many similarities with the increasing ecological consciousness in the GDR and the portrayal of environmental problems in GDR literature.[15] A number of writers are also reassessing the development of industrial production at high environmental cost and the official policy of encouraging consumption, and are thereby questioning what this kind of "progress" means for the quality of life. A statement made by Reimar Gilsenbach at the Ninth Writers' Congress in 1983 could apply also to the problems raised in these literary depictions of illness and disability:

> Wir leisten Erkleckliches, um durch Argumente, Wissen, Erkenntnisse für einen rationalen Umgang mit der Natur zu werben; wir sind zurückhaltend, wenn es sich um die Erziehung der Gefühle handelt, um die Vermittlung von Wertungen, die sich aus dem Mensch-Natur-Verhältnis ergeben; wir sind Stümper, wenn es darum geht, diese Wertungen in Millionen von Menschen so zu verinnerlichen, daß sie zu moralischen Haltungen werden, zu einer sozialistischen Ethik, die das Sich-verantwortlich-Fühlen für die Natur dieses Planeten zu einem Charakterzug des neuen Menschen macht.[16]

For all of the writers discussed here, the path towards creating this new socialist ethics--whether in interaction with other people or with nature--seems to lie in the conscious efforts of individuals, whereby imaginative and informative literature could play a significant part in such a transformation of consciousness.

Notes

[1] Volker Keßling, _Tagebuch eines Erziehers_ (Berlin: Neues Leben, 1980), p. 64.

[2] Susanne Hahn and Achim Thom, _Sinnvolle Lebensbewahrung - humanes Sterben_ (Berlin: Deutscher Verlag der Wissenschaften, 1983), pp. 22ff.

[3] Hahn and Thom, p. 24.

[4] Wolfgang Presber, Rolf Löther et al., _Sozialistischer Humanismus und Betreuung Geschädigter_ (Jena: Gustav Fischer Verlag, 1981), pp. 27ff.

[5] Irene Dölling, _Naturwesen, Individuum, Persönlichkeit_ (Berlin: Deutscher Verlag der Wissenschaften, 1979), p. 132, as quoted in Hahn and Thom, p. 25.

[6] These include: Roswitha Geppert, _Die Last, die du nicht trägst_ (Halle: Mitteldeutscher Verlag, 1984); Gerda Jun, _Kinder, die anders sind. Ein El-_

ternreport (Berlin: Volk und Gesundheit, 1981); Volker Keßling, Tagebuch eines Erziehers (Berlin: Neues Leben, 1980); Klaus Möckel, Hoffnung für Dan (Berlin: Neues Leben, 1983); Sybille Muthesius, Flucht in die Wolken (Berlin: Der Morgen, 1981); Irene Oberthür, Mein fremdes Gesicht (Berlin: Der Morgen, 1984); Wilhelm Thom and Elfriede Thom, Rückkehr ins Leben (Berlin: Neues Leben, 1979; 2nd. ed., 1981); Maxie Wander, Leben wär eine prima Alternative (Berlin: Der Morgen, 1979).

[7] Winfried Völlger, Das Windhahnsyndrom (Rostock: Hinstorff, 1983), p. 296. Subsequent page references will appear in parentheses in the text.

[8] Cf. Michael Rohrwasser, Saubere Mädel, Starke Genossen (Frankfurt: Roter Stern, 1975) on the Red-One-Mark novels of the Weimar Republic.

[9] I will not discuss here the theme of suicide, which has been dealt with extensively in: Michael Rohrwasser, "Das Selbstmordmotiv in der DDR-Literatur," in Probleme deutscher Identität. Zeitgenössische Autobiographien, Identitätssuche und Zivilisationskritik, ed. Paul Gerhard Klussmann and Heinrich Mohr (Bonn: Bouvier, 1983).

[10] Brigitte Martin, Nach Freude anstehen (Berlin: Der Morgen, 1981). Other relevant works by women authors dealing with such psychological stresses and disorders are: Monika Helmecke, Klopfzeichen (Berlin: Neues Leben, 1981), and Muthesius, Flucht in die Wolken.

[11] Jurek Becker, Schlaflose Tage (Frankfurt: Suhrkamp, 1978).

[12] Ulrich Plenzdorf, "kein runter kein fern," in Erzählte Zeit, ed. Manfred Durzak (Stuttgart: Reclam, 1980), p. 451. See Ute Brandes, "Toward Socialist Modernism: Ulrich Plenzdorf's 'kein runter kein fern,'" in Studies in GDR Culture and Society 4, ed. Margy Gerber (Lanham: University Press of America, 1984), pp. 107-25.

[13] "Documentation: Christa Wolf," German Quarterly, 57, No. 1 (1984), p. 93.

[14] Christa Wolf, Nachdenken über Christa T.

(Neuwied: Luchterhand, 1970), p. 64.

[15] Cf. Hubertus Knabe, "Zweifel an der Industriegesellschaft. Ökologische Kritik in der erzählenden DDR-Literatur," in Umweltprobleme und Umweltbewußtsein in der DDR, ed. Redaktion Deutschland Archiv (Cologne: Wissenschaft und Politik, 1985), pp. 201-51.

[16] As quoted in Knabe, pp. 221-22.

Fortschritt in der DDR-Literaturkritik
der 80er Jahre - ein ambivalentes Phänomen?

Gerd Labroisse

Daß der Zustand der Literaturkritik in der DDR ein ernsthaftes und fortdauerndes Problem ist, zeigt die seit den 50er Jahren nicht abreißende Kritik an ihr, am eindringlichsten zum Ausdruck kommend in den Literaturdiskussionen der 60er und insbesondere in der Lyrik-Diskussion zu Beginn der 70er Jahre.

In zeitlichem Zusammenhang mit den Ereignissen um die Ausbürgerung Wolf Biermanns wurde im November 1977 ein Beschluß des Politbüros des ZK der SED veröffentlicht über "Aufgaben der Literatur- und Kunstkritik."[1] Daß auf diesem Gebiet Probleme und Defizite zu verzeichnen sind, sagt nicht nur ein Satz wie: "In weitaus stärkerem Maße sollte die Literatur- und Kunstkritik in der ganzen Vielfalt ihrer Formen und Methoden entwickelt werden" (S. 2). Vor allem die komparativen Formulierungen der Aufgaben dieser Kritik lassen das erkennen: Der Entwicklung der Wirklichkeitsbeziehungen der Schriftsteller und Künstler sollte sie "größere Aufmerksamkeit" widmen; in Rezensionen und anderen Beiträgen müsse "noch sorgfältiger" herausgearbeitet werden, "welche neuen Kunstwerke zur Festigung sozialistischer Überzeugungen und Verhaltensweisen und zur Ausprägung kommunistischer Ideale beitragen und welche nicht" (S. 2). Die ästhetischen Probleme des Kunstschaffens seien dabei "stärker zu berücksichtigen" (S. 2). Die Kritik sollte ihre "fördernde, helfende Rolle noch stärker ausprägen," wozu eine "offene und wirksame" Kritik notwendig sei, "die der kritischen Erörterung nicht ausweicht" (S. 2): Die Kritik solle die "öffentliche Diskussion" über Leistungen und Probleme des literarischen Lebens fördern und dabei "die ideellen, moralischen und ästhetischen Ansprüche unserer sozialistischen Gesellschaft an das sozialistisch-realistische Kunstschaffen noch stärker ausprägen helfen" (S. 3).

Angesichts der in den zitierten Punkten, doch auch in allen anderen Teilen des Beschlusses erkennbaren intensiven Einbindung der Aufgaben der Kritik in die ideologischen Grund- und Rahmenbedingungen des Marxismus-Leninismus stellt sich die Frage, ob hier überhaupt von einem 'Fortschritt' gesprochen werden kann, wenn man--ausgerichtet auf das Problemfeld Literaturkritik--mit Rita Schober unter Fortschritt verstehen will: "ein Fortschreiten im tieferen Erfassen der Phänomene Kunst und Literatur, des Beziehungsfeldes zwischen ihrer Produktion und Rezeption als einer durch Kunstwerke vermittelten Verständigung."[2]

Da im ZK-Beschluß zugleich mit dem starken Gewicht auf Ideologie die Aufgaben der Literaturkritik formuliert sind in Hinblick auf die ästhetischen Probleme, auf die "Kompliziertheit künstlerischer Schaffensprobleme" (S. 2), dürfte es von der jeweiligen _realen_ Kritik abhängen, wie sie die vorgegebene "strategische Orientierung" (Walfried Hartinger)[3] im Einzelfall (taktisch) umsetzt: wie stark sie sich in Richtung ideologische Bedingungen und Bindungen orientiert bzw. wie offen sie ist für die Besonderheiten des Ästhetischen ihres Gegenstandes, ob das Ideologische besonders thematisiert oder überhaupt nicht eigens zur Sprache gebracht wird. Für mich ist das der systemimmanente Ambivalenz-Charakter von Fortschritt in sich realisierenden Sozialismus-Formen auf der Grundlage des Marxismus-Leninismus.

Daß solche Überlegung nicht bloße Hypothese ist, zeigt sich in der kurz darauf im _Sonntag_ publizierten Diskussion von Kritikern über ihr Verständnis dieses Beschlusses.[4] Hier wird, insbesondere von Karin Hirdina, als Kernsatz angesehen, daß die Kritik die öffentliche Diskussion nachhaltig fördern solle, wird die 'Konstituierung von Öffentlichkeit' zum Kernpunkt der sozialen Funktion von Kritik, ihrer Rolle als Vermittler an Leser, kombiniert mit einem bewußten Herausstellen der Subjektivität von Kritiker-Aussagen. Die in dieser Zeit veröffentlichte Leipziger Lyrik-Diskussion vom Vorjahr läßt für die Besonderheiten des Ästhetischen und der dichterischen Produktion große Offenheit erkennen.[5]

Ein ganz anderes Bild als die Kulturpolitik bietet die Entwicklung der Literaturwissenschaft. Der Kürze halber beziehe ich mich hier nur auf die Darstellung von Wolfgang Thierse und Dieter Kliche in ihrem Artikel "DDR-Literaturwissenschaft in den siebziger Jahren,"[6] zumal sie als fundiert und sachlich gelten kann.

Für die beiden Autoren ist diese Zeit "ein Jahrzehnt heftiger methodologischer Wandlungen, Neuerungen, Irritationen und Bereicherungen" (S. 267). So zeichne sich z.B. in der literaturgeschichtlichen Forschung eine Wandlung ab, die "von dominant ideologiegeschichtlich-kritischen und ästhetisch- beziehungsweise humanistisch-normativen Betrachtungsweisen wegführt in Richtung auf die Untersuchung der Geschichtlichkeit der Literatur," wodurch "sozialgeschichtlichen Fakten ein systematischer Ort in den literarischen Produktions- und Rezeptionsprozessen zukommt" (S. 271). Auch in der Realismustheorie sehen sie eine grundlegende Wendung der Fragerichtung: "von der Frage nach Übereinstimmung oder Nichtübereinstimmung zwischen literarischem Werk und der Realität zur Frage nach der nur jeweils historisch bestimmbaren Funktion von Formen und Inhalten literarischer Widerspiegelung, vom realistischen Formideal weg zur realistischen Funktion" (S. 275). Als Signum schlechthin für die DDR-Literaturwissenschaft in den 70er Jahren gilt ihnen 'Literatur als Kommunikation,' zu verstehen als "der Übergang von der darstellungsästhetischen, also rein werkorientierten zu einer kommunikationsästhetischen Sicht" (Rita Schober).[7]

Daß die von ihnen herausgestellten, in die 80er Jahre fortlaufenden und mit internationalen Fachdiskussionen in Verbindung stehenden modernen Entwicklungen in der DDR-Literaturwissenschaft nicht ohne erhebliche wissenschaftliche Kontroversen verlaufen, vermelden Thierse und Kliche, ebenso daß zu den Desiderata der Forschung gerade das Verhältnis Literaturwissenschaft und -kritik gehört. In Zusammenhang damit steht eine ihrer Schlußbemerkungen, wo sie als auffällig angeben: "die Diskrepanz zwischen den wissenschaftlichen Bemühungen um die Bestimmung der ästhetischen Eigenart von Literatur und einer doch dominant ideologiekritisch verfahrenden literarkritischen Praxis" (S. 297).

Auch wenn hier noch vieles offen ist, müßten die neuen Erkenntnisse über Literatur als solche (Besonderheiten ihrer Produktion und des literarischen Werkes) und die Probleme ihrer Rezeption sich in der Literaturkritik abzeichnen, schon wegen der Parallelität, sogar Identität einiger dieser Probleme und nicht zuletzt deshalb, weil viele Wissenschaftler als Literaturkritiker tätig sind.

Zu denken wäre vor allem daran, das Literarische eines Werkes ins Zentrum der Betrachtung zu rücken: seine Sprachform und seine "Problemdifferenziertheit" (Dieter Schlenstedt).[8] Dem steht entgegen, was Walfried Hartinger noch 1984 als Dilemma der Literaturkritik formuliert hat: daß Kritiker einen Text auf etwas befragen, was er zwar auch hervorbringt, was "aber nicht sein ideelles Zentrum ausmacht"; daß sie einen Text "auf einen offenbar leicht herauszupräparierenden, auf den Begriff zu bringenden Sachverhalt hin aufschließen"; daß Auffassungen "von der Priorität, sogar Hierarchisierung der Stoffe" dazu verführen, "im jeweils ausgebreiteten Gegenstand schon die Gewähr oder das Manko für gesellschaftliche Bedeutsamkeit zu sehen."[9]

Was sich in der Literaturwissenschaft als Fortschritt, weil literaturgemäßeres Umgehen mit Literatur erweist und wohl auch durchsetzt, braucht oder kann sich nicht gleich, direkt, linear fortbauend umsetzen in dementsprechenden literaturkritischen Umgang mit Neuerscheinungen. Hier spielen zweifellos die besonderen Bedingungen der Literaturkritik, wie Orientierung auf ein breites, nicht von vornherein speziell gegliedertes Publikum, Umfangsbegrenzungen einer Rezension, Publikationsort und -zeit, doch auch kulturpolitische Schwerpunktsetzungen bzw. gesellschaftspolitische Konditionierungen eine nicht unerhebliche Rolle. Die Frage nach Fortschritt in der Literaturkritik dürfte im Prinzip komplizierter, komplexerer Natur sein, insbesondere wegen der variierenden Abhängigkeit von literatur-externen Faktoren.

Um auf die eingangs gestellte Frage nach Fortschritt in der DDR-Literaturkritik zumindest eine Antwort exemplarischer Art zu geben, werden die drei Sammelbände literaturkritischer Arbeiten untersucht, die die literarischen Publikationen des Jahres 1983 rezipieren: <u>Kritik 83, Positionen 1, DDR-Literatur</u>

'83 im Gespräch.[10] Diese Beschränkung im Material hat den Vorteil einfachen Zugangs, leichter Überschaubarkeit und schneller Überprüfungsmöglichkeit der Aussagen.[11] Mit diesen drei parallelen Publikationen wird neueste Literatur zum ersten Mal in solcher Breite und Mannigfaltigkeit, in zeitlich kürzestem Abstand kritisch rezipiert und für ein breites Publikum zur Diskussion gestellt.

Kritik 83 bringt--als Reihe nun bereits zum neuntenmal--eine Auswahl Rezensionen des im Titel angegebenen Jahres in Wiederabdruck. Der Band bietet 54 Rezensionen aus Tages- und Wochenzeitungen und nicht-germanistischen Zeitschriften.[12] Zu einigen der 41 Titel sind mehrere Rezensionen abgedruckt, womit eine gewisse Meinungs-Vielfalt zum Ausdruck kommt. Eine Auswahlbibliographie (erstmals in Kritik 82) verzeichnet weitere Kritiken zu den im Band vorgestellten Werken.

Positionen 1, vom Titel her auf Fortsetzung angelegt, bringt "Wortmeldungen zur DDR-Literatur" (Untertitel). Von den fünfzehn Beiträgen sind sechs Wiederabdrucke aus Neue Deutsche Literatur und Sonntag (in z.T. erweiterter Form). Neben drei thematischen Überblicken zu Prosawerken (auch Nicht-Neuerscheinungen), einem Aufsatz zu Strittmatters Der Laden und einer kommentierten Sammlung von Leser-Reaktionen auf Görlichs Die Chance des Mannes bietet dieser Band Autoren-Äußerungen: zum eigenen neuesten Werk, über einen anderen Autor (Czechowski über Werner, Kahlau über Streubel), über sie gerade berührende Probleme. Ohne eine schon erkennbare Konzeption, ist das umfängliche Zur-Sprache-Kommen von Autoren auffällig und läßt an eine Wiederbelebung der Ende der 60er/Anfang der 70er Jahre einmal wichtigen Stellungnahmen von Autoren zur Literatur und ihrer Rezeption denken.

DDR-Literatur '83 im Gespräch, ebenfalls konzipiert als Reihe, versammelt eigens hierfür verfaßte Arbeiten zur Literatur dieses Jahres: Gattungs- und Genre-Überblicke, Berichte und zwanzig Werk-Interpretationen (u.a. einzelner Gedichte). Der Band bietet ein breites Spektrum, denn er bezieht auch Essayistik, Kinder- und Jugendliteratur sowie Hörspiele ein, die Beiträge nehmen von unterschiedlichen literaturwissenschaftlichen Ansätzen aus Stellung (eine wissenschaftliche Akzentuierung ist unverkennbar), und eine umfängliche Bibliographie versucht, die literarische Jahresproduktion bis in den Bereich der Heftreihenliteratur zu erfassen.

Die bei einem einfachen Vergleich der behandelten Titel sich als stark differierend zeigende Auswahl besprochener Werke erweist sich bei näherem Hinsehen als nicht so unterschiedlich. In erster Linie ist das eine Folge der Ausgangspositionen: Eine große Anzahl der in Kritik 83 gesammelten Rezensionen betrifft im Vorjahr publizierte Titel (Czechowskis Lyrikband Was mich betrifft bereits 1981), die in DDR-Literatur '83 wegen der Ausrichtung auf das Erscheinungsjahr der Werke somit nicht mehr behandelt werden (Ausnahme: eine Arbeit über Cibulkas Swantow von 1982). Erst der Band Kritik 84 wird über deutliche Verteilungsunterschiede Aufschluß geben können.

Drei mit Rezensionen bedachte Titel werden in DDR-Literatur '83 in den Überblicken behandelt: Peter Gosses Essaysammlung Mundwerk in Joseph Pischels "Welt- und Kunstanschauung im Essay" (S. 28-31), Uwe Saegers Sinon oder die gefällige Lüge und Angela Stachowas Erzählungsband Kleine Verführung in Siegfried Rönischs "Aspekte der Prosa" (S. 87-88). Lediglich vier rezensierte Werke des Jahres 1983 bleiben in DDR-Literatur '83 unerwähnt: Prosa von Elfriede Brüning, Horst Deichfuß, Jan Flieger und Rainer Kerndl.[13]

Umgekehrt bringt der letztgenannte Band auf Grund seiner Überblicke, doch auch einiger spezieller Artikel ein breiteres und vor allem noch vielfältigeres Literatur-Angebot 'ins Gespräch.' Allein die Überblicke zur Kinder- und Jugendliteratur und zur Lyrik behandeln vierzehn bzw. dreizehn Werke, abgesehen von ebenfalls herangezogenen Gedicht-Abdrucken in Zeitschriften. Zudem ist hier als Besonderheit zu verzeichnen, daß die Überblicke und die je zwei Einzelarbeiten zu Drama und Hörspiel die mediengebundene bzw. -nutzende Literatur einbeziehen und dabei auch Werke zur Sprache bringen, die (noch) nicht als Buchpublikation vorliegen, wie Jürgen Groß' "Denkmal," Christoph Heins "Ah Q" oder Irena Liebmanns Hörspiel "Sie müssen jetzt gehen, Frau Mühsam."

In einen solchen Vergleich ist Positionen 1 nicht ohne weiteres einzubeziehen, insbesondere wegen der starken Ausrichtung auf Autoren-Äußerungen. Drei der abgedruckten Gespräche beziehen sich dazu auf bereits 1982 erschienene Werke, die allerdings in Kritik 83 mit zwei oder sogar drei Rezensionen vertreten sind.[14] Die im Zentrum des Gesprächs mit Eberhard Panitz stehende Erzählung Eiszeit (1983) wird sonst nicht weiter erwähnt.[15]

Eine gute Ergänzung ist auf jeden Fall Karin Hirdinas Artikel "Soziale Erkundungen in der Literatur der DDR" (S. 78-105), in dem sie kontrastiv vorgeht und z.B. Charlotte Worgitzkys Meine ungeborenen Kinder Fritz Rudolf Fries' Alexanders neue Welten gegenüberstellt oder Günter Görlichs Die Chance des Mannes Christoph Heins Der fremde Freund (alle mit Rezensionen in Kritik 83), dabei Winfried Völlgers Das Windhahn-Syndrom einbeziehend (nur in DDR-Literatur '83, als Einzelbeitrag ebenfalls von Hirdina), oder Hanns Cibulkas Swantow in Beziehung setzt zu Franz Fühmanns Saiäns-Fiktschen (erstes in beiden Sammelbänden, letztes in keinem).

Bei der Feststellung von Auswahl und Verteilung der Titel ist die Häufigkeit ihrer Nennung bzw. Behandlung wohl ein Indiz für die Beachtung, die sie erfahren, aber mehr nicht--außer es werden auch Gründe zur Sprache gebracht oder erkennbar. Zwei Textvergleiche sollen das verdeutlichen.

In den Rezensionen zu Günter Görlichs Die Chance des Mannes hebt z.B. Klaus Höpcke die Hauptgestalt Wolfgang Weiß, Ratsvorsitzender einer norddeutschen Kleinstadt, besonders hervor, dessen vierseitiger Monolog über seine Arbeit als Staatsfunktionär es "vertragen [würde], als Traktat zum Thema 'Wie arbeite ich als guter sozialistischer Staatsfunktionär?' gesondert veröffentlicht zu werden."[16] Kritisch wendet Höpcke ein, daß der Autor seine Gestalt nicht auch ihren Vorsätzen gemäß handeln lasse, fragt, ob ihm gegenüber nicht die Ehefrau Monika versagt haben könnte (zu dieser Frage wurde er durch ein Gespräch mit Leserinnen angeregt). Er verweist zudem auf Ungereimtheiten in der Entwicklungsgeschichte Monikas. Doch trotzdem ist Höpckes Schlußfolgerung markant-positiv:

> Im Leben von Funktionären unserer Partei und unseres Staates das glückliche Aufblühen der eigenen Person in der Hingabe an die Interessen der Arbeiterklasse und des

ganzen Volkes künstlerisch zu gestalten,
dazu gehört ... der Mut eines überzeug-
ten kommunistischen Künstlers und die ge-
dankliche Kraft, die geistigen Spannungsbö-
gen im Leben solcher Helden aufzufinden,
sowie die Meisterschaft, deren Brisanz zum
Angelpunkt spannender künstlerischer Gestaltung werden zu lassen. Ich meine, wir
können Günter Görlich für einen Beitrag
danken, der solche Zeichen trägt. (S. 96-
97)

Ganz anders Michael Hinze,[17] dem sich das, was er als Roman lesen wollte, "mehr und mehr als Lektüre dreier Personalakten" anbot (S. 89), der vor allem kritisiert, daß man nicht erfährt, warum diese Menschen Illusionen und Hoffnungen aufgeben mußten. Das Verhalten der aus dieser Ehe ausbrechenden Monika bleibe "seltsam steril" (S. 89). Bis zum Schluß sei ihm unentdeckt geblieben, welche Chance Wolfgang habe; so wie er geschildert sei, habe er überhaupt "keine Chance zur Umkehr mehr" (S. 90). Es sei nur zu hoffen, daß sich Monikas Traum vom Neubeginn erfülle. Demgegenüber hebt auch Horst Haase die Position der Hauptgestalt als 'Leiter' hervor und ist der Meinung, daß Görlich mit den Problemen, in denen eine solche Gestalt heute in ihrer Tätigkeit und ihrem Privatleben stehe, eine Dialektik der Entwicklung in der DDR sichtbar mache, die dem Buch eine weitere Dimension gebe.[18] Haase hat Einwände gegen die oft saloppe Sprache, gegen Klischees bei der Charakterisierung der ins Negative umschlagenden Ordentlichkeit von Wolfgang Weiß. Seinem weiteren Einwand, daß häufig "doch noch ausdrücklich gesagt wird, was eigentlich schon klar ist" (S. 87), gibt er jedoch sofort eine positive Wendung: selbst darin erkenne man Görlichs Bestreben, "den Leser in Diskussionen einzubeziehen, deren parteiliche Klärung von Bedeutung ist" (S. 87).

Auch für die von Marianne Krumrey[19] vorgestellten Leser-Echos--im Zusammenhang mit einem Vorabdruck von der Frauenzeitschrift Für Dich organisiert--gilt, daß es in den Reaktionen "nicht um Gestaltungsfragen" geht, vielmehr die Leser diese Ehegeschichte als "ein Stück Realität" nehmen, wie "einen authentischen Fall" behandeln (S. 106) und dazu unterschiedlich Stellung beziehen. Krumrey sieht denn auch das Positive darin, daß es Görlich gelungen sei, "wichtige Fragen unserer gesellschaftlichen Entwicklung, Fragen der Lebensweise, der Partnerschaft und des Zusammenlebens der Geschlechter aufzugreifen" (S. 116). Margot Gerischs Gespräch mit dem Autor bringt keine Aufschlüsse,[20] weder darüber, was die Hauptfigur so hat werden lassen, noch welche Chancen ihr bleiben, außer man gibt sich mit Görlichs Antwort zufrieden, sie beständen darin, "über seinen im persönlichen Leben erlittenen Verlust ernsthaft nachzudenken" (S. 120). Er verbindet das mit dem Hinweis, Lenin habe trotz allen Weitblicks, trotz aller Sachlichkeit "Zeit für so viele Kleinigkeiten" gefunden, "herzlichen Anteil am Einzelschicksal" genommen (S. 120).

Allein Karin Hirdina bringt argumentierend vor, warum sie nicht der verbreiteten Meinung ist, Görlich habe wichtige Probleme richtig aufgeworfen, nur etwas schludrig geschrieben.[21] Zudem stellt sie die Frage, was Görlich über Gerti Tetzner, über Helga Schütz, "über die schon gehabten Geschichten hinaus" erkunde. Sowohl Görlich als auch Haase attackierend, heißt es über Monika Weiß:

> Sie verläßt den "goldenen Käfig" (Zitat, nicht ironisch!), um - wie Horst Haase schreibt - "sich selbst treu zu bleiben". Was ist dieses Selbst, das der Denkleistung, dem Rationalen entgegengesetzt wird; wer ist sie, diese Monika, "als Mensch"? Daß sie eine begabte Studentin war, eine gute Wissenschaftlerin hätte werden können, behauptet der Ich-Erzähler - glauben kann man das kaum. (S. 86)

Mit einer längeren Textstelle belegt sie ihren Vorwurf, Görlich wisse über Monika Weiß nur banalste Äußerlichkeiten mitzuteilen, und fährt fort:

> Diese Monika Weiß ist eine Illustrierten-Schönheit, mehr nicht. Ihr Anspruch auf "Selbst"-verwirklichung bleibt leer, weil sie leer bleibt. Damit aber fällt ihr Emanzipationsanspruch in sich zusammen. (S. 87)

Für Hirdina unterscheidet sie das von der Hauptfigur in Heins Der fremde Freund, die auch leer bleibe, was aber dort genau das Thema sei. Gegen Haases Auffassung von einer sichtbar werdenden Entwicklungs-Dialektik wird vorgebracht, daß das nur falsche Alternativen seien. Görlich erzähle "in einem Dilemma der

Inkonsequenz: Allzu schlecht darf er diesen Mann nicht erzählen, denn er ist schließlich ein hoher Funktionär. Aber er muß ihm Menschlichkeit absprechen, sonst fällt die Konstruktion des Buches zusammen" (S. 87-88). Die Folge sei:

> Modische Entgegensetzung von Rationalität, Sachlichkeit, Funktionalität und Emotionalität, Gemütlichkeit, Menschlichkeit. Nicht nur Klischee statt Erkundung, sondern Ignoranz gegenüber der Existenz einer Literatur – ich denke nur an die Sowjetliteratur von Aitmatow bis Granin, von Trifonow bis Tendrjakow –, die Maßstäbe gesetzt hat in der Behandlung eines hier nur angeahnten Problems. (S. 88)

Mit dieser vernichtenden Kritik an Struktur und Differenzierung der Problemlage, an Erzählweise und Sprache führt Karin Hirdina weg von einer Einschätzung, die sich lediglich an einer Aktualität des Inhalts und an parteilichem Ideengehalt orientiert, aber unberücksichtigt läßt, daß es sich hier doch um Literatur handelt, handeln soll.

Ein Beispiel anderer Art ist die Rezeption von Christoph Heins Novelle Der fremde Freund. In seiner Rezension skizziert Klaus Hammer einzelne Züge des von Hein gegebenen "literarische[n] Porträt[s] einer Egomanin," einer Ich-Figur, die "systematisch alle Empfindungen abgebaut" hat, die dahinlebt "ohne Erwartung, ohne Glücksanspruch."[22] Hein mache an dieser Figur deutlich, "wie eine große Chance, nicht nur des Lebens schlechthin, sondern der sozialistischen Gesellschaft im besonderen, verpaßt wurde" (S. 103). Er moralisiere nicht, er gebe aus völliger Distanz eine Diagnose: Er greife als Autor nicht in seine Geschichte ein, "die Blindheit seiner Ich-Figur wird nicht direkt demontiert, sie soll die Bewußtheit des Lesers, die Überprüfung seiner eigenen Lebenshaltung und sein Bedürfnis nach Veränderung herausfordern" (S. 103).

Karin Hirdina sieht das Überzeugende der Novelle nicht in den Versuchen, die erschreckende Kälte dieser Frau aus Verletzungen in ihrer Mädchenzeit zu erklären, nicht darin, "Kälte und Deformation anderer" als Erklärung hinzuzuziehen, sondern in dem konsequenten Porträt dieser Frau: "in der Spannung zwischen ihr Bewußtem und Verdrängtem," Handeln und Selbstinterpretation, im Nichteingestehen von vorhandenen Sehnsüchten "aus Angst vor Verletzungen, aus Angst, überrumpelt zu werden von den Problemen anderer," in ihrer Berührungsangst.[23] Hirdina spricht von der Kongruenz zwischen Porträt und nüchterner, lapidarer Schreibweise, die suggeriere, was diese Frau von sich glaube: sicher zu sein,--obwohl dahinter Unruhe und Leidenschaft stehe, wie das im Text in ein Bild gefaßt sei: "Hinter den Gesichtern auf den Hochzeitsfotos sieht sie die Anarchisten" (S. 89). Für Hirdina ist dieser Text Literatur, "ein zusammengefaßtes, verallgemeinertes Bild von Möglichkeiten in der Wirklichkeit. Eine Warnung. Eine zugespitzte Beschreibung dessen, was wir in Ansätzen auch in uns verdrängen" (S. 90). Durch die Konsequenz seines Erzählens löse Hein, anders als Görlich, "eine gesellschaftliche Selbstverständigung aus, die im noch ungesicherten Raum erfolgt," deshalb "zu inneren Entscheidungen" zwinge (S. 90).

Was bei Hirdina als hervorgerufene 'Widerstände' bei Lesern anklingt, wird in Hans Kaufmanns Aufsatz "Christoph Hein in der Debatte" im einzelnen zur Sprache gebracht:

> Die meisten öffentlichen Kritiker mißbilligen die dem Leser dargebotene Innenwelt Claudias; die wenigsten beachten, daß von den übrigen Figuren der Erzählung, die es mit der Außenwelt der Heldin, mit ihrem Handeln und Verhalten zu tun haben, kaum jemand von ihr erwartet, sie möge anders sein . . .[24]

Kaufmann sieht bei Hein das Auseinanderfallen des Menschen in einen 'Privatmann' und eine öffentliche Person als Problem auftauchen. Da dieses Auseinanderfallen von Marx als spezifisch bürgerliches Verhältnis enthüllt worden sei, versteht er, daß hier Kritiker die Frage stellen, ob das eine Beschreibung der sozialistischen Gesellschaft sein soll. Er zitiert Ursula Wilkes Forderung, Hein solle "ein Quantum mehr Totalität hereinholen," da ohne diese die Novelle "unwahr" würde (S. 46). Für Kaufmann ist Claudia dagegen "eine echt epische Gestalt" (S. 46), die nicht einfach recht oder unrecht habe. Das gelte auch für ihre Selbstcharakteristik. Ihr mit fast pathetischem Nachdruck betontes Distanzhalten werde vom

Autor zusätzlich verdächtig gemacht, z.B. durch den Traum-Prolog. Kaufmann faßt zusammen:

> Nur mit einer rein mechanistischen Auffassung vom Widerspiegeln kann man Hein unterstellen, er bilde einfach einen allgemeinen Zustand ab. Er beschreibt etwas in Wirklichkeit Mögliches. Ein Warnbild liefert er insofern, als sich der Leser einen Zustand, in dem Beziehungen wie die geschilderten vorherrschend sind, mit Schrecken vorstellt. Aber es gibt sie, und sie haben eine Basis. (S. 47)

Daß einige Kritiker Mißtrauen hegen gegen den Verfasser, versteht Kaufmann als eben die "Berührungsangst," die sie an Claudia entdecken:

> Glaubt man ihnen, so sind "wir" anderen alle hochsensibel, wahre Samariter des Seelenlebens unserer Mitmenschen, während diese da platterdings ein "Monster" ist, das man - sensiblerweise - "im Leben links liegen lassen" würde [zitiert nach Gabriele Lindner]. Die Vermutung erscheint nicht abwegig, daß Hein auch gegen solche Selbstgerechtigkeit angeschrieben hat. (S. 48)

Fragt man gerade angesichts eines so offenkundig 'problematischen' Textes, ob der hier vorgelegten Rezeption Repräsentanz zuzusprechen ist, so kann das nicht ohne weiteres bejaht werden (was nicht für andere Themenkomplexe zu gelten braucht). Bringen auch weitere Zeitungsrezensionen nichts Neues,[25] die Übersicht von Hans Kaufmann hat erhebliche Lücken. Zwar nimmt er mit den Meinungs-Wiedergaben von Ursula Wilke und Gabriele Lindner Bezug auf die Beiträge zu Der fremde Freund in den Weimarer Beiträgen,[26] doch fehlt dabei vor allem ein Hinweis auf Bernd Leistner,[27] der durch eine Behandlung der Dichte von 'Motiven' diese Novelle als ein "herausragendes Stück künstlerischer Prosa in der neueren Literatur der DDR" auszuweisen weiß (S. 1642). Unverständlich ist-- gerade wegen seiner intensiven Kritik an Kritikern[28]--daß Kaufmann nicht Brigitte Böttchers Rezension beachtet,[29] die ganz konzentriert die Literarizität dieses Textes zur Sprache bringt: ihn als 'Modell' begreift, seine Struktur--auch in Beziehung zum Novellen-Charakter--herausarbeitet, ohne dabei die eigene gesellschaftliche Position außer acht zu lassen.

Was diese drei Bände alles in allem wichtig macht, ist nicht die Menge der behandelten Literatur und nicht unbedingt eine Repräsentanz. Das ist auch nicht die mit ihnen gegebene Möglichkeit, die reale bzw. realisierte Rezeption in ihren unterschiedlichen Abhängigkeiten kennenzulernen, seien es äußere Publikationsformen, gesellschaftspolitische Gegebenheiten oder Probleme des literarischen Objekts und seiner Erfassung. Es ist vielmehr die Verbindung eines breiten Spektrums an Literatur mit den vor allem durch die Mehrfach-Aussagen, durch die Überlappungen zutage tretenden Unterschieden und Widersprüchlichkeiten der Aussagen, die einen Leser geradezu nötigen, Stellung zu beziehen, eigene Meinung herzustellen. Diese in vieler Hinsicht 'kommunikationsästhetische' Ausrichtung und Potenz--die Bände werden fortgesetzt--darf als Fortschritt in der DDR-Literaturkritik bezeichnet werden, unabhängig davon, inwieweit das auch für das literaturkritische Verständnis als solches gilt.

In dieser Beziehung sind Zweifel anzumelden, zeigen die Arbeiten doch--man rekapituliere nur einmal die eben vorgeführten--ein ambivalentes Literatur-Verständnis: traditionelle Sichtweisen stehen einer modernen Literatur- und Rezeptions-Auffassung gegenüber, und das in erheblichem Umfang. Erstere finden sich häufig in Zeitungsrezensionen, da hier die Informierung des Lesers, die Aufgabe, ihn mit Thema, Inhalt, Handlungsverlauf des neuen Werkes bekanntzumachen, im Vordergrund steht, so daß Angaben zu Sprachform, Strukturierung usw. sporadisch bleiben, wobei oft schwer ausmachbar ist, welche Bedeutung ihnen zugemessen wird. Andererseits finden sie sich auch in den Überblicken. Allem Anschein nach führt, verführt der Versuch, Werke in größere Zusammenhänge einzuordnen, zu Globalaussagen, bei denen ein Werk als literarischer Text, als Singularität, hinter große Linien zurücktritt, für deren Kennzeichnung sich ideologisch-gesellschaftliche Generalnenner eher anzubieten scheinen als gattungs- oder genrespezifische Überlegungen und Beziehungsgeflechte. Siegfried Strellers abwägenden Ausführungen zu Christa Wolfs Kassandra in DDR-Literatur '83[30] stehen stark simplifizierende Verallgemeinerungen in Joseph Pischels und in Siegfried Rönischs Essay- bzw. Prosa-Überblick gegenüber;[31] Christel und Walfried Hartingers Lyrik-Überblick[32] bringt im dritten Abschnitt insofern irritierende ideologische Überlegungen, als ihre Allgemeinheit offen läßt, wer und was damit getroffen werden soll, eine Technik, die sich auch in Eberhard Günthers Gedanken zur DDR-Literatur in <u>Positionen 1</u> findet: Seine sehr allgemeinen, streckenweise modern wirkenden Bemerkungen werden aber ganz traditionell, wenn sie mit einer allgemeinen Unterstellung von "Subjektivismus" Drohhaltung annehmen.[33]

Die moderne, auf Fragen der Literarizität (wie Sprachform oder Problemdifferenziertheit im Sinne Schlenstedts) gerichtete Behandlungsweise findet sich eher bei Arbeiten zu einzelnen Werken, in besonders eindrücklicher Weise z.B. in Frank Hörnigks Versuch über Christoph Heins "Ah Q"[34] und dem Dieter Schlenstedts über ein Gedicht von Steffen Mensching.[35]

Trotz begründeter Bedenken und Vorbehalte würde ich sagen, daß diese Zusammenstellung von Überblicken und Einzelanalysen und die damit gegebenen Querverbindungen eine Mannigfaltigkeit zum Vorschein bringen, die Literaturkritik für den Leser produktiv macht. Nimmt man hinzu, daß in verstärktem Maße in den Fachzeitschriften Diskussionen und Sammelbeiträge zur neuesten Literatur publiziert werden--so "DDR-Literaturentwicklung in der Diskussion" und "Kassandra von Christa Wolf" in den <u>Weimarer Beiträgen</u> <u>1984</u>[36]--, daß in der <u>Zeitschrift für Germanistik</u> eine Rubrik 'Interpretationen' eingerichtet worden <u>ist</u>, begonnen mit der eines Gedichts von Volker Braun[37]--, dann ist auf dem breiten Feld der Literaturkritik eine Entwicklung im Gange, die positiv zu werten ist. Man muß sich aber bei solcher Einschätzung bewußt sein, daß <u>literaturwissenschaftlicher</u> Fortschritt und <u>reale Literaturkritik</u> in keinem linear-direkten Umsetzungsverhältnis stehen, sondern in einem sehr komplexen, auch Zufälligkeiten ausgesetzten Wirkungsgefüge, daß außerdem Literaturkritik in besonderem Maße anfällig ist gegenüber gesellschaftspolitischen Erscheinungen, und daß Fortschritt somit ein ambivalentes Phänomen ist und bleibt.

Anmerkungen

¹ "Aufgaben der Literatur- und Kunstkritik," Sonntag, 31, Nr. 48 (1977), S. 2-3. Auch abgedruckt in Peter Lübbe, Hrsg., Dokumente zur Kunst-, Literatur- und Kulturpolitik der SED 1975-1980 (Stuttgart: Seewald, 1984), S. 460-62 (Dokument 127).

² Rita Schober, "Zur Frage der Bewertung von Literatur," Weimarer Beiträge, 26, Nr. 10 (1980), 23.

³ Walfried Hartinger, "Kritik in der gesellschaftlichen Verständigung," Neue Deutsche Literatur, 32, Nr. 6 (1984), 58.

⁴ "Die erste Runde. Kritikergespräch zum 'Kritik'-Beschluß," Sonntag, 31, Nr. 51 (1977), 3.

⁵ "Zeitgenossenschaft und lyrische Subjektivität," Weimarer Beiträge, 23, Nr. 10 (1977), 80-104.

⁶ Wolfgang Thierse und Dieter Kliche, "DDR-Literaturwissenschaft in den siebziger Jahren. Bemerkungen zur Entwicklung ihrer Positionen und Methoden," Weimarer Beiträge, 31, Nr. 2 (1985), 267-308.

⁷ A.a.O., S. 277, zitiert nach Rita Schober, Abbild - Sinnbild - Wertung. Aufsätze zur Theorie und Praxis literarischer Kommunikation (Berlin/Weimar: Aufbau, 1982), S. 7.

⁸ Dieter Schlenstedt, "Wertung in der Literaturkritik," Weimarer Beiträge, 26, Nr. 10 (1980), 83-90. Seine Auffassung, das literarisch Wertvolle sei "eine beherrschte Sprache," sieht er dem wohl sogar herrschenden Glauben gegenübergestellt, "es sei nicht wichtig, in welcher Sprache und in welcher Form ein Werk daher kommt - so, als könne 'Inhalt' und 'Ideengehalt' unabhängig sein von der Form, die ihn in Wirklichkeit konstituiert" (S. 85-86). Auch einer "Problemdifferenziertheit" (für ihn der "Indikator für Echtheit"), die an den Idealen der Revolution festhält, dabei aber "die sichtbar gewordenen Schranken auch des Sozialismus nicht . . . als 'heilige Grenze' [Marx] auffaßt," sieht Schlenstedt die Meinung entgegenstehen, "man könne vorhandenem unglücklichem Bewußtsein mit Darstellungen begegnen (und so Lebenshilfe vermitteln), die weit unter der bereits

existierenden Problemdifferenziertheit operieren" (S. 86).

9 Walfried Hartinger, "Kritik in der gesellschaftlichen Verständigung," Neue Deutsche Literatur, 32, Nr. 6 (1984), 58f. Als Beispiele verweist Hartinger auf die Behandlung von Joachim Nowotnys Ein gewisser Robel, Christa Wolfs Kindheitsmuster, Franz Fühmanns Prometheus, Joachim Walthers Geschichtensammlung, Irmtraud Morgners Trobadora-Roman, Rolf Schneiders Das Glück (S. 59-62).

10 Kritik 83. Rezensionen zur DDR-Literatur, hrsg. von Eberhard Günther, Werner Liersch und Klaus Walther (Halle/Leipzig: Mitteldeutscher Verlag, 1984); Positionen 1. Wortmeldungen zur DDR-Literatur, hrsg. von Eberhard Günther (Halle/Leipzig: Mitteldeutscher Verlag, 1984); DDR Literatur '83 im Gespräch, hrsg. von Siegfried Rönisch (Berlin/Weimar: Aufbau, 1984).

11 Eigentlich bedarf es einer historisch angelegten, umfänglichen und detaillierten Arbeit, um die Komplexität der Entwicklungsschübe und ihre ideologisch-politischen, literaturtheoretischen und soziokulturellen Verklammerungen und Bezüge in Weite und Varietät erfassen und eine ausgewogene Antwort auf die Frage nach Fortschritt in der DDR-Literaturkritik geben zu können. Der exemplarische Versuch sollte aber zu einer Charakterisierung und Einschätzung der gegenwärtigen Lage imstande sein. Auch wenn ich die von Literaturwissenschaftlern und -kritikern vorgelegten 28 'Versuche' "Aspekte jüngster DDR-Literatur," Teil I/II, Weimarer Beiträge, 29, Nr. 1 (1983), 5-85; Nr. 2 (1983), 260-367, nicht berücksichtige, auch nicht die 'Selbstverständigungsversuche' von Kritikern und Autoren unter dem Titel "Anspruch, Einspruch, Zuspruch. Literaturkritik in der Verständigung," Neue Deutsche Literatur, 32, Nr. 6 (1984), 57-110, einschl. der oben zitierten Arbeit von Walfried Hartinger, so stellen die drei Sammelbände doch eine tragfähige Auswahl zur Verfügung, zumal ich im Fall von Christoph Heins Der fremde Freund einen Querschnitt der Rezeption als Stichprobe anbiete.

12 Die 54 Rezensionen stammen, geordnet nach Häufigkeit, aus: Neue Deutsche Literatur (14), Sonntag (10), Berliner Zeitung (6), Neues Deutschland (5), Die Weltbühne (4), Sinn und Form (3), Tribüne

(3), <u>Wochenpost</u> (3), Beiträge zur Kinder- und Jugendliteratur (2), Junge <u>Welt</u> (1), <u>Leipziger Volkszeitung</u> (1), <u>Der Morgen</u> (1), National-Zeitung (1).

[13] Elfriede Brüning, <u>Wie andere Leute auch</u> (Roman); Horst Deichfuß, <u>Windmacher (Roman)</u>; Jan Flieger, <u>Die ungewöhnliche Brautfahrt und andere Geschichten</u> (Kurzgeschichten); Rainer Kerndl, <u>Ein ausgebranntes Leben</u> (Abenteuerroman); alle erschienen im Mitteldeutschen Verlag, der auch die <u>Kritik</u>-Reihe publiziert.

[14] Jurij Koch zu <u>Landung der Träume</u> (2 Rezensionen); Wolfgang Eckert zu <u>Familienfoto</u> (3), Günter Görlich zu <u>Die Chance des Mannes</u> (3).

[15] Kritisch anzumerken ist, daß bei <u>Positionen</u> 1 nicht deutlich wird, warum gerade Gespräche mit diesen Autoren aufgenommen wurden (abgesehen von der Anna-Seghers-Gesprächszusammenstellung als eine Art Nachruf) und warum nur bei Görlich Leser-Reaktionen einbezogen worden sind. Undeutlich bleibt auch die Funktion der essayistischen Autoren-Beiträge.

[16] Klaus Höpcke, "Chancen eines Stoffes im Roman," in <u>Kritik</u> <u>83</u>, S. 92.

[17] Michael Hinze, "Eine Chance für Wolfgang Weiß?" in <u>Kritik</u> <u>83</u>, S. 88-90.

[18] Horst Haase, "Geschichte einer Ehe, die über private Fragen hinausreicht," in <u>Kritik</u> <u>83</u>, S. 84-87.

[19] Marianne Krumrey, ". . . sich Gedanken machen hinter manchen Türen," in <u>Positionen</u> <u>1</u>, S. 106-16.

[20] Margot Gerisch, "Unser Ideal verwirklichen," in <u>Positionen</u> <u>1</u>, S. 117-20.

[21] Karin Hirdina, "Soziale Erkundungen in der Literatur der DDR," in <u>Positionen</u> <u>1</u>, S. 78-105.

[22] Klaus Hammer, "<u>Der fremde Freund</u> von Christoph Hein," in <u>Kritik</u> <u>83</u>, S. 102.

[23] Karin Hirdina, "Soziale Erkundungen in der Literatur der DDR," S. 89.

[24] Hans Kaufmann, "Christoph Hein in der Debat-

25 Herangezogen wurden die in der Auswahlbibliographie von Kritik 83 (S. 250) aufgeführten Rezensionen in Berliner Zeitung (Helmut H. Schulz), Junge Welt (Ingrid Feix), Der Morgen (Christoph Funke), Tribüne (Sybille Eberlein).

26 Rüdiger Bernhardt, Klaus Kändler, Bernd Leistner, Gabriele Lindner, Bernd Schick, Ursula Wilke, "Der fremde Freund von Christoph Hein," Weimarer Beiträge, 29, Nr. 9 (1983), 1635-55.

27 A.a.O., S. 1642-45.

28 Für das "Mißtrauen gegen den Verfasser" (S. 48) wären zu nennen gewesen: Aussagen von Rüdiger Bernhardt (S. 1638), Klaus Kändler (S. 1640) und Ursula Wilkes bösartige Schlußfolgerung, zur Darstellung "unserer Welt" hätte es "- eben - einer reiferen Weltanschauung" bedurft (S. 1655). Es würde der Orientierung des Lesers zugute kommen, hätte Kaufmann für die ironisierte Belesenheit von Rezensenten und deren Vergleich des Textes mit Camus' Der Fremde die Namen und Titel der Arbeiten von Ursula Wilke, Bernd Schick (nur Name) und Gabriele Lindner (nur Titel), für den Hinweis auf Ehrensteins Tubutsch Ursula Heukenkamps Sammelrezension "Die fremde Form," Sinn und Form, 35, Nr. 3 (1983), 631, genannt.

29 Brigitte Böttcher, "Diagnose eines unheilbaren Zustands," Neue Deutsche Literatur, 31, Nr. 6 (1983), 145-49.

30 Siegfried Streller, "Selbstbildnis im Angesicht des Todes. Christa Wolf, Kassandra. Vier Vorlesungen. Eine Erzählung," in DDR-Literatur '83, S. 190-201.

31 Joseph Pischel, "Welt- und Kunstanschauung im Essay," in DDR-Literatur '83, S. 7-32; Siegfried Rönisch, "Aspekte der Prosa," in DDR-Literatur '83, S. 71-90.

32 Christel und Walfried Hartinger, "Von Horizonten und Grenzen. Zum Charakter zeitgenössischer lyrischer Subjektivität," in DDR-Literatur '83, S. 268-94.

[33] Eberhard Günther, "Aus verlegerischer Sicht - Einige Gedanken zur Entwicklung der zeitgenössischen DDR-Literatur," in Positionen 1, S. 29. Sowohl in Einzelrezensionen als auch Überblicken ist die Technik zu finden, Kritisches derart zu inkorporieren, daß dessen Spezifik wirkungslos wird, keine Konsequenzen hat. Ein treffendes Beispiel, hier sogar für das Inkorporieren der eigenen Kritik, ist Höpckes letztendlich geradezu hymnisches Lob für Görlichs Roman (siehe Anmerkung 16).

[34] Frank Hörnigk, "'Die wahre Geschichte des Ah Q' - ein Clownsspiel mit Phantasie," in DDR-Literatur '83, S. 234-39.

[35] Dieter Schlenstedt, "Die kleine Geste. Zu einem Gedicht von Steffen Mensching ["Auf einem Bein, nachts, nackt"], in DDR-Literatur '83, S. 320-25.

[36] H. Haase, W. Hartinger, U. Heukenkamp, K. Jarmatz, J. Pischel, D. Schlenstedt, "DDR-Literaturentwicklung in der Diskussion," Weimarer Beiträge, 30, Nr. 10 (1984), 1589-1616; "Kassandra von Christa Wolf," Weimarer Beiträge, 30, Nr. 8 (1984), 1353-81.

[37] Ursula Heukenkamp, "Überantwortete Sinngebung. Volker Brauns 'Material I: Wie herrlich leuchtet mir die Natur,'" Zeitschrift für Germanistik, 3, Nr. 2 (1982), 173-88.

Moderne, Avantgarde und Postmoderne:
Zur neueren Rezeption in der
Literaturwissenschaft der DDR

Günter Erbe

In der Literaturwissenschaft der DDR hat in den siebziger Jahren eine intensive Beschäftigung mit der literarischen Moderne und der Avantgarde dieses Jahrhunderts begonnen. Mehrere Einzelstudien und eine Fülle von Aufsätzen in Fachzeitschriften, u.a. über Kafka und Musil, den deutschen Expressionismus, den französischen Surrealismus, den modernen englischsprachigen Roman, den Nouveau Roman in Frankreich, die Strömungen der russischen Avantgarde in der Zeit vor und nach der Oktoberrevolution bezeugen dieses Forschungsinteresse.[1] Dem entsprechen auf literaturtheoretischem Gebiet Auseinandersetzungen mit Benjamin, Bloch und Adorno, dem Formalismus, Strukturalismus und Poststrukturalismus.[2] Bemerkenswert an diesen Arbeiten sind das Bemühen um Differenzierung und der Verzicht auf vorschnelle weltanschauliche Grenzziehungen. Ehe durch einzelne Beispiele die Rezeption bzw. Auseinandersetzung mit der Moderne und Avantgarde vorgestellt wird, soll nach den Gründen gefragt werden, die das verstärkte Interesse der Literaturwissenschaftler an diesem Gegenstand erklären.

Es handelt sich dabei zum einen um ein Problem der Literaturwissenschaft selbst, das sich jedoch erst zuspitzte, als einer ihrer Untersuchungsgegenstände, die DDR-Literatur, die mit ihr befaßte Disziplin zu einem Umdenken nötigte. Immer weniger ließ sich ignorieren, daß die in der DDR entstandene schöne Literatur--ich denke dabei vor allem an die in den letzten Jahren erschienenen Werke von Autoren wie Franz Fühmann, Christa Wolf, Heiner Müller, Günter Kunert, Fritz Rudolf Fries und Wolfgang Hilbig--nicht mit der Elle des Realismus zu messen war. Das begriffliche Instrumentarium dieser Theorie war veraltet und unbrauchbar geworden. Die Konstruktion eines Gegensatzes von Realismus und Modernismus bzw. Avantgardismus erwies sich immer weniger als geeignet, die Entwicklungen in der DDR-Literatur seit den siebziger Jahren zu erfassen und versagte ebenso bei der Aufarbeitung der weltliterarischen Strömungen in der ersten Hälfte dieses Jahrhunderts.

Die Möglichkeit, sich heute unbefangener mit einer literarischen Tradition auseinanderzusetzen, die in den Jahren des Kalten Krieges und auch weitgehend noch in den sechziger Jahren, vor allem wegen ihrer Inanspruchnahme durch die westdeutsche Kulturpolitik, als formalistisch, dekadent, antirealistisch usw. denunziert worden war, hängt ferner zusammen mit einem grundlegenden Wandel der DDR-Kulturpolitik in ihrer Einstellung zum kulturellen Erbe. Für die Literatur bedeutet dies, daß die vormals unter ideologisch-weltanschaulichem Aspekt als destruktiv, nihilistisch oder existentialistisch angesehenen Werke z.B. eines Kafka, Musil oder Eliot heute trotz weiter bestehender weltanschaulicher Vorbehalte in ihrer künstlerisch-literarischen Bedeutung differenzierter beurteilt werden. Der gelassenere Umgang mit Werken von Protagonisten der literarischen Moderne und Avantgarde führte schließlich auch zu einer Neubewertung ihres weltanschaulichen Gehalts. Es genügt heute, einem bürgerlichen Schriftsteller ein humanistisches Anliegen zu attestieren, um ihn in das kulturelle Erbe der sozialistischen Gesellschaft einzureihen.[3] Mit der Leerformel des "Humanismus" läßt sich nun allerdings nahezu die gesamte moderne Weltliteratur dem sozialistischen Erbe zuschlagen. Es dürfte deshalb auch bald an der Zeit sein, daß die Werke Becketts auf den Bühnen der DDR ihren Einstand feiern werden.[4]

Diese Entwicklung mag überraschen angesichts der unverändert scharfen politisch-ideologischen Abgrenzung, die die DDR gegenüber den westlichen kapitalistischen Gesellschaften vornimmt. In den 50er und 60er Jahren war dieses Abgrenzungsbestreben noch Ausdruck eines Selbstbehauptungswillens eines um seine internationale Anerkennung kämpfenden Staates, der alle Mühe hatte, von der eigenen Bevölkerung und von außen anerkannt zu werden. Die Konsolidierung der DDR in den 60er Jahren, ihre ökonomischen und politischen Erfolge, haben das Selbstbewußtsein der politischen

Führung gestärkt und ihre Legitimationsprobleme gemildert. Mit Beginn der Honecker-Ära Anfang der 70er Jahre konnte die DDR auf eine weltweite Anerkennung zurückblicken und--im internationalen Maßstab betrachtet--auf einen beachtlichen Lebensstandard ihrer Bevölkerung verweisen. Mit der Erhöhung des materiellen Lebensstandards korrespondierte ein Anstieg im Niveau der geistig-kulturellen Bedürfnisse, die auch vor der Belletristik nicht haltmachten.

Hier ist auf ein weiteres Phänomen hinzuweisen, das nicht unwesentlich dazu beigetragen hat, eine Öffnung der Literaturpolitik hin zur Tradition der Moderne und Avantgarde zu forcieren: Die nach Erfüllung drängenden Ansprüche einer um den Besitz kultureller Güter bemühten Intelligenzschicht. Die kulturpolitisch Verantwortlichen tragen dieser Situation auf verschiedene Weise Rechnung: Während seit einigen Jahren Werke der vormals als dekadent eingestuften Klassiker der Moderne in größerer Zahl erscheinen können[5] und von der Literaturwissenschaft in differenzierten Analysen gewürdigt werden, begegnen Publikationen von DDR-Schriftstellern, die offensichtlich mit dieser literarischen Tradition verbunden sind, nach wie vor erheblichem Mißtrauen und müssen sich auf eine weltanschauliche Überprüfung gefaßt machen. Erkennt man in den Werken Kafkas und Musils, der Surrealisten und Expressionisten Ansätze zu einer Selbstkritik der bürgerlichen Gesellschaft, so ist man jedoch nur zögernd bereit, die gleiche Haltung Gegenwartsschriftstellern der DDR zuzubilligen. Von ihnen wird nach wie vor ein positives Bekenntnis zum realen Sozialismus verlangt, wenngleich--das muß gesagt werden--die Selbstkritik dieser Gesellschaft implizit und explizit als Infragestellung des marxistisch-leninistischen Weltbildes, des eindimensionalen Technikverständnisses und der Fortschrittsgläubigkeit der marxistisch-leninistischen Philosophie und Weltanschauung in Literatur und Kunst ein beachtliches Niveau erreicht hat. Als Beispiel für das unterschiedliche Reagieren von Vertretern des Kulturapparats und eines Teils der Literaturkritik ließe sich die Kontroverse um Christa Wolfs Kassandra anführen. Während der Altkommunist und frühere Chefredakteur von Sinn und Form Wilhelm Girnus weltanschauliche Bedenken äußerte, war das Echo in der Literaturkritik überwiegend positiv.[6]

Ich gehe im folgenden auf einzelne Beiträge zur

Moderne- und Avantgardeproblematik in der Literaturwissenschaft der DDR ein. Karlheinz Barck, Dieter Schlenstedt und Wolfgang Thierse, die Herausgeber des Sammelbandes Künstlerische Avantgarde, der ersten umfangreicheren DDR-Publikation zur Avantgarde-Problematik, bezeichnen es als ihr Anliegen, auf die Breite der Tradition "demokratischer und sozialistischer Kunst," wie sie sagen, aufmerksam zu machen. Der Band versammelt Beiträge von Autoren aus mehreren osteuropäischen Ländern, die sich darin einig sind, "daß die Entwicklung der revolutionären, der sozialistischen Literatur und Kunst ohne die Berücksichtigung der als Avantgarde (oder links-avantgardistische bzw. linke Strömungen) bezeichneten Richtungen und Gruppierungen nicht erfaßt und verstanden werden kann."[7] Die Absicht dieser Schrift ist weder, eine Theorie der Avantgarde zu entwickeln, noch einen eindeutigen Begriff von Avantgarde vorzustellen. Vorerst handelt es sich nach Auffassung der Herausgeber nur--im Untertitel des Bandes wird es eingeräumt--, um Annäherungen an ein unabgeschlossenes Kapitel. In der Abgrenzung des Gegenstandes werden jedoch Akzentsetzungen deutlich. Die allgemeine Bestimmung, wonach Avantgarde als das jeweils fortgeschrittenste, auf Innovation drängende, künstlerische Bewußtsein aufzufassen ist, tritt zurück hinter eine historisch-spezifische Kennzeichnung künstlerischer Bestrebungen im ersten Drittel dieses Jahrhunderts, für die der Ausdruck historische Avantgarde-Bewegungen in Übereinstimmung mit westlichen Forschern gewählt wird. Ähnlich wie der Bremer Literaturwissenschaftler Peter Bürger in seinem Buch Theorie der Avantgarde[8] begreifen Barck/Schlenstedt/Thierse die Avantgarde als radikalisierten Ausdruck der Funktionskrise traditioneller bürgerlicher Kunst, als einen Versuch, Kunst- und Lebenserneuerung miteinander zu verschmelzen.

Auch in der begrifflichen Unterscheidung von Moderne und Avantgarde knüpfen die Literaturwissenschaftler an Ergebnisse westlicher Forschungen an. Der Begriff Moderne meine etwa bei Adorno die Einheit spezifischer künstlerischer Aktivitäten in der bürgerlichen Gesellschaft seit Baudelaire. Das Besondere der Avantgarde sei hingegen--hier stimmen die DDR-Wissenschaftler mit Bürger überein--, daß sie den Begriff der Kunst selbst herausfordere. Das Ziel des avantgardistischen Impulses, Kunst in Lebenspraxis zu überführen, könne jedoch in verschiedener Weise angegangen werden:

> Dort, wo nach einem Weg für das Zusammengehen von künstlerischer und politischer Avantgarde gesucht wurde, wo die Kritik an den Illusionen bürgerlicher Kunstautonomie geschichtlich konkrete Form erhielt, wo auch die bestehenden Distributionsapparate und neue Vermittlungsarten von Kunst, die Gefahr der Integration und Vermarktung antibürgerlich intendierter Kunstarbeit in der Reflexion erschienen, wurde Avantgarde mehr als nur destruktiver Bürgerschreck oder umgestülpter Ästhetizismus: Umfunktionieren und revolutionärer Umbau der Kunst für eine neue Gesellschaft konnten anvisiert werden.[9]

Barck/Schlenstedt/Thierse sehen hier das Aufkommen einer sozialistischen Avantgarde, deren Aufbrechen des traditionellen Kunstbegriffs und des Autonomiestatus der Kunst bis zum Einsatz didaktisch-agitatorischer Kunstmittel führte. Die bewußte ästhetisch-experimentelle Orientierung auf das Verhältnis von politischer Avantgarde und Kunstfortschritt wird zum entscheidenden Moment der Avantgarde. Die Aktualität der historischen Avantgarden für die oppositionelle künstlerische Intelligenz in den heutigen kapitalistischen Ländern besteht nach Auffassung der Autoren darin, daß mit ihren Leistungen Modelle des Übergangs auf neue politische und ästhetische Positionen vorgelegt wurden, die Alternativen des Verhaltens innerhalb herrschender bürgerlicher Kulturverhältnisse bereitstellen. Diese These korrespondiert mit der Auffassung, die Avantgarde sei, historisch betrachtet, ein transitorisches Phänomen in der Epoche des Übergangs vom Kapitalismus zum Sozialismus.

Im Unterschied zu Bürger, der die Avantgarde primär unter dem Aspekt ihres geschichtlichen Scheiterns betrachtet und dabei vor allem ihre Problematik in den kapitalistischen Gesellschaften vor Augen hat --dies zeigt sich z.B. im Ausklammern der sowjetischen Avantgarde--, stehen die Beiträge des Sammelbandes im Kontext mit Klärungsprozessen innerhalb der ästhetischen Theorie sowjetsozialistischer Länder. Denn auch für die Kunst und Literatur in diesen Ländern, für die Entwicklung der marxistischen Literaturtheorie und für die Programmatik des sozialistischen Realismus sei--so Barck/Schlenstedt/Thierse-- der avantgardistische Impuls anregend. Mithin stelle sich die Frage nach einer theoretischen Verarbeitung unterschiedlicher Strategien eines Zusammengehens von Kunst und sozialer Bewegung wie sie mit den Positionen des von Lukács repräsentierten Realismustyps, dem Literaturprogramm des Bundes proletarisch-revolutionärer Schriftsteller und den Avantgarde-Konzepten vorliegen.

Exemplarisch für die heutige Auseinandersetzung mit der Avantgarde ist der Beitrag Silvia Schlenstedts.[10] Schlenstedt untersucht das Avantgarde-Problem am Beispiel des deutschen Expressionismus. Es sei in der Literaturgeschichtsschreibung umstritten, ob der Expressionismus zur Avantgarde zu rechnen sei. Die Frage der Zuordnung nimmt Schlenstedt zum Anlaß, über die Kriterien eines Begriffs der Avantgarde nachzudenken. Man könne diesem Problem nicht beikommen, indem man eine bestimmte Richtung der Avantgarde, z.B. den Surrealismus, zu einem allgemeinen Typus modelliere oder umgekehrt auf dem Wege ahistorischen Abstrahierens allgemeine Wesensmerkmale hervorhebe (S. 39). Mit Bezug auf die Begriffsgeschichte stellt Schlenstedt fest, daß mit Avantgarde ursprünglich ein Zusammenhang von geschichtlich-sozialem Fortschritt und Kunst gemeint war, der diesen Begriff auch heute noch kennzeichne. In einem bestimmten Spätstadium des Kapitalismus erhalte das Problem der künstlerischen Erneuerung jedoch eine neue Qualität angesichts der Existenz einer revolutionären Gegenkraft zur bürgerlichen Gesellschaft:

> Mit Bezug auf dieses historische Stadium der Kunstentwicklung wird bei mir von Avantgarde die Rede sein; der Begriff wird verwendet und erörtert für eine historische Periode, in der die Ablösung des Kapitalismus auf die geschichtliche Tagesordnung tritt. (S. 41)

In ihrer Untersuchung des literarischen Expressionismus geht Silvia Schlenstedt auf ein Thema ein, das in der marxistischen Literaturwissenschaft bisher kaum beachtet worden sei: Der Zusammenhang zwischen literarischer Avantgardebewegung und dem Stand in der Entwicklung der Arbeiterbewegung. In einer Zeit, in der durch die Massenbewegungen die soziale Revolution auf die Tagesordnung gesetzt worden sei, habe die Avantgarde nicht umhin gekonnt, diese Bewegungen und die soziale Revolution zum Bezugspunkt zu nehmen.

Während jedoch in Rußland die Avantgarde durch die erfolgreiche Revolution zu konstruktiven Lösungen gefunden hätte, sei es in Deutschland infolge des Scheiterns der Revolution zu einer Krise der linken Avantgarde gekommen. Bemerkenswert ist nun, daß Schlenstedt diese Krise auch der KPD anlastet, da sie kein Verständnis für avantgardistische künstlerische Bestrebungen gehabt hätte (S. 51f.). Zu dem Zeitpunkt, als die linksavantgardistische Strömung innerhalb des Expressionismus--u.a. Ernst Toller und Iwan Goll--sich profilierte, sei die gerade gegründete KPD noch stark den kunsttheoretischen Traditionen der II. Internationale (Mehring) verhaftet gewesen. Aus dieser Sicht wurden noch Anfang der 20er Jahre sowohl der Expressionismus wie auch das Avantgarde-Theater Piscators abgelehnt. Schlenstedt stellt fest:

> Es kommt zu Spannungen, Gegensätzen, Konflikten zwischen künstlerischer und politischer Avantgarde (und es kann auch zu Entgegensetzungen von künstlerischer Revolution und politischer Revolution kommen) dann und in dem Maße, wie innerhalb der Arbeiterbewegung bzw. im Konnex mit ihr noch nicht eine historisch-materialistische Theorie revolutionärer realistischer Kunst und Kunst der Übergangsperiode ausgebildet wird. . . . (S. 51-52)

In Deutschland wäre die Avantgardebewegung schon an ihrem Ende angelangt, als sich in Gestalt des BPRS, der Arbeiterkorrespondentenbewegung, des Agitprop die Basis für eine proletarisch-revolutionäre Kultur herausgebildet hätte. Diese Voraussetzungen hätten die Chance entstehen lassen, in Deutschland eine sozialistische avantgardistische Kunst neuen Typs zu schaffen. In John Heartfield sieht Silvia Schlenstedt einen der wenigen Künstler, "die eine Kontinuität von den avantgardistischen Anfängen im Dadaismus zur revolutionären Kunstpraxis des proletarischen Klassenkampfes herstellen konnten" (S. 53).

Barck/Schlenstedt/Thierse sehen--wie bereits angeführt--im Verhältnis von künstlerischer und politischer Avantgarde den entscheidenden Punkt der Avantgardeproblematik. Sie binden die gesellschaftsrevolutionären Vorstellungen linksavantgardistischer Gruppen an eine von den kommunistischen Parteien getragene revolutionäre Praxis. Wenn in einzelnen Beiträgen des Bandes--wie in dem von Silvia Schlenstedt--auch eingeräumt wird, daß die kommunistischen Parteien der zwanziger und dreißiger Jahre in konventionellen künstlerischen Strategien befangen waren und den avantgardistischen Bestrebungen wenig Verständnis entgegenbrachten, greift eine Fragestellung, die künstlerische und politische Avantgarde miteinander verknüpft, ohne das Scheitern der politischen Avantgarde auf das Experiment des sozialistischen Aufbaus selbst zu beziehen, zu kurz. Notwendig ausgeklammert bleibt in dieser Betrachtung, daß der Konservatismus der herrschenden Kunstdoktrin in den sowjetsozialistischen Ländern auch eine Folge des Einfrierens der gesellschaftsrevolutionären Impulse ist. Die Neigung, das Avantgarde-Problem zu historisieren, ohne den aktuellen Standpunkt des Betrachters mit einzubringen, trägt bei aller Differenziertheit der Analysen und kritischen Beurteilung vergangener Kulturpolitik zur Entschärfung eines weiteren Problems bei: Kann das, was mit dem Titel einer sozialistischen Literatur versehen wird, diesen Anspruch überhaupt erfüllen, wenn es hinter den ästhetischen Standard der Avantgarde zurückfällt? Diese Frage drängt sich geradezu auf, wenn die avantgardistische Literatur als ein Phänomen des Übergangs zu Formen einer nichtbürgerlichen Kultur verstanden wird. Ferner ist zu klären, ob der behauptete Zusammenhang zwischen der Funktionskrise der bürgerlichen Kunst in einer bestimmten historischen Phase und dem Aufkommen der Avantgarde-Bewegung nicht mutatis mutandis auf die Situation der Kunst in den sowjetsozialistischen Ländern zutrifft. Zu fragen wäre z.B., ob die Krise der marxistisch-leninistischen Ideologie ein Antriebsmoment für neoavantgardistische Bestrebungen in der DDR sein könnte oder nicht vielmehr für modernistische Bestrebungen im Sinne einer Rückgewinnung der Kunstautonomie. Der von Sascha Anderson und Elke Erb herausgegebene Band <u>Berührung</u> <u>ist</u> <u>nur</u> <u>eine</u> <u>Randerscheinung</u> dokumentiert z.B. das Zusammentreffen beider Tendenzen.[11]

Ich komme noch einmal zurück auf die Frage nach den Motiven und der möglichen Funktion einer Rehabilitierung der Moderne und Avantgarde in der DDR. Für die Möglichkeit, das Forschungsinteresse heute auf diesen Gegenstand zu richten, läßt sich neben den bereits genannten Gründen ein weiterer anführen. Die neuen avantgardistischen Impulse im Westen sind mit dem Niedergang der Studentenbewegung und dem Bedeutungsverlust der Neuen Linken weitgehend erloschen.

Das Terrain wird heute nicht mehr von linken Kritikern des realen Sozialismus beansprucht und kann folglich ideologisch neu besetzt werden. Angesichts der kulturellen Tendenzwende und des Aufkommens der Postmoderne im Westen geraten die alten ideologischen Fronten ins Wanken. Ein Bemühen um Erweiterung des traditionellen Realismuskonzeptes um Elemente der Moderne und Avantgarde ist dadurch gegen den Vorwurf gewappnet, es mache sich die weltanschauliche Position des Klassenfeindes zueigen.

Für die Darstellung der gegenwärtigen Diskussion über Moderne und Postmoderne in der DDR möchte ich die Stellungnahmen von Karin Hirdina, Robert Weimann und Utz Riese heranziehen. In seiner Besprechung einer im Bouvier Verlag Bonn erschienenen Abhandlung von Robert W. Weber über den modernen Roman kritisiert Riese, daß ästhetische Bestrebungen, die eine Zusammenführung von ästhetischer und sozialer Avantgarde zum Ziel hatten und sich anderer künstlerischer Methoden bedienten als Proust, Joyce, Woolf und Faulkner, vom Verfasser vernachlässigt würden.[12] Übersehen würden von Weber auch die tieferliegenden Gründe für das Aufkommen einer vor allem die amerikanische Literaturentwicklung kennzeichnenden Postmoderne, die--so Riese--eine Antwort darstelle auf die Eingliederung des institutionalisierten Kunstbetriebs in die massenhafte Produktion, Verteilung und Rezeption von Kulturgütern. Webers These, die Postmoderne sei eine einfache Fortschreibung der Moderne, sei in jedem Fall zu widersprechen. Riese sieht das entscheidende Kennzeichen der Postmoderne in ihrer Absage an die "Restutopie klassisch-bürgerlicher Humanität sowie überhaupt eines aufklärerischen Geschichtsoptimismus" (S. 507).[13] Die Aufkündigung des Anthropozentrismus durch die Postmoderne stelle ganz neue Fragen an das Verhältnis von Moderne und Realismus. Sie seien weit weniger voneinander entfernt, als ihre Vertreter und manche Theoretiker das glauben machen wollten. Für die Moderne, z.B. Joyce, gelte, daß der vereinseitigten humanistischen Utopie nach wie vor eine ins Werk hineingeschriebene Sinngebung entspreche, während die Postmoderne vor allem die Erzeugung eines epistemologischen Vakuums intendiere (S. 508).

An anderer Stelle geht Riese der Frage nach, warum Klassiker der Moderne wie Joyce, Eliot, Woolf, Kafka, Proust, Musil und Dos Passos lange Zeit in der

DDR auf dem Index standen.[14] Er macht dafür politische Gründe geltend, da die genannten Autoren bis in die 60er Jahre hinein Leitsterne für eine modernistische Ästhetik gewesen seien, deren Antirealismus sich in politischer Hinsicht mit einem Antikommunismus verbunden gesehen hätte (S. 759). Offenbar ist mit dem Klassisch-Werden der Autoren und dem Verlust ihrer Leitsternfunktion in der Ästhetik der westlichen Gesellschaften, an deren Stelle die Postmoderne getreten ist, der Zeitpunkt gekommen--so läßt sich Riese interpretieren--, die früher als dekadent Geschmähten in das Erbe der sozialistischen Literatur einzugliedern.

Mit dem Verhältnis von Realismus und Moderne angesichts des Phänomens einer Postmoderne beschäftigt sich auch ein Beitrag der Kunstwissenschaftlerin Karin Hirdina.[15] Sie geht von der Beobachtung aus, daß in der kunsttheoretischen Diskussion und in der kunstpolitischen Szene der Bundesrepublik in den letzten Jahren das Interesse am Realismus wieder zugenommen habe. Hirdina konstatiert eine Umbewertung der Kunstentwicklung: der Realismus werde gegenüber der Avantgardekunst, wie sie sich in diesem Jahrhundert entwickelte, aufgewertet. Parallel dazu breite sich der Postmodernismus vor allem in der Architektur und im Design aus.

> Realismus wie Postmodernismus werden als Alternative zur Avantgarde der zwanziger und dreißiger Jahre gefaßt - als Absage an deren forcierten Technikoptimismus, als Rückkehr zur Tradition, als neue Qualität von Volkstümlichkeit. (S. 402)

Dieser Vorgang spielt sich nun allerdings zu einem Zeitpunkt ab, da innerhalb der marxistisch-leninistischen Kunsttheorie eine differenziertere Beurteilung der Avantgarde die alten Interpretationsmuster ablöst. An die Stelle bloßer Entgegensetzung von Realismus und Avantgarde oder Moderne ist eine historisch-funktionale Betrachtungsweise getreten. Hirdina weist in ihrem Beitrag darauf hin, daß die Rehabilitierung des Realismus im Westen nichts zu tun hat mit einer Aneignung des Realismusbegriffs der marxistisch-leninistischen Ästhetik. Der Realismus werde entpolitisiert, enthistorisiert und formalisiert. Es würden ihm von westlichen Wissenschaftlern Attribute zugeordnet, die in der DDR bislang als Bestimmungen für Modernismus galten. Realismus, so verstanden, stelle Sinnbilder einer entfremdeten versteinerten Wirklichkeit dar. Für die kunsttheoretische Reflexion in der DDR hält Hirdina fest:

> Es geht heute nicht mehr um eine Legitimation des Realismus gegenüber dem Modernismus, dies Geschäft erledigen andere. Was sie allerdings damit legitimieren und rehabilitieren ist wohl nicht unbedingt, was uns als Realismus gilt. (S. 410)

Innerhalb der marxistisch-leninistischen Ästhetik sei der Realismusbegriff nur in einem geschichtsphilosophischen Zusammenhang als historischer und wertender Begriff sinnvoll zu begründen.

Ein Überdenken des Realismusbegriffs fordert auch Robert Weimann.[16] Der Realismus befinde sich weltweit in einer Phase der Veränderung und Bezugserweiterung und sei einbezogen in einen internationalen Paradigmenwechsel, "in dessen Verlauf der Modernismus abgelöst wird durch jenen postmodernen Wandel in Stil, Funktion und Theorie der Künste, der von der Literatur über die bildende Kunst bis zur Architektur reicht" (S. 942). Auch Kunst und Kunsttheorie in der DDR seien mit der "abgrundtiefen Krise des Modernismus" konfrontiert. Von dieser Entwicklung sei der alte Gegensatz von Realismus und Modernismus betroffen. Ebenso wie Riese und Hirdina meint Weimann, daß beide Strömungen aus postmoderner Sicht näher aneinander heranrücken würden.

> Aus postmoderner Erfahrung ergeben sich zwischen den Antipoden von ehedem (sagen wir: zwischen Balzac und Joyce) ungeahnte Gemeinsamkeiten in der Sozialfunktion und Weltaneignung, historisch übergreifende Verkehrseffekte und Sinngebungen, die einstmals - im blendenden Lichte des modernistischen Experiments - übersehen wurden. (S. 942)

Der Realismus trete in einen neuen ambivalenten Funktionskontext. Das Ende des avantgardistischen Impulses mache ihn im Westen hoffähig. Der Realismuseffekt im Westen sei sehr schillernd. Er trete in konservativem wie auch in gesellschaftskritischem Gewande auf. Im Unterschied zum konservierenden Realismus sei dessen postmoderne populäre Funktionserweiterung nicht einfach zu negieren. Weimann nennt als Beispiele den Fotorealismus und eine bestimmte Art, nun allerdings nicht gerade populärer Texte, in denen die Kategorie der Bedeutung problematisch geworden ist.

> Re-präsentation findet nicht statt: Objektivität dokumentiert nichts anderes als sich selbst. Alle Dinge, alle Farben, alle Motive sind gleich bedeutend. Damit ist - anders als im konservierenden Realismus des Westens - die Kategorie der Bedeutung selbst in die Krise geraten. Das Semantische wird von der Pragmatik des Zeichens amputiert. Das Widerspiel von Sein und Schein, von Realität und Fiktion bestärkt jenes "epistemologische Vakuum", das die Kunst (wie die Kunsttheorie) selbstreflexiv macht. Die Zerstörung aller Hierarchien von Wert und Form und Farbe hat dann - hier wie dort - nur noch eine Konsequenz: den Anthropozentrismus aus der Kunst zu vertreiben. (S. 944)

Hier sei der Punkt erreicht, wo die Kluft zur sozialistischen Kunst unüberbrückbar werde.

Das Bemerkenswerte an Weimanns Position ist, daß die konstatierte Abwesenheit des Menschen in Produkten der postmodernen Kunst nicht einfach als unrealistisch oder als Verfallserscheinung interpretiert wird, da die Maßstäbe klassischer bürgerlicher Humanität heute unserer Welt utopisch entrückt seien und ein daraus abgeleiteter Realismusbegriff heutigen Welterfahrungen nicht mehr gerecht werde. Das Phänomen des Verschwindens des Menschen aus der Kunst lasse sich nicht allein der westlichen Kultur zuschreiben, da die Postmoderne auch die DDR unaufhaltsam in Theorie und Praxis erreiche. Weimann spricht von der Realität des internationalen Kunstprozesses, der Bedingungen schaffe, daß man auch in der DDR "vor dem unsagbaren Schmerz in Becketts verstummenden Stimmen nicht die Ohren verschließen" dürfe (S. 945). Er fordert eine sachliche Analyse dieser Kunstprodukte, wobei stets die konkrete soziale Funktion der Werke zu berücksichtigen sei.

In der poststrukturalistischen Literaturtheorie sieht Weimann eine produktive Herausforderung des

Realismusgedankens, die bei aller notwendigen historisch-materialistischen Kritik des gesamten Gedankengebäudes die Perspektive eröffne, einen modernen Realismusbegriff jenseits der klassisch-romantischen Kunsttradition zu entwickeln.[17]

Der differenziertere Umgang mit der Moderne, das Bemühen um eine Neubewertung der historischen Avantgardebewegungen und die auf einem hohen Niveau sich zutragende Auseinandersetzung mit der Postmoderne in den Literatur- und Kunstwissenschaften der DDR blieben bei den Kulturverantwortlichen nicht ohne Resonanz. In einer Rede über "Tradition und Fortschritt" vor der Akademie der Künste stellte der für Kultur und Wissenschaft zuständige ZK-Sekretär Kurt Hager fest:

> Unser Hauptaugenmerk gilt der Literatur und Kunst des sozialistischen Realismus, aber wir verschließen unsere Augen nicht vor dem Wertvollen, das in anderen humanistisch fundierten künstlerischen Richtungen entstanden ist. Pauschale Aburteilungen etwa expressionistischer und avantgardistischer Werke als "dekadent" oder "formalistisch" haben sich, wie bekannt, nicht als förderlich für das Verständnis dieser Richtungen und die Intentionen der Schriftsteller und Künstler erwiesen.[18]

In der Auseinandersetzung mit den verschiedenen Strömungen bürgerlich-modernistischer Kunst und Literatur käme es darauf an, zwischen "humanistischen Intentionen und damit verbundenen künstlerischen Errungenschaften" und "politisch-weltanschaulichen Begrenztheiten und ästhetisch-künstlerischen Irrwegen" (S. 450) zu unterscheiden. Wie zu zeigen versucht wurde, sind die Literaturwissenschaften in der Sondierung des Terrains schon sehr weit gegangen, so daß die Rehabilitierung "ästhetisch-künstlerischer Irrwege" als ein nächster Schritt nicht ausgeschlossen werden kann.

Anmerkungen

1 Erwähnt seien hier nur: Brigitte Burmeister, Streit um den Nouveau Roman (Berlin: Akademie-Verlag, 1983); Gudrun Klatt, Vom Umgang mit der Moderne (Berlin: Akademie-Verlag, 1984); Künstlerische Avantgarde. Annäherungen an ein unabgeschlossenes Kapitel, hrsg. von Karlheinz Barck, Dieter Schlenstedt und Wolfgang Thierse (Berlin: Akademie-Verlag, 1979); und Wolfgang Wicht, Virginia Woolf, James Joyce, T.S. Eliot (Berlin: Akademie-Verlag, 1981). Zu Kafka vgl. den Bericht über die Berliner Konferenz am 28. Juni 1983 in Zeitschrift für Germanistik, 5, Heft 3 (1984), 319-21.

2 Vgl. u.a. Gudrun Klatt, "'Rettende Kritik' - Walter Benjamins Baudelaire-Studien (1938/39)," in Vom Umgang mit der Moderne, S. 178-211; Günther K. Lehmann, "Stramin und totale Form. Der Kunstphilosoph Georg Lukács und sein Verhältnis zu Ernst Blochs Ästhetik der Hoffnung," Weimarer Beiträge, 31, Heft 4 (1985), 533-57; Literarische Widerspiegelung. Geschichte und theoretische Dimensionen eines Problems (Berlin: Aufbau, 1981); Robert Weimann, "Mimesis und die Bürde der Repräsentation. Der Poststrukturalismus und das Produktionsproblem in fiktiven Texten," Weimarer Beiträge, 31, Heft 7 (1985), 1061-99.

3 In einem im Neuen Deutschland erschienenen Aufsatz zum 100. Geburtstag Franz Kafkas bezeichnete Dieter Schiller den Dichter als einen bedeutenden Vertreter der humanistischen Literatur unseres Jahrhunderts. Vgl. Neues Deutschland vom 2./3. Juli 1983. Für Jürgen Engler bietet Kafkas Werk auch für Sozialisten "überreichlich Stoff zur Selbstprüfung, zum Nachdenken über die Möglichkeit, in dieser Welt redlich das Notwendende zu tun," Neue Deutsche Literatur, 31, Heft 6 (1983), 118. Im Nachwort zu einem Band mit Aufsätzen, Vorträgen und Essays von T.S. Eliot resümiert der Herausgeber Wolfgang Wicht, daß vieles, was Eliot schrieb, "wenn auch nicht immer vorbehaltlos anzuerkennen, so doch in der sozialistischen Gesellschaft rezipierbar" sei (Nachwort zu T.S. Eliot, Ausgewählte Aufsätze, Vorträge und Essays [Berlin: Volk und Welt, 1982], S. 402). Zu Musil vgl. den Essay von Siegfried Rönisch, "Robert Musil. Ein Versuch über sein Leben und Werk," Weimarer Beiträge, 30, Heft 6 (1984), 926-53.

[4] Vgl. dazu Alfred Dreifuß, "Asterix kontra Godot," *Die Weltbühne*, 80, Heft 24 (1985), 750-51.

[5] Werke von Eliot, Joyce und Musil erschienen bei Volk und Welt in Berlin, Kafka bei Reclam und Kiepenheuer, Woolf und Proust ebenfalls bei Kiepenheuer und Insel in Leipzig. Von Kafka ist außerdem eine Neuauflage des erzählerischen Werks bei Rütten & Loening in Berlin erschienen. Klaus Hermsdorf besorgte eine Erstausgabe seiner "Amtlichen Schriften" im Ostberliner Akademie-Verlag.

[6] Vgl. Wilhelm Girnus, "Wer baute das siebentorige Theben?" *Sinn und Form*, 35, Heft 2 (1983), 439-47, und Hans Kaufmann, "Wider die trojanischen Kriege," *Sinn und Form*, 36, Heft 3 (1984), 653-63.

[7] *Künstlerische Avantgarde*, S. 18.

[8] Peter Bürger, *Theorie der Avantgarde* (Frankfurt/Main: Suhrkamp, 1974).

[9] *Künstlerische Avantgarde*, S. 10.

[10] Silvia Schlenstedt, "Problem Avantgarde. Ein Diskussionsvorschlag. Bezugsfeld deutscher Expressionismus," in *Künstlerische Avantgarde*, S. 39-54.

[11] Sascha Anderson und Elke Erb, Hrsg., *Berührung ist nur eine Randerscheinung. Neue Literatur aus der DDR* (Köln: Kiepenheuer & Witsch, 1985).

[12] Utz Riese, "(Rezension) Robert W. Weber: Der moderne Roman (Bonn: Bouvier, 1981)," *Weimarer Beiträge*, 30, Heft 3 (1984), 505-08.

[13] Vgl. auch Utz Riese, "Zwischen Realismus und Postmodernismus," *Weimarer Beiträge*, 31, Heft 3 (1985), 517-23.

[14] Utz Riese, "(Rezension) Wolfgang Wicht: Virginia Woolf, James Joyce, T.S. Eliot (Berlin: Akademie-Verlag, 1981)," *Weimarer Beiträge*, 29, Heft 4 (1983), 759-64.

[15] Karin Hirdina, "Realismus in der Diskussion," *Weimarer Beiträge*, 30, Heft 3 (1984), 401-15.

[16] Robert Weimann, "Realität und Realismus,"

Sinn und Form, 36, Heft 5 (1984), 924-51.

[17] Eine grundlegende Kritik am Poststrukturalismus hat Weimann im Nachwort des Buches Structure and Society in Literary History (Baltimore: Johns Hopkins, 1984) formuliert; in deutscher Übersetzung erschienen unter dem Titel "Mimesis und die Bürde der Repräsentation," vgl. Anm. 2.

[18] Kurt Hager, "Tradition und Fortschritt," Sinn und Form, 37, Heft 3 (1985), 449.

The Museum of Hope:
The Poems of Richard Pietraß

Anna Chiarloni

Until now, Richard Pietraß has been little discussed in the West. This is, I believe, essentially a matter of chronology. Pietraß belongs to the "halfway" generation born soon after the war, a generation that does not readily fit into the standard scheme of literary history. In fact, a distinction is generally drawn between the highly ideological generation born in the 1930s--that of Braun or Biermann--and the generation born in the 1950s, for whom the confrontation with the socialist specific is solely a "Randerscheinung," as is indicated in the title of a recent anthology of young GDR writers, Berührung ist nur eine Randerscheinung.[1] In contrast, Pietraß's generation is still concerned with political events--its points of reference are the building of the Berlin Wall (1961) and the events in Prague (1968); at the same time, it manifests a distinct detachment from the rhetoric of the Aufbau period. This detachment is however not so much a sign of dissent as of a gradual withdrawal from the ideological vocabulary of the GDR, without losing sight of its real landscape. In this study of Richard Pietraß, I will highlight six essential stages of his lyrical journey, the discussion of each of which is prefaced by a line from one of his poems.

1. Im Stichjahr meiner Geburt

Richard Pietraß was born in Lichtenstein, Saxony in 1946. On leaving school, he was employed first as a metal worker and then as a hospital attendant; from 1968 to 1972 he studied psychology at Humboldt University. His first collection of poems appeared in

1974 as an issue of Poesiealbum under the editorship of Bernd Jentzsch.[2] His subsequent collections, Notausgang and Freiheitsmuseum, were published by Aufbau Verlag in 1980 and 1982.[3]

Pietraß belongs to a postwar generation no longer marked by the "deutsche Vergangenheit." For Pietraß, fascism and World War II are but a faint memory enshrined within his family, a memory which he has evoked in tender portrayals of his father, who was a refugee from the Eastern part of the Reich ceded to Poland after the war. Pietraß is even too young to have experienced the torments of the 1950s, the contradictions faced by the intellectuals, bound as they were by Ulbricht's cultural policy to a firmly based, smoothly flowing ideological constructivism. His entry onto the literary scene coincides with that of the Werthers in blue jeans, when the new course steered by Honecker left room for a literature that was more complex and problem-oriented. Pietraß is aware of the advantages of having been born after the war. To borrow an expression from one of his poems, he can swim with fast strokes across the face of history. He still hears, however, the tragic murmur of the past:

> Wär ich ein Fisch,
> Ging ich der Geschichte auf den Grund.
> So schwimm ich mit raschen Zügen drüberhin.
> Aber Stimmen hör ich,
> Drunten, Lorengequietsch und, leise,
> Detonationen.   ("Nachtrag," PA, p. 3)

Pietraß represents a generation that is still cultured, with a relatively high level of education, unlike its immediate successor in the 1950s (Kolbe, Anderson, Papenfuß, Döring, Faktor, Lorek), whose background is that of TV, discos, and pop music. Peter Böthig rightly remarks that Pietraß's poetry is "hochgradig Gemachtes."[4] He is clearly an author who has consciously absorbed the lessons of contemporary European poetry, thanks to a period spent in a publishing house (Neues Leben) and his editing of the Poesiealbum series from 1977 to 1979. Even so, his poems are neither contrived nor erudite. They turn on subtle differences, on a subdued, often nocturnal contraposition with a bewildering, rule-bound Umwelt which is never concretely described, but rather metaphorically evoked, as it were, through negation.

2. Drachensteigen

The result is a plain, allusive language, drained dry of any ideological expression. In his first collection of poems published in Poesiealbum, for example, Pietraß uses a bird metaphor to convey fragments of an inner state that flares up within the brief space of a single night:

> Am Abend verwandeln wir uns
> und werden Vögel, Mauersegler, die mit schrillen
> Schreien den ungeteilten Himmel befliegen,
> und lautlos streichende Eulen, steigen
> unter die höchsten Türme, nisten
> des Nachts und bleiben ertappte Vögel, denen
> der Morgen die geborgten
> Federn nimmt.   ("Am Abend," PA, p. 6)

The image of flight lends Pietraß's work an ascending, lyrical expression that seems to convey the need to break out of a suffocating perimeter, to widen the confines of a daily routine cramped within the narrow gage of the urban intellectual.

In "Im November," the doves swoop down at dawn into the chilly autumn courtyards; the poem itself is printed in the form of spiral, a single verse that lies on the page like a bright wedge that brings to mind an ancient harmony between heaven and earth:

> IM NOVEMBER SCHAFFT ES DIE SONNE NICHT
>   MEHR,
>   den Tau vom Zement des hochummauerten
>   Hofes zu lecken. Ihre Strahlen
>   tasten nur die Kante der
>   Dächer und melden so:
>   Es wird Tag. Die
>   ewig blauen
>   Tauben aber
>   schwingen
>   sich hin-
>   unter in
>   den Schlund
>   und fressen
>   den Weizen
>   vorm Fenster
>   des neuen
>   Mieters. Es
>   heißt, er

>   kommt vom
>   Land.   (PA, p. 7)

In a similar way, Pietraß's second collection opens with the image of a magpie building its windswept nest at the top of the trees in a "Niemandsland" that escapes the violence of the hunters (NA, p. 7). But in this second volume, the patches of sky gradually diminish, the horizon draws tighter, and the Berlin courtyard weighs oppressively like a "Stickkammer getäuschter Hoffnung" (NA, p. 9). The lyrical voice again finds its identity in a bird, a thrush ("Drossel"). This time, however, it is wingless, featherless, stiff, and incapable of song:

> Bin die Drossel beschäftigt
> Kürze mein hastiges Lied
>
> Bin und schweige entkräftet
> Von dem was um mich geschieht
>
> Singe nicht mehr bin nackt
> Flügellos in flatternden Räumen
>
> Bin steif meine Federn kleben
> In vielen zu bunten Bäumen.   (NA, p. 54)

The metaphor of flight gradually wings its way out of Pietraß's poetry. In the third collection, <u>Freiheitsmuseum</u>, the doves are permanently swallowed up in a spectral suburb behind sinister, walled-up windows ("Abriß," FM, p. 34). From a striving upwards, metaphorically expressed in the gesture of flying a kite, dangerously, perhaps, in the direction of Western skies ("Drachensteigen," PA, p. 8), one passes--in <u>Notausgang</u>, which brings together texts written from 1972 to 1977--to a painful shrinking of horizons, expressed in the dry images of an inner amputation:

> Beschnitten.
> Mein Winter drängt.
>
> Die Himmelsleiter:
> An den Nagel gehängt.
>
>   ("Beschnitten," NA, p. 45)

And even if the close alludes to a necessary pruning

"um Frucht zu treiben," recalling the bitter leitmotiv of Müller's Mauser--"das Gras noch / müssen wir ausreißen, damit es grün bleibt"[5]--the lyric measure becomes more bitter and more painful. The ironic tone, the open rejection of socialist-style consumerism[6] and of the opportunism of official historiography[7] that stride boldly through Pietraß's early verse give way to more circumspect reflexion that willingly lingers in closed spaces, digging--with a fully homey vocabulary--behind the facade of real socialism.

3. Gras redend, träumen wir Stein

When Pietraß examines the role of the poet in contemporary society, he reflects a process discernible in GDR writing in general in the 1980s, a process one could define as the breakup of the collective unit. This needs a word of explanation. The "collective unit" does not mean here society alone, but rather the Apparat that determines the official attitude towards events, with its penchant for soothing language designed to supply a picture of glowing solidity. The breakup practiced by Pietraß is essentially linguistic, pursued through a patient search for words that have so far escaped the bureaucratic maw.

Let us examine the elements of this process. Poesiealbum closes with two poems which focus on language. "Replik" (p. 30), dedicated to Enzensberger, plays on the opposition between sagen and reden; it deals with the difficulty of a manner of speaking that does not come easily, an incomplete, defensive vocabulary. In "Das Wort," on the other hand, which is dedicated to Boccaccio, Pietraß, while aware of the provisional, fragile nature of words, which are sometimes no more than an attempt at rapprochement ("tastende Hand am Leib der Dinge") ends with a tercet that has a substantially positive note and sees words as a more effective weapon than silence.

> Messer an der Zunge des Sängers
> ist es doch größer
> als das Schweigen.   (PA, p. 31)

At the beginning of the 1970s, the poet's intention was clear: to create for himself a language that walked hand-in-hand with things, apart from the automatic phrases of the times and loaded with the contradictions typical of real life. Notausgang is the expression of this search.

In keeping with this approach, the great horizons fall away, dragging with them the monumental portraits, the "men of marble." "Proletarisches Porträt," with its uneven rhyming, is marked by the rhythm of urgent necessity and has the tone of an inevitable condemnation:

> Ich kenne keine Ruhe
> Ich trage schwer.
> In meiner Lage ist man
> Schnell hinüber.   (NA, p. 82)

The poet's gaze is now directed to the day-to-day dimension of living. His inventory is limited, but it is one he can trust. The lyrical voice shrinks from any public gesture, almost fearful of losing its way in "the labyrinth of the collective unit."[8] When asked to contribute to an anthology on the events in Chile in 1973, Pietraß replied by denouncing the insufficiency of the protest of the Solidaritätsgedichte[9] and the indifference towards violence displayed by modern man:

> Während ihr aufschreit   Unter scheelen Gewehren
> Schlägt mein Herz   Monoton in die Nacht.
>
> ("Ein Weiteres," NA, p. 35)

This retreat from the militant internationalist poetry, the standard of the GDR's old intellectual guard, is clearly not an escape from a political commitment. It stems from the poet's wish to take a first-hand look at the realities of his immediate surroundings. To cry "Scandal!" upon the occurrence of a distant event lacks, in his view, credibility; it is a reaction destined to "drown in the waters of the Atlantic." Hence, by contrast, the close-up analysis of the deep Ego, nocturnal, oneiric, that often spreads itself in the wir, reconstructing an entirely novel imagery:

> Abends stürzt unser Tag vom Scheitel.
> Die Nächte werden dem Lager
> Kurz. Aber Beischlaf findend, hoffen wir Liebe.
> Gras redend, träumen wir Stein.

Immer sind wir weiter als gewußt wird.
   Leuchtender Staub:
Krönt uns die Nacht.

   ("Einführung in die Metaphorik," NA, p. 34)

4. <u>Meine</u> <u>Haut</u> <u>ist</u> <u>dünn</u>

The moving spirit in these poems is primarily centripetal, to the exclusion of the outside world, which is perceived as a consuming, diurnal dust ("Tagesstaub"):[10]

Der Vorhang fällt, die Kerze engt das Zimmer.
Was uns die Welt war, schließt sich dunkel zu.
Fern wacht der Bleitod unterm Sternenflimmer.
Das Doppelbild des Fensters schneidet Ruh.

("Lebensraum," NA, p. 56)

To draw the blinds and close one's eyes seems indispensable to the laborious search for one's own self. A journey that may even cast doubt on the identity of the lyrical voice:

Ich begegne mir im Fenster einer Drogerie
und schließe die Augen
Geschlossenen Auges begegne ich einem Skelett

Es geht vorbei   ("Auf der Straße," NA, p. 40)

Once his inner security is lost, man exists solely in his physical being. Any intellectual operation awakens suspicion. The biological dimension is the only one in which to place one's trust:

Im Zimmer sitze ich im Mantel. Draußen wirbt
Ein Frühling, der mich entblößen wird.
Ich zähle die Finger. Zehn, noch eben.
Der Spiegel weist die Zunge, jede Knospe:
                              ein Spalt.

("Die Dämmerung," NA, p. 70)

Beyond the merely physical perception of self there begins the world where deception is possible. Even one's own name is suspect: a shadow or a "banner," it never coincides with the lyrical voice, which remains bare, unarmed, and, above all, betrayed: "In meinem

Namen bringt man Brüder um" ("Schatten," NA, p. 73).

Still, it is this very path away from the fragmentary magma of productive life, from the "Sumpf der Zwecke" (NA, p. 56), which allows the poet to strip off the "Lebenshornhaut,"[11] the calluses which, aided and abetted by the individual, proliferate on his skin and render him prone to compromise. When Pietraß declares: "Meine Haut ist dünn" ("Barometer," NA, p. 67) he is in effect asserting an ethical choice, the wish to remain on the outskirts of the system, assailed, perhaps, by the doubt of knowing himself to be a loser, vulnerable, yet for this very reason intolerant of malaise; a possibly marginal accessory, but the watchful, sensitive indicator of an unimpaired conscience:

> Ich zeige den Druck
> der auf euch lastet
> während ihr unbeschwert
> zu Flugzeug und Straßenbahn hastet.

("Barometer," NA, p. 67)

It is from this position as an outsider, then, that Pietraß commences his solitary journey. With Benjamin-like attention to the linguistic spirit that haunts the concrete world, he carries out a re-exploration of the hidden reality by means of an unconfined use of language. In a continuous round of interlockings and variations, he is intent on reasserting human experience as an ambiguous, fugitive, and contradictory complexity.

5. <u>Gespielt</u> ist <u>gezielt,</u> <u>gebettelt</u> <u>verzettelt,</u> <u>benannt</u> <u>gebannt</u>

Behind this social shield of language, the notion of the Ego begins to be rethought, I mean reconstituted, in the unpredictable play of word and sound combinations that characterize the poet's latest collection of poetry, <u>Freiheitsmuseum</u>, published in 1982. Take, for example, "Generation," dedicated--with forethought--to Velimir Chlebnikov, the Russian futurist poet:

> Ausgeschlupft.
> Schlupfgehupft.

> Hupfgebuttert.
> Buttbemuttert.
>
> Muttgeschaffen.
> Schaffgeschlaffen.
>
> Schlaffgeflippt.
> Flippgestrippt.
>
> Stripbegradigt.
> Gradbegnadigt.
>
> Gnadverkalkt.
> Kalkgewalkt.
>
> Walkhinieden.
> Niedgeschieden.
>
> Schiedgehimmelt.
> Himmelgebimmelt.   (FM, p. 26)

Here sounds split up words into forms that are ever new and different, as though to indicate the multiplicity of possible orders that can be found or even created through artistic activity. And it is at this point that the interaction between poetry and society is rendered evident. Pietraß, standing aside from the <u>Aufbau</u> concept, as some critics have complained,[12] reveals a widespread need for literary "deprovincialization," a linguistic reacquisition of reality not far removed from that expressed by the futurists and the dadaists at the beginning of the twentieth century. Pietraß, in a word, reasserts a function of art, namely that of representing a voice that flees from the political strategies that would control the individual: art as the "Selbstbefreiung des einzelnen und der vielen."[13]

Removed from the bedlam of everyday life, the poet questions himself and carves out a niche where the meaning of words is carefully filtered. Poetry thus becomes a "Freiheitsmuseum," the untouched home of unrenouncable hopes, the "kingdom of freedom."[14] It is also an instrument of knowledge, capable of detecting in the reflection of appearance "das Doppelgesicht allen Fortschritts: das des Befreiers und greisen Sklavenhalters."[15]

The image of the "Freiheitsmuseum" shows for the

first time, albeit in a coded form, a clear detachment from the social "ship of progress" adumbrated in Notausgang.[16] But if Pietraß was here describing an individual deviation, a drawing upon poetry as on a personal emergency exit, the term "museum" adds a public dimension, one that is anchored in an individual dream, but which by its very nature acquires historical value.

Furthermore, the sallies of the lyrical voice from artistic separateness towards the magma of daily life, the incursions into the "swamp of the useful," also interpenetrate this collection. Now, however, the answers are clear and definite. "Lektor," for example, is an outstanding illustration of eikastic descriptiveness:

> Meine Praxis. Ein wackliger Stuhl.
> Die Waage. Das kühle Blut.
> Das Zünglein mein tauber Geschmack.
> Am Haken der griffbereite Hut.   (FM, p. 23)

This poem is dated 1976, the year in which, after the expulsion of Biermann, the publisher of Poesiealbum, Bernd Jentzsch, had decided to stay in Switzerland. Pietraß, too, declared himself ready to leave, but also ready to put up a passive resistance, to retire to bed, if too hard pressed by the galloping "Tagesbefehl."[17]

> Immer öfter hinter zugezogenen Gardinen bemerke,
>   ertappe
> ich mich in der Horizontalen. . . .
>
>
>   Mein Horizont,
> gewiß! enthält wenig besetzbaren Boden, nurmehr
>   Himmel.
> Die Füße, wie immer zuletzt genannt, nehmen das
>   Gesicht
> aus dem Staub und zeigen ihr bergmännisches
>   Lächeln.
>
>   ("Nicht rühren!" FM, p.42)

Here the tone is one of ironic amusement, provocatively prosaic, a sort of Jean Paul grimace at those who seek to gear their inner lives to the rhythm of industrial production.

6. Ich weiß kein Lied

In other poems, one senses the desperation of a person crushed by the contradictions of recent GDR history. In "Anzeige"--the quatrain that precedes "Lektor"--Pietraß publicly declares his total bewilderment:

>Gern wär ich sonstwer. Schlei vor der Angel.
>Kieselstein. Dem keiner droht.
>Wessen stiller Freund in der Kadermangel.
>(Herz, von stockendem Blut durchloht.)

(FM, p. 20)

This denial of decision-making, which Pietraß explicitly associates with daily life in the GDR by using the word "Kadermangel," is illustrated in other poems by a series of equally unequivocal references. In "Was mir zum Glück fehlt" (FM, p. 11), for example, his list of desires includes: "Verse, die mir nicht die Butter kosten" and "Eine Zeitung, die nicht gedruckt lügt." The reasons for this distress are thus enunciated.

At this point, some questions spring spontaneously to mind. Is something changing in the GDR's cultural policy? Is room being made for voices, like that of Pietraß, which do not sing the praises of the socialist wir? And can we assume that the trauma following the expulsion of Biermann and the massive exodus to the West in 1984 have taught something to those bureaucrats who wish to reduce literature to a work program, so as to avoid every danger, also existential?

It is too early yet to hazard an answer. Particularly since it is difficult to assess the success of these younger writers in the GDR. I recently asked a famous author living in East Berlin what he thought of Richard Pietraß. "Never heard of him," was the reply. I will refrain from making any predictions. Even so, I feel that those whose interest lies in the GDR and its literature should, over and above the names bruited abroad by the Western sound-box, lend an ear to the persistent, subtle voices that from the depths of the Berlin Hinterhöfe speak both of "night journeys" and "arrest warrants" and of "steps of courage" and the "art of living."[18]

It is true that Pietraß's Homo Novus, unlike the neuer Mensch of socialist stamp, is wholly unsuited for a flight towards great theatrical goals. Indeed, his horizon is an individual figure that coincides with "the life-line on the hand."[19]

Yet it is precisely by means of this almost physiological loyalty to his own need to express himself that Pietraß stubbornly shelters his poetry from the mechanical ideologic mantle, even at the cost of near aphasia. Lying on the grass, the poet remarks, from this recurrent, provocative, "horizontal" viewpoint:

> Der Unrat, dem ich unterstehe
> Verpuppt sich für das siebte Glied.
> Ich schaue auf. In blauer Höhe
> Die Lerche fehlt. Ich weiß kein Lied.

("Freies Feld," FM, p. 60)

Notes

[1] Sascha Anderson and Elke Erb, eds., Berührung ist nur eine Randerscheinung (Cologne: Kiepenheuer & Witsch, 1985).

[2] Richard Pietraß, Poesiealbum 82 (Berlin: Neues Leben, 1974). In the following the title abbreviation PA will be used when citing page references to this edition.

[3] Richard Pietraß, Notausgang (Berlin/Weimar: Aufbau, 1980); Freiheitsmuseum (Berlin/Weimar: Aufbau, 1982). Subsequent page references will appear parenthetically in the text. The title abbreviations NA and FM will be used to indicate the volumes.

[4] Peter Böthig, "Richard Pietraß: Freiheitsmuseum," Weimarer Beiträge, 30, No. 9 (1984), 1546. Other reviews of Pietraß's books: Jürgen Engler, "Notausgang - Eingang für Leser?" Neue Deutsche Literatur, 29, No. 11 (1981), 150-53; Rainer Zekert, "Ernste Spiele," Neue Deutsche Literatur, 32, No. 1 (1984), 155-57.

[5] Heiner Müller, "Mauser," Alternative, 19, No. 110/11 (1976), 182.

[6] "Aussicht," in Poesiealbum, p. 10.

[7] "Von einem Kaiser und seiner Nachtigall," in Poesiealbum, p. 20.

[8] "Portrait P.R.," in Notausgang, p. 33.

[9] See Pietraß's interview with Karin Köbernick, "Herzschlag Hornhaut," Neue Deutsche Literatur, 30, No. 4 (1982), 117.

[10] "Du wirst zum Raum, in dem ich mich entfalte, / sobald der Tagesstaub mich nicht mehr frißt" ("Lebensraum," in Notausgang, p. 56).

[11] See interview with Karin Köbernick, p. 118.

[12] For example, Ingrid and Klaus-Dieter Hähnel, "Junge Lyrik am Ende der siebziger Jahre," Weimarer Beiträge, 27, No. 9 (1981), 135.

[13] "Lesezeichen," in Freiheitsmuseum, p. 99: "Literatur, trotz ihrer geringen Kraft, begreife ich als Beitrag zur Selbstbefreiung: des einzelnen und der vielen."

[14] Ibid.

[15] Ibid.

[16] "Epistel," in Notausgang, p. 28.

[17] "Amulett," in Freiheitsmuseum, p. 30.

[18] See titles of the different sections: "Berliner Hof," "Nachtfahrt," "Steckbrief," "Stufen des Mutes" in Notausgang; "Die Kunst zu leben," "Homo Novus," "Die Bilder" in Freiheitsmuseum.

[19] "Opposition," in Freiheitsmuseum, p. 17.

Wolf Biermann and "die zweite deutsche
Exilliteratur": An Appraisal after Nine Years

Dennis R. McCormick

It has been almost ten years now since the sensational expulsion of Wolf Biermann began an exodus of writers, actors, musicians, and other intellectuals of such proportions that the sixteenth of November, 1976 is destined to mark the beginning of an important chapter in the history of GDR literature and culture. Within a year of Biermann's expulsion the flood of fellow artists who found themselves more or less involuntarily in the West had become so great that at least one commentator spoke of an "Aderlaß und . . . Austrocknen der DDR-Kulturlandschaft,"[1] and others, such as Fritz J. Raddatz, began to speak of a "zweite deutsche Exilliteratur."[2] While the first assertion can be dismissed out of hand in light of subsequent developments, i.e., the cultural landscape of the GDR has not dried up, Raddatz's formulation, though certainly questionable, cannot be so easily discounted. Although a good number of writers, including Reiner Kunze, Günter Kunert, Sarah Kirsch, Thomas Brasch, and Hans-Joachim Schädlich, have for a variety of reasons consistently and categorically rejected the term "exile" for their status in the West, Wolf Biermann rejected Heinrich Böll's ironic label of an "in-die-Heimat-Vertriebener" and insisted vociferously that he was indeed in exile:

> Ich würde mich weniger im Exil befinden, wenn ich zum Beispiel mit Gewalt nach Moskau verfrachtet worden wäre. Dort hätte ich zwar das Problem der Sprache, aber ich würde die Gesellschaft besser verstehen.[3]

The two major questions I will address in this study are: to what extent was Biermann justified in initially claiming the term "exile" to describe his situation in the West, and can he be regarded today in light of his subsequent development in the West in any meaningful sense as a GDR writer-in-exile?

Before one can even begin to answer the first question, it is essential to recognize the difficulties entailed in employing a loaded term such as "exile" to describe the move from East to West Germany. It is useful, I believe, to distinguish at least two fundamental dimensions of the term: a material, physical, and geographical dimension; and a more complex ideological, literary one. Together they correspond roughly perhaps to the Marxist concepts of "base" and "superstructure."

Whichever of these dimensions one chooses to examine, the question of the appropriateness of the term "exile" for individuals such as Biermann immediately becomes encumbered with the entire weight of historical baggage known collectively as the "German Question." Let us tackle the problem first in its material, geographical, and political dimension; how --to put the issue somewhat crudely--can a German be exiled from Germany to Germany? The delicacy and political sensitivity of the matter is illustrated by the linguistic acrobatics contained in a recent book on the phenomenon of the inner- (or inter-?) German emigration: <u>Von Deutschland nach Deutschland: Zur Erfahrung der inneren Übersiedlung</u>,[4] published by the Federal Office of Political Education in Bonn. The term "Übersiedlung," one suspects, was chosen in order to avoid the word "emigration," not only because the phrase "innere Emigration" clearly carries a rather specific meaning in quite another context, but also because of a desire to avoid any term contradictory to the official West German view on the significance of the German-German border. To some degree, then, the appropriateness of the term "exile" depends upon one's view of the German Question, upon whether one accepts the formulation of one German nation consisting of two German states. A major reason for Biermann's vehement insistence that he <u>was</u> in exile, in fact, was to demonstrate forcefully <u>his</u> rejection of that formulation. In the "Vorworte" to the second half of the volume <u>Preußischer Ikarus</u> Biermann clearly articulates the common attitude which he deplores:

188

> Was heißt hier Exil! Ein Deutscher in
> Deutschland! - Ja, das wäre Exil zu nennen:
> Verfolgt von der Fremdenpolizei! verhun-
> gert! ohne Obdach! ohne Arbeitserlaubnis!
> ohne Kenntnis der Sprache! - aber ein DDR-
> Mensch in der Bundesrepublik, automatisch
> Bundesbürger, mehr so ein Heim-ins-Reich-
> Fall, das ist doch kein Exil! So einer soll
> doch dankbar sein! Das reden hier viele.[5]

That the view which Biermann rejects, however, is held not only by the West German "reactionaries" whom he wished to irritate but also by some of his fellow writers was perhaps most forcefully illustrated by Hans-Joachim Schädlich, who insisted at a gathering of former GDR authors held in West Berlin in February, 1984 under the motto "Flüchtlingsgespräche" or "Gedanken über die Dauer des Exils" that he most definitely does not consider himself to be in exile:

> Fühle ich mich deshalb als Emigrant? Be-
> finde ich mich im Exil? . . . Welcher
> Emigrant in welchem Exil-Land ist am Tag
> seiner Ankunft faktisch Staatsbürger dieses
> Landes?[6]

Similarly, shortly after coming to the West in 1978, Sarah Kirsch saw herself "keine Sekunde lang" as being in exile and found her "Grenzübertritt" far too banal to support a concept which forty-five years earlier had designated life-and-death political conflicts.[7]

Legal and political considerations aside, however, there is no reason to doubt that Wolf Biermann's return to the West was extremely traumatic. Whether he would really have found the society of the Soviet Union less alien than that of the FRG may be debatable, but even the editors of Von Deutschland nach Deutschland concede that "Die Übersiedlung von einem Teil Deutschlands in den anderen ist mehr als ein Umzug in eine andere Stadt, es ist ein Schritt von einer Welt in die andere."[8] The differences between the two Germanies in social, political, and economic systems and institutions are clearly so great that a common language (and even that assumption is not unchallenged) and, until 1945, a common history cannot guarantee an easy adaptation to the new environment in the West, particularly for a writer whose entire sense of personal and artistic identity was drawn so strongly from his status as a citizen of the GDR, albeit an uncomfortable one. A widespread, though by no means universal feeling of shock and alienation can be amply documented in the works of numerous GDR writers shortly after their arrival in the West. Jürgen Fuchs's poem "Vielleicht / gibt es viele Zuhause," for example, concludes with the lines: "Aber hier // in einer Fremde / Die meine Sprache spricht // Hier?"[9] Like the heroine of Christa Wolf's <u>Der geteilte Himmel</u>, they feel in the West, at least initially, "auf schreckliche Weise in der Fremde."[10] Even Schädlich, in his Berlin statement, which is bluntly entitled "Ich bin nicht im Exil," agrees with this point:

> Zwar fühlte ich mich lange Zeit fremd; die gleiche Sprache, die gleiche Kultur, die gleiche Stadt täuschten mich über Unterschiede hinweg, die umso heftiger zutage traten.[11]

The significant point to be noted, however, is that all such descriptions seem invariably to refer to <u>initial</u> reactions and feelings in the West. Insofar as the term "exile" implies a more or less permanent condition of ideological and political homelessness combined with a longing or waiting to return to the home country, it seems inevitably to lose its appropriateness with the passage of time and the progressive assimilation of GDR writers into West German society. Not even Biermann is as adamant in claiming to be in exile as he once was; he remarked at the Berlin conference, "Jetzt ist es schwieriger, das Wort zu gebrauchen."[12] Moreover, GDR writers as a group have neither formed a "colony," founded a journal, nor attempted in any way to speak with a common voice, as groups of exiles typically do, so it is difficult at best to see Biermann, or any other former GDR writer, for that matter, as part of a "zweite deutsche Exilliteratur."

Up to this point, I have been considering only the material dimension of the term exile, that is, the geographical, social, and political aspects of the move from East to West. The initial shock described by many writers is essentially the same as that experienced by any former citizen of the GDR upon emigrating to the Federal Republic. The question as to the appropriateness of the term "exile" becomes even more complex when considered in its ideological, literary dimension. Just as the issue could not be considered in its material sense without conjuring up the question of the unity of the German nation, any consideration of its specifically literary dimension leads directly to the question of the unity of German literature. How many German literatures are there? If the formulation "zwei deutsche Staaten - eine deutsche Nation" is especially true, or, as Günter Grass never tires of arguing, <u>only</u> true when one leaves the material sphere and considers the unity of the "deutsche Kulturnation,"[13] then the term "exile" clearly loses much of its meaning when applied to German writers as writers. The writer may be in political exile, but if he continues to write, he is still a part of German literature, or so the logic of this argument would have it.

While it is difficult to accept a view the logical implication of which is that there is no such thing as GDR literature, it is nevertheless important to acknowledge that the old debate over the unity of German literature and culture has never been definitively settled and is still going on. Since the early seventies, in fact, the argument for the unity of German literature has drawn significant new impetus from the phenomenon usually referred to as "convergence." According to this view, GDR writers in the Honecker era have increasingly broken out of the mold prescribed for them by GDR cultural policymakers and begun to address matters of common concern in both German states. Christa Wolf's <u>Kindheitsmuster</u>, for example, demonstrates that the German past is problematical even for citizens of that German state which officially claims to have overcome it. Problems associated with modern industrial societies in general also begin to receive attention: environmental pollution, lack of individual fulfillment in the face of stultifying regimentation and sex-role expectations, dissatisfaction with rampant materialism, etc. In the political arena, parallels are drawn between the reaction in the West to the student revolts of 1968 and the reaction in the GDR to the Prague Spring of the same year. Writers in both Germanies were confronted with a form of restoration, bourgeois and capitalist, on the one hand, Stalinist, on the other. According to this view, writers on both sides were thus reunited in the experience of a failed revolution, the traditional <u>deutsche</u> <u>Misere</u>. Finally, the meetings of writers from East and West organized by Stephan Hermlin have reminded participants on both sides of their analogous difficulties in their position between the superpowers and of their shared responsibility for peace arising out of a common past.

The relevance of these considerations for the question at hand is apparent. If this convergence phenomenon could be shown to demonstrate at least a certain commonality of German literature, and if Biermann's writings both before and after his expulsion could be shown to be a part of this phenomenon, then clearly there would be little sense in regarding him as a GDR writer-in-exile. Such an hypothesis might strike some as far-fetched, but that there is, in fact, good reason to view <u>some</u> former GDR writers as part of a diverse literary culture that is best described simply as <u>German</u> is proven, I believe, by the case of Günter Kunert. Kunert is just such a writer who had never regarded himself primarily as a representative of an autonomous GDR literature, but rather as a cosmopolitan, German, even international writer with residence in the GDR. In a radio interview shortly after his move to Itzehoe near Hamburg, Kunert clearly stated his view that the literature of the GDR and that of the Federal Republic comprise one German literature: "Es ist deutsche Literatur. Das ist ja ganz unleugbar; denn was sollte es wohl sonst sein?"[14] Later in the same interview Kunert went on to make remarks strongly suggestive of his own adherence to the convergence hypothesis:

> Die industriellen Zivilisationen, wie wir sie kennen, also die sozialistische wie die bürgerliche, haben ja trotz vieler Gegensätze und grundlegender Unterschiede Probleme und Schwierigkeiten, die aus denselben Gründen resultieren, und ich glaube, daß diese Gründe, die die Schwierigkeiten herstellen, immer bedrängender werden, so daß die kommenden Probleme, von denen ich annehme, daß sie uns fast an den Rand unserer Existenz . . . bringen werden, andere überdecken und andere in den Hintergrund treten lassen werden. (p. 1229)

This analysis simply does not work in the case

of Biermann, however, for his writings prior to his expulsion reflect not pan-Germanic, but rather very specific GDR concerns viewed from within that system. Biermann had, in fact, so identified himself with these concerns that he stated in an interview just two weeks before his expulsion, "daß ein Leben im Westen für mich das Ende meiner schriftstellerischen Arbeit bedeuten würde."[15] If Biermann's worst fears had proven to be justified, one would not, of course, have to debate whether he should be considered a GDR writer-in-exile today, for in that case he would no longer be considered a writer at all. But he has continued to write in the West, about as prolifically as before his expulsion. Before returning to the original question, therefore, I would like to insert at this point a necessarily brief overview of Biermann's literary production and development in the West.

If Biermann was to continue to write in the West, his greatest problem was to find a stance, to begin to interact with FRG society and not become a Berufsdissident who continued to write about GDR reality of which he was destined to have ever less first-hand knowledge. Nor did he wish to dwell on the past, for it was obvious that that theme would soon grow stale. Besides, Biermann had already said what he wanted to say on that account. In his own words:

> Ich . . . kam nicht in den Westen mit einem Sack voll ungesagter Wahrheiten über den Osten. Ich muß hier nun nichts ausbreiten, aufarbeiten und entlarven. Was ich in der DDR dachte und fühlte, habe ich auch in der DDR gesagt, da ist für mich nichts nachzuholen.[16]

But what should Biermann then write about and from what standpoint? His situation in the GDR had always provided him with his subject matter, issues which Biermann had turned into some excellent poems but which, as Reinhard Baumgart has pointed out, were limited to certain basic themes:

> Außer den sinnlichen Freuden der Liebe . . ., dem Ärger mit der Partei . . . und einem unbeirr- oder unbelehrbaren Glauben ans irdische Himmelreich des Kommunismus . . . kommt da kaum irgend etwas zur Sprache.[17]

Moreover, Biermann's problems were not those normally associated with "exile," for, in many respects, he was already an emigrant while he was living in the GDR. As Thomas Rothschild put it:

> Was ist ein Emigrant? Ein Ausgewiesener, der von seinen Landsleuten und der Öffentlichkeit ferngehalten wird, der allenfalls über die Grenzen wirken kann. Heine in Paris, Brecht in Hollywood, Biermann groteskerweise in der Chausseestraße.[18]

Although Biermann insisted after his expatriatrion that he was an emigrant in the West, his real problem, I would argue, was to find a stance in a society that refused to treat him like one.

For a while, Biermann simply took advantage of the opportunity to perform old material after so many years of Berufsverbot. His first publication after his expulsion was Nachlaß I (1977), a collection of his previously published works up until the expulsion, which, as the title implies, Biermann regarded as a major caesura, a kind of death.[19] His self-professed immediate goal was, "So schnell wie möglich in einen Stoffwechsel mit dieser Gesellschaft sich einlassen. Sich verbünden mit den fortschrittlichen Kräften im Westen."[20] Finding any kind of alliance with the splintered West German Left exceedingly difficult, Biermann flirted with Euro-Communism and even joined the Spanish Communist Party. As the outraged conservative press never tired of pointing out, Biermann's initial earnings from old material in the West were considerable, allowing him to purchase a house in his native Hamburg. Gradually, he began to accommodate himself to the necessity of remaining in the West, and he began to write.

Biermann's first publication with works written in the West was the volume Preußischer Ikarus (1978). The book is divided into two halves separated by a "wall," a blank sheet of paper. The poems of the first half were all written in the East; those of the second, in the West. The Western poems in this collection have a tentative quality about them, indicative of a poet still unsure of his stance. There is still a great deal of self-absorbed reflection on his own situation, especially in the "Vorworte" to the second part and in the poem "Deutsches Miserere" with the famous (or infamous) "Jauche" metaphor.[21] Several poems castigate the factionalized Left, but Biermann does not exclude himself from criticism, either. The poem "Mag sein, daß ich irre" reveals the uncertainty and precariousness of the author's position, as do the lines from "Linkes Liedchen": "Von rechts winkt noch müde das große Geld / Und links winkt das Ghetto mir."[22] A few poems are very personal, such as a love poem to his wife ("Kleiner Brief") and a greeting in Hamburg dialect to his new daughter ("Nelli"), but one also finds the first poems devoted to topical West German themes: a strike on the Hamburg docks ("Die Streikposten vor Euro-Kai"), nuclear power ("Gorleben Lied"), and several on the terrorism issue. On the whole, the volume did little to answer questions about Biermann's development in the West, though it did show that he did not intend to fall silent.

With the release of the record album "Hälfte des Lebens" in 1979, however, Biermann's artistic direction appeared to some to have taken a startling turn. The album contains Biermann's musical compositions to twenty-seven texts, most of them not by himself but by 18th, 19th, and 20th century poets as diverse as Hölderlin and Van Hoddis. Recorded in the bourgeois comfort of the living room into which he had allegedly withdrawn, these all too beautiful songs include love and nature lyrics, travel impressions, and other less-than-overtly-revolutionary verses. For some, it was clear: Biermann had abandoned his roots as a political activist to the pursuit of purely artistic glory.

Acting forcefully to dispel this charge, Biermann writes in the accompanying text to his next album, "Eins in die Fresse, mein Herzblatt":

> Nach der noblen "Hälfte des Lebens"-LP
> . . . fürchteten manche, hofften andere,
> ich sei nun in die höhere Kunst abgestiegen. Nun, mit der neuen "Eins in die Fresse" . . . geht es wieder in den tagespolitischen Dreck der Epoche.

The album is a live recording of Biermann's preelection concert tour in the spring of 1980 under the motto "es grünt so grün," but the new songs in this album are not so much pro-"Green" as they are anti-

Strauß. Though he is far more favorably disposed toward them today, Biermann originally mistrusted the "Greens" and feared they might prove to be "ein Gemisch . . . von deutschnationalen Salatfressern und frustrierten K-Gruppenresten."[23] Although the album clearly indicated that Biermann had no intention of avoiding political themes, it did provide some cause for concern about the quality of his poetry in the West. A few of the songs first released in this album, such as "Starfighter" or "S & S," are lacking in the dialectical wit and Brechtian poignancy that had marked the best of his political verses in the East. <u>Spiegel</u> editor Christian Schultz-Gerstein finds the Biermann of this concert tour a very poor political singer, "wenn denn politische Lieder mehr sein sollen als Vereinshymnen für den Anti-Strauß-Fan-Club. . . ."[24] It is regrettable that Schultz-Gerstein goes on to impugn not only the quality of the texts but Biermann's motives as well: "So singt er auch nicht politische Lieder, sondern Lieder, deren ganzer Inhalt sich darin erschöpft zu beweisen, daß er nach wie vor der linke Barde ist."[25] They <u>are</u> political songs, but some are not very good ones.

Following the 1980 tour, Biermann withdrew from the public eye for a time, in his own words, "weil ich spürte, daß eine Phase in meinem Leben beendet ist, meine erste Westphase."[26] With the publication of the volume <u>Verdrehte Welt - das seh' ich gerne</u> (1982)[27] and two record albums entitled "Wir müssen vor Hoffnung verrückt sein" (1982) and "Im Hamburger Federbett" (1983), the general outlines of the next phase began to emerge. Biermann's latest poetry has become somewhat more personal, more reflective, less strident, and not so optimistic and self-assured. At the same time, his political views appear to have undergone a slight rightward shift, at least insofar as he offended many on the left by stating, for example, that he would no longer return to the GDR even if he could,[28] by mocking "Berufsrevolutionäre ohne Beruf und ohne Revolution"[29] who cannot bring themselves to criticize repression in Poland, by suggesting that the peace movement, which Biermann very much supports, is sometimes manipulated by DKP-controlled hypocrites,[30] and by admitting with increasing frequency to moments of doubt about the inevitable victory of humanistic socialism.[31]

Because of this, articles began to appear which

spoke of resignation, melancholy, and withdrawal into the private, biographical realm, epitomized by a Zeit interview with Fritz J. Raddatz entitled "Nächtlich bei Biermann" with its key words "zurückgezogen," "melancholisch," and "still."[32] Der Spiegel, a journal which Biermann, at the Berlin "Flüchtlingsgespräche" conference, referred to as "Bild am Montag," immediately seized upon the interview and mocked Biermanns's withdrawal from the political arena: "Dem 'Zeit'-Feuilletonchef Raddatz beichtete er bei Kerzenschein und Rotwein, daß er nur noch schreiben wolle, 'was meine Sache ist.'"[33] Fans of the socialist Bürgerschreck and political agitator were, of course, horrified. Biermann, now in his mid-forties, had sold out, had degenerated into a mere poet. If Biermann's worst fears about his fate in the West, namely that he would no longer be able to write, had not come true, the situation was even worse. The fondest hopes of his antagonists in the GDR had been realized: Biermann was just another comfortable bourgeois poet.

In truth, the charge that Biermann is no longer concerned with political issues is patently absurd and can only be supported by carefully gerrymandering the evidence. What has really happened, I believe, is that Biermann has begun to take a longer-range view of the effect of political poetry and believes his final Nachlaß will be an important political document only to the extent that it is also an important literary document. He has vehemently denied the conclusions of the Raddatz article[34] and repeatedly explained that he intends henceforth only to avoid a superficial treatment of topical themes in which he has too little personal stake to write good poems. Biermann has described his own development in the West as follows:

> Als ich neu im Westen war, lebte ich unter dem verheerenden Druck, beweisen zu müssen, daß ich hier nicht politisch, moralisch und künstlerisch kaputtgehe und daß ich in dieser westlichen Marktgesellschaft nicht untergehe. Da habe ich, weil ich ja nun auch meine alten DDR-Wunden nicht ewig lecken wollte hier im Westen, ... da habe ich eben über politische Themen geschrieben, die wichtig waren oder die ich für wichtig hielt: Terrorismus, Baader-Meinhof,

> Streik der Hafenarbeiter hier in Hamburg. Nichts dagegen, gute Absicht soll sein. Aber inzwischen, seit ich hier wieder meinen eigenen Stoffwechsel mit dieser Gesellschaft habe, bin ich fest entschlossen und habe das auch in den letzten Jahren getan, wieder so zu leben und zu arbeiten, wie ich es immer getan habe in den Jahren vor meiner Ausbürgerung aus der DDR. Nämlich nur und nur über politisch wichtige Dinge zu schreiben dann und in dem Maße, wie sie sich mit meinem wirklichen Leben überschneiden, nur, wenn sie wirklich schmerzhaft oder lustvoll einbrechen. Anders sind wohl lebendige Lieder und Gedichte nicht zu schaffen. Jedenfalls ich kann es nicht anders.[35]

Biermann now believes that the best songs and poems can only originate "wo sich das Familienalbum berührt mit dem Geschichtsbuch. Wo die allerprivateste Ebene sich überschneidet mit dem gesellschaftlich Bedeutsamen."[36] Wherever Wolf Biermann is able to sustain this creative tension between the autobiographical, personal, and the historical, political sphere--as he was usually able to do in his earlier works but apparently had to relearn after the shock of his expulsion--then he has shown himself to be capable of writing songs and poems that are as good as anything he has ever written.

Returning to the question of Biermann's status as a "GDR writer-in-exile" however, it is clear that precisely his success in becoming involved, in entering into a "Stoffwechsel" with West German society, has called the suitability of such a designation very much into question. To be sure, because his themes are so often autobiographical, Biermann's latest poems contain constant reminders of his background and experiences in the East, as seen in the poems "Ich leb mein Leben, sagt Eva-Marie," "Kleines Lied für R.[obert] H.[avemann]," and the marvelous "Bei Flut."[37] But it is not contemporary GDR reality that is reflected, except perhaps in "Grünheide, kein Wort," written after a deathbed visit to Robert Havemann in East Berlin, permitted only after Biermann promised not to write anything about Havemann. In an ironic variation on Brecht, the poem concludes:

> Was sind das für Zeiten, da ein Gespräch
> über Menschen fast ein Verbrechen ist
> aber von den Bäumen, nicht wahr, Genosse
> Honecker, von den Bäumen werde ich reden.[38]

On the whole, then, it would seem that Biermann can no longer be regarded as being in exile or as a part of contemporary GDR literature. But the entire issue of a "zweite deutsche Exilliteratur" is fraught with complexities that defy all-too-facile answers. If Biermann cannot be considered part of GDR literature, for example, because he no longer writes about contemporary GDR reality, then what about a writer such as Erich Loest, who stated at the Berlin "Flüchtlingsgespräche" conference: "Mein Stoff liegt in meiner alten kalten Heimat, und vielleicht bin ich doch im Exil."[39] Is Loest still a GDR writer so long as he writes about the GDR? Or is it a question of audience? Is Biermann not a GDR writer because he is not published in the GDR? He was not published there for years before his expulsion either, so just when did he cease being a GDR writer? And is Jurek Becker, for example, who _has_ published new works in the East since coming West, still a GDR writer, but are none of the others now in the West who have not? The entire issue defies categorical answers precisely because it is as complicated as the German Question itself. If Biermann is no longer a part of contemporary GDR literature, he still cannot be classified as just another West German writer, for the twenty-three years he spent in the GDR will presumably continue to resonate strongly in his poetry. And although Hans-Joachim Schädlich may want to free himself of clumsy labels such as "former GDR writer" as quickly as possible, dropping that label in Biermann's case may be possible only because his background is so well-known that the label is unnecessary. Biermann himself captured much of the ironic complexity of his situation in these lines from "Deutsches Miserere (Das Bloch-Lied)":

> Und als ich von Deutschland nach Deutschland
> Gekommen bin in das Exil
> Da hat sich für mich geändert
> So wenig, Ach! und so viel[40]

Notes

¹ Harald Kleinschmid, "Zum VIII. Schriftsteller-Kongress der DDR," Deutschland Archiv, 12, No. 7 (1978), 676.

² Fritz J. Raddatz, "Die zweite deutsche Exil-Literatur," Die Zeit, 12 August 1977.

³ Wolf Biermann, "Die wissen genau, wie sehr sie bedroht sind," Der Spiegel, 22 November 1976, p. 36.

⁴ Gerhard Finn and Liselotte Julius, eds., Von Deutschland nach Deutschland: Zur Erfahrung der inneren Übersiedlung (Bonn: Bundeszentrale für politische Bildung, 1983).

⁵ Wolf Biermann, Preußischer Ikarus (Munich: Deutscher Taschenbuchverlag, 1981), pp. 110-11.

⁶ Hans-Joachim Schädlich, "Ich bin nicht im Exil," Die Zeit, 30 March 1984, p. 46.

⁷ "Gleicher Abstand zu beiden Seiten," Der Spiegel, 17 July 1978, p. 144.

⁸ Von Deutschland nach Deutschland, p. 9.

⁹ Jürgen Fuchs, Tagesnotizen (Reinbek: Rowohlt, 1979), p. 8.

¹⁰ Christa Wolf, Der geteilte Himmel (Munich: Deutscher Taschenbuchverlag, 1973), p. 174.

¹¹ Schädlich, "Ich bin nicht im Exil," p. 46.

¹² Quoted from my notes on the conference. Another aspect of Biermann's present position is revealed in the statement from the same conference: "Wir sind im Exil, und arbeiten daran, diese Gesellschaft in eine Heimat zu verwandeln."

¹³ See, e.g., Grass's discussion of a series of lectures he delivered in China on this topic in Kopfgeburten (Darmstadt: Luchterhand, 1980), p. 8. He describes the main thesis of these lectures as follows: "Als etwas Gesamtdeutsches läßt sich nur noch

die Literatur nachweisen; sie hält sich nicht an die Grenze, so hemmend besonders ihr die Grenze gezogen wird." For a further discussion of related issues, see Anneli Hartmann, "Was heißt überhaupt noch 'DDR-Literatur'?" in Studies in GDR Culture and Society 5 (Lanham: University Press of America, 1985), pp. 265-80.

14 "Gespräch mit Günter Kunert. Interview des Deutschlandfunks," Deutschland Archiv, 14, No. 11 (1980), 1229.

15 Quoted in Exil: Die Ausbürgerung Wolf Biermanns aus der DDR, ed. Peter Roos (Cologne: Kiepenheuer & Witsch, 1977), p. 15.

16 Preußischer Ikarus, p. 116.

17 Reinhard Baumgart, "Ende des Familienkrachs," Der Spiegel, 22 August 1977, p. 134.

18 Thomas Rothschild, Wolf Biermann: Liedermacher und Sozialist (Reinbek: Rowohlt, 1976), p. 42.

19 Wolf Biermann, Nachlaß I (Cologne: Kiepenheuer & Witsch, 1977).

20 Preußischer Ikarus, p. 116.

21 The refrain to this song reads: "Hier fallen sie auf den Rücken / Dort kriechen sie auf dem Bauche / Und ich bin gekommen / ach! kommen bin ich / vom Regen in die Jauche" (Preußischer Ikarus, p. 201). The outrage and animosity these lines provoked in some quarters of West German society are epitomized in an article by Thomas Engel entitled "Jauche über unseren Staat" in the Bayernkurier of 20 October 1979. Engel's article concludes: "Toleranz ist eine großartige Sache. Aber wenn ein Zugereister aus dem Arbeiter- und Bauernstaat das Maul so voll nimmt, verdient er zumindest einen kräftigen Tritt in den Hintern, damit er sich an seiner eigenen Wortwahl verschluckt."

22 Preußischer Ikarus, p. 164.

23 "Ich bin kein Punk: Ein Gespräch mit Wolf Biermann," Die Tageszeitung, 19 October 1982, p. 11.

24 Christian Schultz-Gerstein, "Lieder für die Anti-Strauß-Fans," Der Spiegel, 12 May 1980, p. 215.

25 Schultz-Gerstein, p. 215.

26 Wolf Biermann as quoted in the article "Bei Flut drückt die See den Fluß in das Land," Kölner Stadt-Anzeiger, 25/26 September 1982.

27 Wolf Biermann, Verdrehte Welt - das seh' ich gerne (Cologne: Kiepenheuer & Witsch, 1982), p. 165.

28 See, for example, the lines from the poem "Ich leb mein Leben, sagt Eva-Marie": "Schön ist Hamburg auch im Regen / und ich mag / Nicht zurück woher ich kam, nicht / einen Tag" in Verdrehte Welt - das seh' ich gerne, p. 14.

29 Verdrehte Welt - das seh' ich gerne, p. 165.

30 Biermann's strongest articulation of this view is contained in "Leute dabei, die nur für Abrüstung im Westen sind," Saarbrücker Zeitung, 15 October 1982, p. 4. See also "Wolf Biermanns politisch-hygienische Erkenntnisse," Die Welt, 1 October 1982, p. 6.

31 See particularly the poem "Totgeburt," which contains lines such as: "immer noch unter dem Herzen / fault mir der Kommunismus, trüb / in der Fruchtblase schwimmt mir / kerngesund der Kadaver im Geiste" in Verdrehte Welt - das seh' ich gerne, p. 183.

32 Fritz J. Raddatz, "Nächtlich bei Biermann," Die Zeit, 21 August 1981, p. 29.

33 "Öder Stern," Der Spiegel, 24 August 1981, p. 169.

34 See particularly Biermann's statement, "In eigener Sache," Der Spiegel, 28 September 1981, pp. 248-49.

35 "Ich bin kein Punk," p. 11.

36 "In eigener Sache," p. 248.

37 All contained in Verdrehte Welt - das seh' ich gerne.

38 _Verdrehte Welt - das seh' ich gerne_, p. 27.

39 To be sure, Loest has more often taken the opposing position and claimed not to be in exile and that he cannot continue indefinitely to write about GDR themes: "Denn meine Erfahrungen mit Leipzig, mit der DDR, verblassen, sie sind alt, sie sind nun bald drei Jahre alt." Quoted from "Interview des Deutschlandfunks mit Erich Loest, 14. August 1983," reprinted in Erich Loest, _Der vierte Zensor_ (Cologne: Verlag Wissenschaft und Politik, 1984), p. 86. Of course, Loest's position on the issue is immaterial to the hypothetical argument being advanced here.

40 _Preußischer Ikarus_, p. 201.

Contributors to Studies in GDR Culture and Society 6:

Pieter A. Boot, Economist, Assistent, Department of Microeconomics, Universiteit van Amsterdam.

Anna Chiarloni, Germanist, Professore Associato, Facoltà di Lettere, Università di Torino.

Mike Dennis, Senior Lecturer in Interdisciplinary Studies, School of Humanities, Wolverhampton Polytechnic, England.

Irene Dölling, Kulturtheoretikerin, Professor, Sektion Ästhetik und Kulturwissenschaft, Humboldt Universität, Berlin.

Günter Erbe, Sociologist, Dozent, Researcher at the Zentralinstitut für sozialwissenschaftliche Forschung, Freie Universität Berlin.

Gerd Labroisse, Germanist, Professor, Studierichting Duitse Taal- en Letterkunde, Vrije Universiteit Amsterdam.

Lyman H. Legters, Historian, Professor, School of International Studies, University of Washington; Senior Fellow, William O. Douglas Institute, Seattle.

Dennis R. McCormick, Germanist, Professor and Chairman, Department of Foreign Languages and Literatures, University of Montana, Missoula.

Rüdiger Pieper, Lecturer, Paul-Löbe Institut, Berlin; Institut für Unternehmensführung, Freie Universität Berlin.

Carol Poore, Germanist, Assistant Professor, Department of German, Brown University, Providence, RI.

Karl-Heinz Röder, Jurist, Professor and Vice-Director, Institut für Theorie des Staates und des Rechts, Akademie der Wissenschaften der DDR, Berlin.

Christiane Zehl Romero, Germanist, Professor, Department of German and Russian, Tufts University, Medford, MA.

Arthur A. Stahnke, Political Scientist, Professor, Department of Government, Southern Illinois University, Edwardsville.

Dietrich Staritz, Political Scientist/Historian, Professor, Arbeitsbereich Geschichte und Politik der DDR, Institut für Sozialwissenschaften, Universität Mannheim.

Editors

Margy Gerber, Germanist, Professor, Department of German, Russian, and East Asian Languages, Bowling Green State University, Ohio.

Christine Cosentino, Germanist, Professor, Department of German, Rutgers University, Camden, NJ.

Volker Gransow, Political Scientist, <u>Dozent</u>, Fakultät für Soziologie, Universität Bielefeld; <u>Privatdozent</u>, Institut für Soziologie, Freie Universität Berlin.

Nancy A. Lauckner, Germanist, Associate Professor, Department of Germanic and Slavic Languages, University of Tennessee, Knoxville.

Christiane Lemke, Sociologist, Researcher at the Zentralinstitut für sozialwissenschaftliche Forschung, Freie Universität Berlin.

Arthur A. Stahnke (see above)

Alexander Stephan, Germanist, Professor and Chairman, Department of Germanic and Slavic Languages and Literatures, University of Florida, Gainesville.

LIBRARY OF DAVIDSON COLLEGE